"In *Reformed Means Missional*, Dr. Sam Logan brings together both well-known authors and some hidden jewels of the church who labor, Jesus-like, in dark places, and serve the least and the lowest. Refreshingly, the theorists are also practitioners, while the practitioners think biblically and theologically about how God's mission shapes their work. The result? This wide-ranging volume, which is calculated to give mind, conscience, and yes, emotions also, a serious, gospel workout."

Sinclair B Ferguson, Theologian; author; and professor, Redeemer Theological Seminary, Dallas, TX

"Building on 'Mission and Evangelism' in the WRF Statement of Faith, *Reformed Means Missional* brings theological substance to 'missional,' ensuring the term doesn't become a passing fad. A collection of the world's top Reformed thinkers have provided rich, compelling insights as to how the church in the twenty-first century must change the way it thinks and behaves as it is sent into the world to proclaim the Good News of Jesus Christ and promote the expansion of His Kingdom."

Jeffrey Jeremiah, MDiv, PhD, Stated Clerk, Evangelical Presbyterian Church

"*Reformed Means Missional* is a foundational and strategic call to all in the Reformed tradition to truly be *His* church, on *His* mission taking the Whole Gospel to the Whole World. My friend, Sam Logan, understands this reality and articulates this call, both in terms of its theological groundings and its global implications, more persuasively than anyone I know. This book is required reading for any leader in the Reformed tradition who wants to be able to participate in twenty-first century conversations with respect to the Reformational church and the core of Christ's calling."

Dr. S. Douglas Birdsall, President of the American Bible Society; former Executive Chair of the Lausanne Movement.

"I have sometimes been annoyed when twenty-first century leaders trumpet the mantra that their ministry is 'missional'—as if no one else had ever discovered this concept before. However these essays, edited by Dr. Logan, focus on God's own mission for his church, immersed in a shape-shifting culture. Here are arrows that fly from the Spirit's own bow, still quivering from a bull's-eye impact!"

Dr. Michael A. Rogers, Senior Pastor, Westminster Presbyterian Church, Lancaster, PA

"God is a missionary God. He reaches out to claim and bless His people and through them to bless others. When God called Abraham, He said to him: 'I will bless you… so that you will be a blessing…and in you all the families of the earth shall be blessed.' We are called by God to be missionaries, to be 'missional.' We cannot all reach all families of the earth; but we can reach some families near or far. This book will help you become intentional in your focus to be missional in some area where you can have influence. Where are you a blessing? Where are you missional?"

Robert C. (Ric) Cannada, Jr., Chancellor Emeritus, Reformed Theological Seminary

"The heartbeat of Reformed theology (at its best) has always been its missional thrust. This extraordinary collection of essays explores from many angles how the gospel translates into God's people serving as his instruments of redemptive healing in a very broken world. It will help us follow Jesus more faithfully into his world that his kingdom may come on earth as it is in heaven."

Leo R. Schuster III, Lead Pastor, East Side Congregation, Redeemer Presbyterian Church

"What is it after all to be 'missional'? Finally, this remarkable book shows us the way. We recognize our calling to build upon our Reformed heritage *and* to passionately look ahead. By God's grace we will fulfill our calling to bring *both* the gospel and long-needed change in our world, engaging issues too-long neglected. Some will need to leave their denominations, others not, but we will labor together. This book unites us and stretches us at the same time—a must read to equip us for our Lord's vast and deep calling to us all."

D. Clair Davis, Professor and Chaplain, Redeemer Seminary, Dallas

"This is the book to read if you are serious about being part of God's mission of reaching the world through the proclamation of the gospel. Articles by experienced missionaries from four continents, focusing on twenty-four different aspects with one conclusion: *Reformed means missional*! A thorough, biblically sound, God-centered, focus. I pray that thousands, through reading it, would be equipped and encouraged to fulfill their calling in the coming of his kingdom!"

Henk Stoker, Professor in Apologetics and Ethics, North-West University, Potchefstroom, South Africa

"Our Lord Jesus Christ said, 'I am the way, the truth and the life.' 'Reformed' usually connotes for us a commitment to the truth. But our sovereign Lord commissioned his followers to apply this truth to all of life. This new book presents challenges from some of the best Reformed thinkers who also are leaders in application of our faith to a great variety of needs in our world."

William S. Barker, Professor of Church History Emeritus, Westminster Theological Seminary; former Moderator of the General Assembly, Presbyterian Church in America

"The European Reformers followed Jesus, the eternal Creator who lived in time-space history as a provincial carpenter-turned-rabbi, into their particular worlds half a millennium ago. In exemplary fashion, our reforming forefathers were both faithful to God's enduring covenant and relevant to their contemporary settings. This volume's heartening example of *semper reformans, semper reformanda* ("always reformed, always reforming") serves today's world Christian movement well toward following Jesus in faithful, relevant, and 'missional' ways."

Rev. Dr. J. Nelson Jennings, Executive Director, Overseas Ministries Study Center; Teaching Elder, Presbyterian Church in America

"At a time when some people are asking how to be Reformed and missional at the same time, this book comes to show that being Reformed IS to be INTRINSICALLY missional. Written from different perspectives, with specific foci, the book is honest to its title as it challenges us to see, in practice, just how true it is that being really Reformed and being really missional are one and the same!"

David Charles Gomes, Chancellor, Mackenzie Presbyterian University, Sao Paulo, Brazil

"The reach of Jesus is as we sing, 'far as the curse is found.' Jesus calls his Body into all spaces of earthly life–as sick, ruined, and corrupt as they may be. Sam Logan has assembled a book that reminds those of us within the Reformed tradition that our attention to truth is always in some practical sense for the sake of the world—not as an abstract proclamation, but to embody in real, though incomplete and imperfect, ways his future now. This collection of essays not only reminds us of the missional aim of Christ, but helps us imagine the reach of Christ—far as the curse is found."

Tuck Bartholomew, Pastor, City Church, Philadelphia, PA

"Searching for gold to enrich your convictions about being Reformed *and* missional? Here's a robust mine in which the most imminently qualified Reformed scholars and practitioners help you discover the reasons, ways, and specific venues our missional God is glorifying himself in this broken world. It is difficult to imagine a more comprehensive, compassionate, compelling, theo-centric, accessible, scholarly, biblically-grounded, and inspiring treatment of the complex dimensions of the missional landscape."

Mike Sharrett, Pastor, Redeemer Presbyterian Church, Lynchburg, VA

REFORMED MEANS MISSIONAL

FOLLOWING JESUS
INTO THE WORLD

Edited by Samuel T. Logan, Jr.

New
Growth
Press

www.newgrowthpress.com

New Growth Press, Greensboro, NC 27404

Cover Design: faceoutstudio, faceoutstudio.com
Typesetting: Lisa Parnell, lparnell.com

ISBN 978-1-938267-75-8 (Print)
ISBN 978-1-938267-99-4 (eBook)

Library of Congress Cataloging-in-Publication Data
Reformed means missional : following Jesus into the world / Samuel Logan, editor.
    pages cm.
  ISBN 978-1-938267-75-8 (alk. paper)
  1. Mission of the church. 2. Reformed Church—Doctrines. I. Logan, Samuel T., 1943–
BV601.8R45 2013
266'.42—dc23
                                                            2013008267

Printed in Canada

20 19 18 17 16 15 14 13   1 2 3 4 5

For Susan

"My love is like a red, red rose."

CONTENTS

WHAT DO WE MEAN BY "MISSIONAL"?

CHRISTOPHER J. H. WRIGHT

Strictly speaking, the word "missional" means "pertaining to, or characterized by, mission"—in the same way that "covenantal" relates to "covenant," or "tribal" to "tribe." The real question is, Whose mission are we talking about when we refer to an activity, community, strategy as being "missional"?

Our tendency has been to think primarily of "missions"—that is, of things that *we* do, activities we plan and execute "for God," to help him get to places he seems to have difficulty reaching. I would like us to reconsider that definition.

In my book *The Mission of God*,[1] I argue that we need to shift our perspective to see that, like salvation, mission belongs to our God. Let me say that again: *Mission is not ours; mission is God's.* It is not so much that God has a mission for his church in the world; rather, God has a church for his mission in the world. Mission was not made for the church; the church was made for mission—God's mission. "Missional church," therefore, is something of a tautology (like "female women"); if it isn't missional, it isn't church. A "church" may be a group of people doing religious things together, but if it is not participating in the purposes of God in the world and for the world, it has lost the plot and forgotten the reason for its own existence.

Such an understanding of what it means to be missional derives from the way the Bible communicates the mission of God. The Bible presents itself to us as an overarching narrative in four great movements: creation, fall, redemption, and future hope. There is one God at work in the universe and in human history, and that God has a mission—a mission that will ultimately be accomplished by the power of his Word and for the glory of his name. That mission, according to Paul, includes the unifying of all creation under Christ (Ephesians 1:9–10), and the reconciliation of all creation through the cross and resurrection of Christ (Colossians 1:15–20). Within that, it includes the blessing and healing of the nations, as the good news of the redeeming work of Christ and all its implications is made known to the ends of the earth.

Missional living starts with a missional reading of the Bible, and that means reading every part of the Scriptures:

- in the light of God's purpose for his whole creation, including the redemption of humanity and the creation of the new heavens and new earth;
- in the light of God's purpose for human life in general on the planet, and of all the Bible teaches about human culture; social, economic, and political relationships; ethics; and behavior;
- in the light of God's historical election of Old Testament Israel, their identity and role in relation to the nations, and the demands he made on their worship and ethics;
- in the light of the centrality of Jesus of Nazareth, his messianic identity and mission in relation to Old Testament Israel and the nations, and his cross and resurrection;
- in the light of God's calling of the church, the community of believing Jews and gentiles who constitute the extended people of the Abraham covenant, to be the agent of God's blessing to the nations in the name and for the glory of the Lord Jesus Christ.

When we grasp that the whole Bible constitutes the coherent revelation of the mission of God, then we find our whole worldview impacted by this vision. The Bible is The Story, which tells us where we have come from, how we got to be here, who we are, why the world is in the mess it is, how it can be (and has been) changed, and where we are ultimately going. And this whole story constitutes the mission of this God. God is the originator of the story, the teller of the story, the prime actor in the story, the planner and guide of the story's plot, the meaning of the story, and the story's ultimate completion. He is its beginning, end, and center. The Bible is the story of the mission of God—of this God and no other.

Now such an understanding of the mission of God as the very heartbeat of all reality, all creation, and all history generates a distinctive missional worldview that is radically and transformingly God-centered. It turns inside out and upside down some of the common ways in which we are accustomed to think about the Christian life. It is certainly a very healthy corrective to the egocentric obsession of much Western culture—including, sadly, even Western *Christian* culture. It constantly forces us to open our eyes to the big picture, rather than shelter in the cozy narcissism of our own small worlds:

- We ask, "Where does God fit into the story of my life?" when the real question is: Where does my little life fit into this great story of God's mission?
- We want to be driven by a purpose that has been tailored just right for our own individual lives, when we should be seeing the purpose of all life, including our own, wrapped up in the great mission of God for the whole of creation.
- We talk about "applying the Bible to our lives." What would it mean to instead apply *our* lives to the *Bible*, assuming the Bible to be the reality—the real story—to which we are called to conform ourselves?
- We wrestle with "making the gospel relevant to the world." But in *this* story, God is about the business of transforming the world to fit the shape of the gospel.
- We argue about what can legitimately be included in the mission that God expects from the church, when we should be asking what kind of church God wants for the whole range of his mission.

- I may wonder what kind of mission God has for me, when I should be asking what kind of *me* God wants for *his* mission.

The paragraphs above are drawn from my book, *The Mission of God*. But it would be good to conclude this foreword with a short extract from The Cape Town Commitment, from the Third Lausanne Congress on World Evangelization in Cape Town, 2010—a document quoted frequently throughout this book. Its section, "We love the mission of God," makes the following statement and challenge. Here, in a nutshell, is missional theology:

> We are committed to world mission, because it is central to our understanding of God, the Bible, the Church, human history and the ultimate future. The whole Bible reveals the mission of God to bring all things in heaven and earth into unity under Christ, reconciling them through the blood of his cross. In fulfilling his mission, God will transform the creation broken by sin and evil into the new creation in which there is no more sin or curse. God will fulfill his promise to Abraham to bless all nations on the earth, through the gospel of Jesus, the Messiah, the seed of Abraham. God will transform the fractured world of nations that are scattered under the judgment of God into the new humanity that will be redeemed by the blood of Christ from every tribe, nation, tongue and language, and will be gathered to worship our God and Savior. God will destroy the reign of death, corruption and violence when Christ returns to establish his eternal reign of life, justice and peace. Then God, Immanuel, will dwell with us, and the kingdom of the world will become the kingdom of our Lord and of his Christ and he shall reign for ever and ever.
>
> *A) Our participation in God's mission.* God calls his people to share his mission. The Church from all nations stands in continuity through the Messiah Jesus with God's people in the Old Testament. With them we have been called through Abraham and commissioned to be a blessing and a light to the nations. With them, we are to be shaped and taught through the law and the prophets to be a community of holiness, compassion and justice in a world of sin and suffering. We have been redeemed through the cross and

resurrection of Jesus Christ, and empowered by the Holy Spirit to bear witness to what God has done in Christ. The Church exists to worship and glorify God for all eternity and to participate in the transforming mission of God within history. Our mission is wholly derived from God's mission, addresses the whole of God's creation, and is grounded at its centre in the redeeming victory of the cross. This is the people to whom we belong, whose faith we confess and whose mission we share.

B) The integrity of our mission. The *source* of all our mission is what God has done in Christ for the redemption of the whole world, as revealed in the Bible. Our evangelistic task is to make that good news known to all nations. The *context* of all our mission is the world in which we live, the world of sin, suffering, injustice, and creational disorder, into which God sends us to love and serve for Christ's sake. All our mission must therefore reflect the integration of evangelism and committed engagement in the world, both being ordered and driven by the whole biblical revelation of the gospel of God.[2]

Because this is what being "missional" involves, I am pleased to commend this present volume to all who desire to be part of the mission of God.

INTRODUCTION

WHY THE WORLD REFORMED FELLOWSHIP SEEKS TO ENCOURAGE MISSIONAL THEOLOGY AND PRACTICE

SAMUEL T. LOGAN, JR.

Chris Wright, in his foreword, explained exactly what "missional" means—or more specifically, what it *should* mean to us. Armed with this new definition, I would now like to briefly describe why the World Reformed Fellowship (WRF) seeks to be missional. I will start my description by using what I call "The Parable of the Two Librarians." Of course, this parable is not inerrant or infallible. It is, however, historical.

Susan and I have had the privilege of spending four sabbaticals in Cambridge, England. During one of those sabbaticals, my research subject was the causes of theological change at Christ's College, one of the constituent colleges of Cambridge University. In 1590, Christ's College was one of the leading Puritan institutions in the world. By 1680, it was one of the leading latitudinarian institutions in the world. What happened?

In my research, I worked with two librarians—the librarian at Christ's College and the librarian at the "UL" (university library). The librarian at Christ's College acted as though it was his mission in life to protect the books at Christ's from people. Every time a person touched a book there was the chance of it being damaged, or at least of it acquiring dirt and grime from the hands touching the book. There was never an outright refusal to hand over a requested volume (so long as the request slip was completely accurate!). But there was a clear sense that he (and the library) would be much happier if I would just go away and let the books and other materials stay exactly as they had been for four hundred years.

The librarian at the UL, on the other hand, acted as though it was her mission in life to get the information in the books "out." When she discovered my research subject, she suggested materials for me to read that I didn't even know existed. She communicated a positive eagerness, that the question I was asking be answered. Now, she did take precautions—did she ever! I was not allowed to bring any writing instrument of any kind into the reading room; she provided #2 pencils and blank paper (this was years before laptops and iPads). I was never left alone with a manuscript; a librarian or sublibrarian was always present and always watching. But the sense one had was that the most important thing was the research—and that, to me at least, made all the difference.

I have come to believe that missional theology embodies the spirit of the UL librarian. Every kind of precaution imaginable is taken to preserve the precious and priceless original source material. But the ultimate goal is not preservation; it is propagation. More than anything else, we want to get the knowledge of Jesus as Savior and Lord "out," so that he receives the honor and worship that is his due.

Of course, even the best "missional librarians" may differ among themselves about both specific preservation measures and specific propagation strategies. But they will all agree that both are critically important, and they will all agree that there is no point in having the most magnificent library imaginable if it is inaccessible to everyone except the librarian himself. Just so, there are different perspectives presented in this volume— different perspectives on church unity and diversity, on missions and evangelism strategies, and on a whole host of other things. We see those different perspectives as enriching the whole, and yet it is critically important to remember that each of those perspectives is presented by an author who has affirmed both his or her personal commitment to one of the great historic Reformed creeds of the church and his or her personal commitment to the following WRF statement: "The Scriptures of the Old and New Testaments are the God-breathed Word of God, without error in all that it affirms."

Perhaps another parable, this one genuinely both inerrant and infallible, will further elucidate the motives of the WRF in the nature and the implications of our missional stance. This parable occurs at the end of Luke 15, but first we need some context.

In Luke 15:1–2, we read this: "Now the tax collectors and sinners were all drawing near to hear him [Jesus]. And the Pharisees and the scribes grumbled, saying, 'This man receives sinners and eats with them.'" Why all the grumbling?

We do need to be fair to the Pharisees and scribes. All through the Old Testament, God's people were urged to come out from amongst the pagans and be separate. For example, the first two chapters of the book of Judges describe God's anger when Israel mixed with the Canaanites. The Pharisees in Luke 15 are just reflecting that reality in their reaction to Jesus. For that matter, this grumbling isn't totally different from Peter's reaction when first invited to eat those wild and unclean animals—"'By no means, Lord; for I have never eaten anything that is common or unclean'" (Acts 10:14).

And we must not forget Luke's *inerrant* statement that these people with whom Jesus was spending time were sinners! There is a clear indication from the text that these people were *notorious and public sinners*. And yet, Jesus actually seems to welcome them, if not blatantly seek them out! This flew in the face of the Jewish culture of that time.

Behind the grumbling of the Pharisees lay many things—and some of them were anchored solidly in appropriate biblical tradition. Of course, in no way did Jesus's "receiving" and "eating with" sinners imply an endorsement of their sin. But it did reveal the essence of his way of responding to their sin. So, no matter how much theoretically good tradition might lie behind the grumbling, it was just that—grumbling.

In response to this grumbling, Jesus tells three parables—not three doctrinal postulates, nor three historical narratives, but three short stories.

Luke 15:3–7 is often called "The Parable of the Lost Sheep," but in light of the way the chapter begins, the better title would be "The Parable of the Seeking Shepherd." Verse six is the key: "And when he comes home, he calls together his friends and his neighbors, saying to them, 'Rejoice with me, for I have found my sheep that was lost.'" The point of this first story: This is just the kind of shepherd you would want if you were a lost sheep.

The parable in Luke 15:8–10 is often known as "The Parable of the Lost Coin," but perhaps a better title would be "The Parable of the Searching Woman." We can see this in verse nine: "And when she has found it, she calls together her friends and neighbors, saying, 'Rejoice with me, for I have found the coin that I had lost.'" The point of our second story, therefore: This is just the kind of owner you would want if you were a lost coin.

And now we come to one of the most famous parables in Scripture. Luke 15:11–32 is often called "The Parable of the Prodigal Son," but once more, in light of the way this chapter begins, the better title would be "The Parable of the Running Father." This time, our key is in verses 20–24.

> "And he [the Prodigal Son] arose and came to his father. But while he was still a long way off, his father saw him and felt compassion, and ran and embraced him and kissed him. And the son said to him, 'Father, I have sinned against heaven and before you. I am no longer worthy to be called your son.' But the father said to his servants, 'Bring quickly the best robe, and put it on him, and put a ring on his hand, and shoes on his feet. And bring the fattened calf and kill it, and let us eat and celebrate. For this my son was dead, and is alive again; he was lost, and is found.' And they began to celebrate."

The point of this third story? *That this is just the kind of father you would want if you were a disobedient and wayward child.*

All three of the stories in Luke 15 are about the person who seeks and carries and sweeps and searches and runs and rejoices, and all three are Jesus's response to the grumbling of the Pharisees. All three stories constitute Jesus's defense of the fact that he "receives sinners and eats with them," and all three stories describe the essence of why Jesus entered the world as the incarnate Son of God. All three of these stories, therefore, describe Jesus's "missional mission."

And the really neat thing is that these three parables are, *in themselves,* instances of fatherly running. The Pharisees grumble, and Jesus responds patiently with stories designed to help them change their grumbling to relishing so they, too, can participate in the family celebration—to help them see that these "sinners" are brothers who were thought to be dead and are now alive, sons who were lost and now are found. In this sense, therefore, in the Parable of the Running Father, the Incarnate Heavenly Father is running to meet the scribes and Pharisees—just as he had already run to meet sinners and tax collectors.

To what end? What did Jesus ultimately want to see happen in the lives of those scribes and Pharisees? Not just that they would cease their grumbling, not just that they would stop criticizing Jesus, but that they would join him in receiving and eating with sinners—to the end that sinners, including those very scribes and Pharisees themselves, might return to their Father and bring delight to his heart. As Martin Allen says in his chapter, "[The Father's] heart throbs and beats with compassion for the ends of the earth." Ours must, as well.

Yes, when one receives and eats with sinners—or when one encourages the (careful) use of centuries-old manuscripts—one engages in behavior which can be (and, far more frequently, can be seen *as being*) dangerous. But what counts is the mission—in the one case, the mission of getting the knowledge in the manuscripts out; and in the far more important case, the mission of maximizing the delight of the Father.

At the WRF General Assembly in Edinburgh in 2010, a new Statement of Faith was received by the members. (The statement is available, in numerous languages, at www.wrfnet.org.) Questions have been raised about the need for such a statement, and some explanations are provided in Andrew McGowan's introduction to the statement. But there is a missional reason for the statement as well. When most of the great historical Reformed confessions were written, the part of the world those confessions sought to serve was considered "Christendom," at least in a broad sense. One searches in vain for the words "mission," "missions," or "evangelism" in such documents as The Westminster Confession of Faith, The Thirty-Nine Articles, The Canons of Dordt, or The Heidelberg Catechism. Those documents focused almost entirely on differentiating Protestant, Reformed Christianity from other Christian churches. The world has changed since those documents were written.

Of course, as Chris Wright has reminded us, "missional" is not synonymous with "missions," or even with "evangelism." But there is an outward face to all of these words—a sense of going out to the world as the running father went to his prodigal son. And that is one main reason for the WRF Statement of Faith: to provide an outward perspective within historic Reformed orthodoxy. The entirety of Section Ten of the Statement ("Mission and evangelism") expresses that outward face, and its specific subsections express well some of the things involved in that outward, missional face:

1. Our calling to be God's witnesses through word and deed
2. The extent of the call to mission
3. The compassion of Christians for the world
4. The transformation of human community

To a significant degree, the present book seeks to give concrete expression to these affirmations.

We start the book with three discussions of the theological foundations of the "outward, missional face" of Reformed theology. We classify these chapters as "Laying the Foundation." We then move to the second section, "The Church Reaches the World." It is here that we explore in greatest detail some of the things that might be involved if the church, and Christians in the church, become serious about living out what Jesus teaches us in The Parable of the Running Father.

The e-book version of this collection (available at newgrowthpress .com) includes an additional section, "Building the Church." This section talks more directly about the church itself, and especially about the thorny problem of what to do when one perceives that his or her church is abandoning its biblical foundations and the complex scriptural teaching regarding church unity.

The book concludes by pulling all these concerns together in Andrew McGowan's "Crafting an Evangelical, Reformed, and Missional Theology for the Twenty-First Century." In all of this, we are seeking to describe how—and why—to be both missional and Reformed.

I have had the privilege for the past couple of years to work as special counsel to the president at Biblical Seminary in Hatfield, Pennsylvania. That institution has, as its vision statement, "Following Jesus into the World." The world can be a frightening place. It is a place of secularism and relativism; it is a place where sexual abuse and child abuse occur; it is a place of pain and poverty and disease; it is a place of sexual dysfunction. It is the kind of place to which Jesus came, and we do him honor as we follow him into that world.

This is what the WRF seeks to do, and it is what this book seeks to do.

Section One
Laying the Foundation

1.

WHAT A MISSIONAL CHURCH LOOKS LIKE

MARTIN ALLEN

What does church look like? There are, of course, different levels at which we can answer this question, just as there are many different dimensions of possible answers—as future chapters in this volume will reveal.

My grandchildren, ages ten and seven, answer this question at a very elementary level. When sitting at the meal table with us, they often point to a model building resting on the kitchen windowsill beside them. The model is made of wool; it was a gift to me upon retirement, two and a half years ago. When they point at it, it is a cue for us to say all together, "There's the church, there's the steeple, open the door and there's the people!"

I would guess that in many cultures, and certainly in Scotland's, it is at this most elementary level that most would answer the question, "What does a church look like?"—in terms of a traditional building, with a familiar shape. But *you* know what question is really being asked: What are the marks of a true Christian church? And, in keeping with the theme of this volume: What are the marks of a truly *missional* Christian church?

Our initial question was a very important one at the time of the Scottish Reformation, and the answer the Reformers and others came up with have been passed down the centuries. It is still one of the most quoted answers to the question today, some 450 years later. What are the marks, the "notae," of any true Christian church? According to the popularly worded historical reply, there are three such marks:

1. the proper preaching of the gospel;
2. the proper administration of the sacraments; and
3. the proper use of discipline.

But for many Christians, it has always been puzzling that a fourth mark was omitted from this standard statement passed down the ages. For, according to the directive of the Lord Jesus, there is surely an additional mark which appears to be a primary and predominant characteristic of a true church—namely, *the proper engagement in mission*.

Indeed, one New Testament commentator, writing on Acts 1, says "the church does not have a mission, it *is* a mission!"[1] That is to say: Mission, evangelism, and witness is of the essence of the true Christian church, for Christ the king and head of the church, in Acts 1:8, says this to the first representatives of his church, "you will be my witnesses in Jerusalem, and in all Judea and Samaria, and to the ends of the earth" (NIV 1984).

So what does a church look like, according to our Lord Jesus? Well, it looks like it's on the move—on the move to the outskirts of the community in which it is placed and ultimately, in principle, to the ends of the earth. On the move, that is to say, in mission, witness, and evangelism. A mark of the true Christian church is its commitment to Christian mission.

And it's not as though the words of Acts 1:8 were a singular mandate for mission in the New Testament. Luke has already underlined this principle in his first book, the Gospel of Luke. He reminds us in verse 1, "In my former book, Theophilus, I wrote about all that Jesus began to do and to teach" (NIV 1984). The word "book" should, perhaps, be more accurately rendered as "account," "narrative," or "installment." This gives us the hint that Luke sees himself as writing only one book about Jesus, but in two parts, and that there is the clearest possible overlap between parts one and two of this book. Part two of

Luke's book, then, begins, "you will be my witnesses" (Acts 1:8, NIV 1984), just as part one ended, "You are witnesses of these things" (Luke 24:48, NIV 1984).

What things? Well, the things to which the Lord has just opened their minds: "Then he opened their minds so they could understand the Scriptures. He told them, 'This is what is written: The Christ will suffer and rise from the dead on the third day, and repentance and forgiveness of sins will be preached in his name to all nations, beginning at Jerusalem. You are witnesses of these things'" (Luke 24:45–48, NIV 1984). This is, in effect, another statement of the Lord's authorization of the mission of his church.

Additionally, we have the apostle John's record toward the end of his Gospel of Jesus commissioning the disciples. On the evening of the day of the resurrection, our Lord says, "'As the Father has sent me, I am sending you.' And with that he breathed on them and said, 'Receive the Holy Spirit. If you forgive anyone his sins, they are forgiven; if you do not forgive them, they are not forgiven'" (John 20:21–23, NIV 1984). It is probably best to understand these words as an acted parable that can be linked with Acts 1:8 and point ahead to the Day of Pentecost. For on that day, the Spirit-filled apostle Peter bore witness to a message that held out forgiveness for those who responded by repentance and public faith (Acts 2:38). Here, then, is yet another charge concerning mission, directly the lips of our Lord.

And supremely, there is in the New Testament what has become known as the Great Commission of our Lord, recorded by Matthew at the end of his Gospel. Just six words in the original language of Matthew 28:19: "Going therefore, disciple all the nations." Again, Acts 1:8 is no singular mandate for mission, but one which continually echoes Jesus's own mandate to his disciples.

"The church *is* mission." In Acts 1:8, Luke underlines that the task of bearing witness and making disciples begins on our own doorstep, namely, in our own "Jerusalem." Therefore, we are faced with certain implications and forced to respond to certain questions with respect to our churches and localities today. For example:

- Is mission a conspicuous mark of the church today?
- Does a missional mentality prioritize our energies, or is a maintenance mind-set more or less in total control of our congregational agendas?
- Do we largely operate with what is sometimes referred to as the Old Testament idea of mission—namely, waiting for the outsiders to come in to us—rather than the New Testament model of going out to them?
- Is there a reluctance nowadays—yes, even a deep-seated aversion—for church membership to engage in door-knocking, visiting, contacting, relating to, identifying with and getting alongside non-church members in the name of Christ and for the gospel's sake?

The late church historian D. F. Wright, in his last published writing, asked, "Why is it in Scotland that we have churches, which are biblical and orthodox to a fault, but evangelistically quite ineffective, yet keen supporters of overseas missions?"[2]

In recent years, there has been an upsurge in new studies of the modern era in the United Kingdom by a number of secular historians. A. N. Wilson, Peter Hennessy, David Kynaston, Andrew Marr, Andy Beckett, T. M. Devine and others have and are engaging in creating detailed, lengthy volumes dealing with the last forty-plus years of social and political life in this country. In most, if not all, of these surveys there is virtually no reference to the Christian church—at all! The lack of comment is particularly striking in Devine's seminal work, *The Scottish Nation 1700-2000*. It is as though the Church of Scotland, in particular, is a nonentity whose significance is virtually non-existent—at least in the eyes of these analysts! What a contrast with the times of the Scottish Reformation. Harry Reid, in his recently published book *Reformation—The Dangerous Birth of the Modern World*, argues quite effectively that those times experienced the massive public impact and influence of a church "on the move" in mission and outreach.[3]

Where today is to be found the missionary passion of a man like John Knox who, we are told, consistently climbed the stairs up to his little bedroom in his house on the Royal Mile in Edinburgh, got down on his knees, and in unwearied intercession cried out to almighty God, "Give me Scotland or I die!" Where is such passion today—in Scotland, the United States, or anywhere else in the West? A mark of the church? It is its *mission*! This seems clear about the church of Acts 1:8.

But, pushing the application of this text a bit further, *what are the marks of the church's mission*? At least four need to be highlighted.

1. This mission is essentially *the work of Christ*.

"You will be *my* witnesses." It is *Christ's* mission! This is a very elementary point to which Luke surely alerts us in the opening verse of the Acts to which I have already referred: "In my former book, Theophilus, I wrote about all that Jesus began to do and to teach until the day he was taken up to heaven." The clear implication is that Jesus, having begun his work in the Gospel, is carrying it on in the Acts.

There are some twenty-eight references in the book of the Acts to the Lord Jesus initiating activity in the lives of other people. Throughout the book of Acts, the Lord himself is cited as being the primary "actor." Most famous, of course, is the narrative in chapter nine, which describes the appearance of Lord Jesus to Saul of Tarsus on the Damascus road. There, Jesus confronted Saul, humbled him, and called him to be led helplessly into the city and submit to the instructions he would receive—and the rest, as they say, is history!

And so, the Lord is continuing to do and teach from heaven what he began to do and teach on earth. The church's mission is essentially the work of Christ.

And the simple lesson for us? First of all, we must *never* give up on the church. We must *never* despair of the church. And we must never do so because it is Christ's church, to which our Lord Jesus Christ has bound himself with his life-giving Spirit. The Lord declared while on earth, "'I will build my church, and the gates of hell shall not prevail against it'" (Matthew 16:18). And that building of the church, despite hell's opposition, is a main theme of the story of Acts.

In the mission of the church today, we must keep our eye firmly fixed on the church's builder. Our perspective should be framed by the nonnegotiable truths concerning Jesus alluded to in Luke's opening section of in the Acts, namely the following:

- He is risen—he "gave many convincing proofs that he was alive" (Acts 1:3, NIV 1984).
- He is reigning—"He appeared to them over a period of forty days and spoke about the kingdom of God" (Acts 1:3, NIV 1984).
- He is returning—"This same Jesus, who has been taken from you into heaven, will come back" (Acts 1:11, NIV 1984)

We must never give up on the church and its mission—because both are the work of Christ.

2. This mission involves *witness to Christ*. "You will be my *witnesses*." The word "witness" is used thirteen times in the book of Acts and always with the precise sense of giving a public eyewitness account of the story of Jesus. The term is almost a legal concept in Acts. Whenever we read the word "witness" in Acts, we should be thinking "witness box." We should be thinking: hand on Bible, to "tell the truth, the whole truth and nothing but the truth, so help me, God!" We are dealing with a public act of witness, by particular eyewitnesses. Acts 1:8 could perhaps be paraphrased, "You apostles should be my eyewitnesses in Jerusalem and in all Judea and Samaria, and to the ends of the earth."

So, what happened after the first eyewitnesses died? The wording on John Wesley's gravestone is appropriate: "God buries his workmen, but carries on his work!" God's work goes out to the ends of the earth and down to the end of the age (Acts 1:11). The apostles are dead and buried, but the church in every age clearly has had a lot of work to do. The primary reference in verse 8 is to the apostles' witness. The secondary reference is to all who follow them—the Christian church, down the centuries to the present time.

Therefore, we have a job to do. It is not to tell our story, but to tell their story—that is, the story of the eyewitnesses. Our job is to tell the world precisely what the eyewitnesses said and what the eyewitnesses preached. So, what was their story?

"You will be my witnesses." Literally, the text reads, "witnesses *of* me"; we might say more precisely, "witnesses *to* me." Christ himself is the great subject matter of the church's mission.

This is illustrated most clearly in Peter's sermon on the day of Pentecost, recorded in Acts 2. To be sure, this is a unique sermon that cannot be copied and repeated. Some sermons can be repeated—and are! But not the Pentecostal sermon. Only once in history could a preacher say to a congregation, "This man was handed over to you by God's set purpose and foreknowledge; and you, with the help of wicked men, put him to death by nailing him to the cross" (Acts 2:23, NIV 1984). It was a once-in-a-lifetime sermon in salvation history. And yet it is also a timeless sermon *for* church history.

New Testament scholar Chris Green writes, "Here in Acts 2 Peter preaches the first sermon of the Christian church as a *representative* sermon, starting at Jerusalem."[4] Our world needs more sermons like this one! For this representative Pentecostal sermon is strikingly Christ-centered in content. Obviously, we only have notes and headings of the sermon recorded here in the book of Acts. That must be the case; otherwise Peter's preaching on the Day of Pentecost would have lasted about three and a half minutes! We are told in verse 40 that "With many other words he warned them" (NIV 1984). While we have only notes from the sermon, those notes make it clear that its subject, from beginning to end, was Jesus.

Peter began by highlighting the Jesus of history, with the words, "Men of Israel, listen to this: Jesus of Nazareth..." (Acts 2:22, NIV 1984). Peter starts with Jesus in and of history, and this is precisely where the church's missional message must begin today. There is a massive cluelessness in contemporary society about the Jesus of history. People around us in Edinburgh or Philadelphia or Sao Paulo or Seoul or even Nairobi are likely to know more about *Jesus Christ Superstar* than Jesus Christ of Nazareth!

Peter's Pentecostal sermon begins with Jesus, and then goes on to explain his work in history in four stages: Jesus's life and ministry (v. 22); his suffering and death (v. 23); his triumph and resurrection (vv. 24–32); and finally, his exaltation and reign (vv. 33–36). Peter's sermon gives the explanation of Jesus in history, and then the application of the same Jesus to the human hearts right there in front of him: "'Repent and be baptized, every one of you, in the name of Jesus Christ for the forgiveness of your sins. And you will receive the gift of the Holy Spirit'" (Acts 2:38, NIV 1984).

We need missional sermons like this today—sermons which describe the Jesus of history and then, and only then, apply that Jesus to the hearts of those listening. The church's mission, therefore, involves witness to Christ.

3. This mission requires *a warrant from Christ*. Jesus speaks about this warrant or empowering in Acts 1:8, "You will receive power when the Holy Spirit comes on you; and you will be my witnesses..." (NIV 1984). This empowering is called a baptism (v. 5); it is referred to by the Lord as a gift promised by the Father (v. 4); and its fulfillment clearly occurred on the day of Pentecost (v. 5). And on that day, Peter states that in heaven, the Father's gift is first handed to the Son, who in turn gives it to his people to empower their witness: "Exalted to the right hand of God, he [the Son] has received from the Father the promised Holy Spirit and has poured out what you now see and hear" (Acts 2:33, NIV 1984). Thus, the gift is indispensable. This mission requires a warrant from Christ.

The Holy Spirit is mentioned fifty-two times in the book of Acts. The references do not occur uniformly throughout the book, but in clusters. Chapter 1 represents one such cluster. While there is some debate as to the work of the Holy Spirit in Acts, it does seem to be the case that each cluster of references indicates the link between the Spirit and mission, either directly or indirectly. Consequently, the Spirit brings power to the church in mission. One scholar, James Read, writes, "In Acts it is as the Spirit exercises transforming power within the church, that He empowers her for witness outside the church as a light to the nations."[5]

So the good news is: In mission, the church is not cast upon its own resources for success. We are *not* dependent upon our own ingenuity, creativity, or communicating skills. We are *not* reliant on the quality of our strategies, programs, and novel enterprises. We are *not* putting our trust in charismatic personalities, dynamic leadership, and the "gift of gab"—the ability to be eloquent and to talk and talk and talk! We don't pin our hopes, ultimately, on anything of the human and the earthly, but rather the divine and the heavenly. Our only hope for empowering for Christ's mission is Christ and the gift of his Spirit.

We express this hope, confidence, trust, reliance, and dependence preeminently in the activity of prayer, and sometimes prayer along with fasting. It is no coincidence that the promise of power in verse 8 is followed closely by the description of the church in verse 14, "They all joined together constantly in prayer" (NIV 1984).

Does the church in our day "major" on prayer in its mission to the world? One preacher of a former era is reported as saying, "Preaching without prayer is like a sword without a cutting edge, a fire without flame, a well without water, a corpse without life. Such preaching may please the intellect and entertain the hearers, but it will never save sinners, or slake the thirst of sin-sick souls."

Is the empowering of the Spirit for preachers only? Surely not! On the day of Pentecost, Peter begins his message by quoting the prophet Joel's words, "'In the last days, God says, I will pour out my Spirit on all people. Your sons and daughters will prophesy... Even on my servants... and they will prophesy'" (Acts 2:17–18, NIV 1984). "Prophesy" surely refers to the Old Testament sense of God making himself known in his Word. And in this sense all God's people, all Christian believers, are now prophets and evangelists. Christian believers come to know God through his Word, and as believers they make God known by his Word.

How are our nations to be evangelized? Solely through crusade evangelists, professional clergy, and pulpit preachers? No! By all God's people—that is, by individual believers, through the power of the Spirit, finding their evangelistic tongues! That's how it was in the Acts of the Apostles. "Those who had been scattered preached the word wherever they went" (Acts 8:4, NIV 1984). In other words, they "gossiped the gospel" in the ordinary networks and relationships of weekly life. Thus it has always been, in times of growth for the church.

Bengt Sundkler and Christopher Stead, in their important study *A History of the Church in Africa*, observe, "The new convert did not keep the discovery for individual consumption, but took the message to others. Thus it was that the message could spread as ripples on the water."[6] Ripples on the water—what a powerful description of the missional church!

But the mission begins with a warrant from Christ. At Pentecost, one sermon resulted in 3,000 converts—that's power. And yes, it does seem nowadays that in many Western countries it takes about 3,000 sermons to get just one convert! But it was not always so. The year 2009 marked the 150th anniversary of the 1859 revival in Scotland, when about 300,000 people professed faith in Christ and joined the Christian church in one year. *That* is missional power!

The church's mission is essentially the work of Christ. It involves witness to Christ, and requires a warrant from Christ.

4. This mission *embraces the world for Christ*. "You will be my witnesses in Jerusalem, and in all Judea and Samaria, and to the ends of the earth." Many have pointed out that Acts 1:8 is a key for understanding Luke's structure of the unfolding story of the church's mission in the rest of the book: chapters 1–7 describe events in Jerusalem; chapters 8–12 outline, among other things, the spread of the gospel in Judea and Samaria; and chapters 13–28 record Paul's missionary expeditions and his journey to Rome, "the eternal city"—from the ancient perspective, the center for the "ends of the earth."

So, God is on the move to the ends of the earth! That's one way of grasping the story of Acts. Luke gives us several summary statements about the spread of the church's mission. Interestingly, each summary statement appears to mark some particular stage of outreach being accomplished before the next stage of expansion is described:

> "And the word of God continued to increase, and the number of the disciples multiplied greatly in Jerusalem" (Acts 6:7).
>
> "So the church throughout all Judea and Galilee and Samaria had peace" (Acts 9:31).

"But the word of God increased and multiplied" (Acts 12:24).

"So the churches were strengthened in the faith, and they increased in numbers daily" (Acts 16:5).

"So the word of the Lord continued to increase and prevail mightily" (Acts 19:20).

"proclaiming the kingdom of God and teaching about the Lord Jesus Christ with all boldness and without hindrance" (Acts 28:31).

And as some like to put it, "Acts 29"—the ongoing mission of the church—then begins, as we join God on his way to the ends of the earth! We continue our witness in this "day" of mission until the great and final day of the Lord's coming.

John Wesley famously said, "The world is my parish." Is it mine and yours? It should be! It *must* be! John Stott wrote, "Mission is the global outreach of a global people of a global God."[7] Is this our view of mission? It should be! It *must* be! This mission embraces a world for Christ.

Some missiologists have pointed out a basic pattern in the story of Acts, which has been repeated to some extent throughout the history of the church. The pattern is as follows: The gospel cause flourishes, and then decays, in the heartlands. And so the gospel is taken to the margins and flourishes there—and so the margins become the heartlands. In Scotland the gospel once flourished as the heartlands— "the land of the book," it was called. But in this land (and in Europe and in North America), there has been decay and declension in the heartlands. The gospel cause, then, moved to the so-called margins of the globe and has flourished there—in parts of South America, Africa, and Asia— to such an extent that in our time, we surely recognize that these are thrilling days for Christian people to be alive in this world.

Some two years ago, *The* (London) *Times* carried a seven-page article on the spread of the Christian gospel and church in China. The writer provided the statistical "guesstimate" that there are now more members of the Christian church in China (one hundred million) than there are members of the Communist party (seventy-five million). So the word of God has spread!

David Smith, in his book on world mission *Against the Stream*, underlined the fact that at the 1910 World Missionary Conference in Edinburgh, there was not a single representative from Africa present. He then told of an extended visit to western Africa in 2002 and of his preaching in a church in Bukuru, in western Nigeria. The service involved dynamic worship, with more than a thousand present. However, at one point, they sang a Victorian hymn from the Sankey song book, which made reference to "the heathen far away." Smith says that he and his colleague began to shake with laughter at the sheer incongruity of it. And yet as he reflected, in modern Africa today the words *do* make sense, for the heathen are indeed far away—in London, New York, and Berlin![8]

So, from the church in these and similar places, there may arise a new Macedonian call to the church in China and Uganda and Nigeria, "Come over and help us." How we need this help! And how powerfully such help would fulfill the goal of the World Reformed Fellowship—"that the strengths of some might become the strengths of all in the service of Jesus Christ."

As Sam Logan suggested in the introduction to this volume, a missional church is one which runs into the world in the name of and for the sake of Christ. "The world for Christ we sing, the world to Christ we bring." So, returning to our opening question, what does such a church look like? Well, it looks a little like the Lord of the church—that "running Father" of Luke 15 whose heart throbs and beats with compassion for those at "the ends of the earth."

2.

WHAT'S THE POINT IN BELIEVING AND DOING THE RIGHT THINGS?

A Missional, "Edwardsean" Approach to Orthodox Belief and Moral Behavior

SAMUEL T. LOGAN, JR.

One of the first major projects of the World Reformed Fellowship was the production of a Statement of Faith, in which we sought to affirm the core of historic Reformed orthodoxy as we shape our understanding of, and response to, uniquely twenty-first century challenges. Even as we maintain our faithfulness to orthodoxy, however, we must keep an equally strong emphasis on "living out" our theology—an emphasis on acting upon what we believe.

Indeed, the more one talks about "missional theology" and "the missional church," the more one bumps up against one of the "stickiest wickets" in all of Reformed theology—the relationship between orthodox belief and moral behavior, often explained in terms of a perceived tension between biblical teaching on justification and sanctification.

This conundrum lay at the heart of the very first full-fledged theological debate on American soil—the antinomian controversy—and it continues to haunt Reformed communities today.[1] Before we move to discuss some specific "missional" applications of Reformed theology, we should take time to consider a way of getting at the essential issues in this debate, which may provide just enough of an explanation to allow us to proceed.

Do I have the answers to all the questions about the relationship between faith and good works? Of course not. But I do believe that one American Reformed theologian points us in a helpful direction, and it is his way of getting at the problem that I'd like us to briefly examine. Jonathan Edwards wrote some of the most profound theological treatises the church possesses. However, he was also a leading participant in the greatest revival America has ever known; a missionary to the Indians of western Massachusetts; and, all too briefly, president of one of the first great American colleges, the College of New Jersey, now known as Princeton University. I would suggest that it was precisely because he was *all* of these things, that he was able and qualified to make theological explanations that can address the issue before us.

One of the most fundamental of all theological questions, both in Edwards's day and in our own, is this one: *What makes a person a Christian?* Understood correctly, this question captures the heart of the debate about the relationship between justification and sanctification, and at the same time gets at the heart of some of the most trenchant fears about "the missional movement." Further, understood correctly, this question addresses directly the question I have posed in the title of this chapter, "What's the Point in Believing and Doing the Right Things?" Finally, this question captures the essence of what Edwards was seeking to express in all of his theology and ministry.

The question "What makes a person a Christian?" must be understood and appreciated in at least these two syntactical senses: 1) What, ontologically, causes a person to become a Christian? And, 2) how is a person recognized as being a Christian?

With regard to the first of these, what is it that moves a person from spiritual death to spiritual life? What moves him from being a member of the kingdom of darkness to being a member of the kingdom of God? Or, to frame the question in terms that most interested Edwards, who gets the credit for the change? The question is not about influences or contexts or missions or evangelism; it is about the specific power which causes the change. Most fundamentally, the question is this: does man cause the change, or does God cause the change?

With regard to the second sense of our question, what are the signs that a person is a Christian? Or, again to frame the question in Edwards's terms, what *must be* the characteristics of a person who claims that she is a Christian? Does it really matter how the person lives? To anticipate later chapters in this volume, does it matter if the person cares for the sick (Susan Post's chapter) or ministers to the poor (Flip Buys) or seeks to end child abuse (Boz Tchividjian)? And if it does matter, how and why does it matter? Is missional living in any sense the *cause* of a person's salvation? And if it is not the cause, is it important at all?

FROM JUSTIFICATION TO AWAKENING

"In the Fall of 1734," writes Edwards in his introduction to *A Faithful Narrative of the Surprising Work of God*, "began the great noise in this part of the country, about Arminianism, which seemed to appear with a very threatening aspect upon the interest of religion here."[2] Edwards then goes on to add that, because of this "noise," "There were some things said publicly on that occasion, concerning justification by faith alone."[3] Those "things said publicly" were, in fact, Edwards's own sermons, which were later collected into what we now regard as Edwards's treatise on justification by faith alone.

Edwards's justification treatise has appropriately received extensive attention; I will not try here to deal with all of the intricacies of that treatise. It is important, however, to recognize that Edwards was deeply concerned about the relationship between belief and behavior from the earliest years of his ministry; he was thirty-one years of age when he preached those 1734 sermons on justification. But it was not until 1746, at the ripe old age of 43, that he came to his final answer to the question, what makes a person a Christian?

Between 1734 and 1746, the American colonies experienced revival and awakening on an unprecedented scale and Edwards was himself at the heart of much that happened. The church went through extraordinary spiritual upheaval during that decade, the likes of which it remains difficult to discover in any other similar period in our nation's history. I am not sure that those of us who talk about the great spiritual changes taking place in our day fully appreciate the magnitude of some of the spiritual changes that occurred in earlier days. Christopher Hill, in *The World Turned Upside Down* (1972), presents a strong case that the 1640s in England was the most crucial decade in determining the religious and political shape of the modern Anglo-American world; Bernard Bailyn's Pulitzer prize-winning book *The Ideological Origins of the American Revolution* makes a similarly powerful case about the period between 1740 and 1776 in the American colonies.

The primary occasion for the upheaval was the Great Awakening, a series of revivals which swept the colonies in what was probably the first "national event" in America's history. From Maine to Georgia, preachers saw hundreds, even thousands, of people professing faith in Jesus Christ, testifying that they had become Christians. On one occasion in October of 1742, the evangelist George Whitefield is said to have preached to a crowd of 30,000 on the Boston Common—and at that time Boston, the largest city in the colonies, had a total population of only 10,000!

But as so often happens during periods of spiritual intensity, reports of the experiences of those impacted by the Awakening became more and more extreme as the years passed; this made the identification of "genuinely gracious" experiences increasingly difficult and increasingly important. In numerous sermons and treatises during the late 1730s and the early 1740s, Edwards worked toward his final position on the correct relationship between orthodox belief and moral behavior, framing his concerns more and more precisely. We first get a glimpse of Edwards's mature position at the very beginning of Part IV of his "Thought on the Revival" (1742): "If we look back into the history of the church of God in past ages, we may observe that it has been a common device of the devil, to overset a revival of religion; when he finds that he can keep men quiet and secure no longer, then he drives them to excesses and extravagances."[4] This observation then becomes the foundation of all that Edwards has to say in his most important work, *A Treatise Concerning Religious Affections*.

EDWARDS: *A TREATISE CONCERNING RELIGIOUS AFFECTIONS*

Published in 1746, the same year in which the college Edwards would lead briefly in the last year of his life was founded, the *Affections* builds extensively on what Edwards had said before. As in "Thoughts on the Revival," Edwards begins the *Affections* by identifying the most serious problem facing the Christian church: "It is by the mixture of counterfeit religion with true, not discerned and distinguished, that the devil has had his greatest advantage against the cause and kingdom of Christ. It is plainly by this means, principally, that he has prevailed against all revivals of religion, since the first founding of the Christian church."[5]

Edwards then sets himself the task, in this his most significant work, of separating the genuine from the counterfeit: "Therefore, it greatly concerns us to use our utmost endeavors, clearly to discern, and have it well settled and established, wherein true religion does consist. … What I aim at now, is to show the nature and signs of the gracious operations of God's Spirit, by which they are to be distinguished from all things whatsoever which are not of a saving nature."[6]

By framing the issue as he does, Edwards asserts a vitally important principle—that the *nature* of the operations of God's Spirit and the *signs* of the operations of God's Spirit are directly related. To put it in the terms of the question with which we began this discussion, what causes a person to *be* a Christian and what signs *identify* a Christian are inextricably related. In making this claim, Edwards, in effect, asserts an essential unity between justification and sanctification—a unity which neither the justification disputants in the 1630s in Boston nor many modern justification disputants seem to have fully understood and appreciated. Nonetheless, it was a unity which provided Edwards with the foundation for both his Reformed theologizing and his missional preaching and evangelizing.

The ground of this unity resides in the very nature of that which defines every person's "true religion," whether that religion is Christian or not, and to that discussion Edwards turns immediately in Part 1 of the *Affections*. In fact, what Edwards actually does in Part 1 is offer a definition of personhood, not in the sense of distinguishing a human being from a being that would not be called human but in terms of identifying exactly who any individual person actually *is*.

Understood in this way, Part 1 of the *Affections* sets a mammoth agenda. Some may question whether Edwards fully accomplishes his agenda here, but without doubt he lays an anthropological foundation based directly upon his understanding of Scripture. He then proceeds, in Parts 2 and 3 of the *Affections*, to build upon that foundation his full and final answer to the question: What makes a person a Christian?

As he builds his case in Part 1, Edwards takes into account all manner of earlier philosophical and theological arguments about human identity. Norman Fiering's study remains the best analysis of the scope of this ideological background of the *Affections*.[7] Stated simply, Edwards is asking the question, what is it that makes me who I am? In effect, Edwards considers commonly affirmed answers and rejects them. I am not, argues Edwards, defined solely by what I think (though what I think is very important). Neither am I defined solely by what I feel or do (though both of these are very important). To anticipate where Edwards is going with this argument—neither right thoughts alone (orthodox theology), right experiences alone (religious passion), nor right actions alone (moral behavior) make me a Christian in *any* sense.

Many who have read Part 1 of the *Affections* with great sympathy wish that Edwards had spent the time on this section that he did on similar issues in *Freedom of the Will*. Part 1 of the *Affections* needed more explication in order to make its arguments watertight. Edwards himself seems to have sensed that Part 1 could have been clearer: "It must be confessed, that language is here somewhat imperfect, and the meaning of words in a considerable measure loose and unfixed, and not precisely limited by custom, which governs the use of language."[8]

But whatever its problems, Part 1 certainly did not need anything more to make Edwards's fundamental argument crystal-clear. If we do not identify a person solely by what she thinks, by what she feels, by what she does, how *do* we identify that person? In the language of the book from which Edwards took his fundamental insight, we identify a person solely by what she "seeks first" (see Matthew 6:28–33). What that person seeks first, Edwards calls that person's "affections." Further, Edwards goes on to argue, *one's religion, whatever that religion, is always defined by one's affections.*

> What has been said of the nature of the affections makes this evident, and may be sufficient, without adding anything further, to put this matter out of doubt; for who will deny that true religion consists in a great measure, in vigorous and lively actings of the inclination and will of the soul, or the fervent exercises of the heart?
>
> That religion which God requires, and will accept, does not consist in weak, dull, and lifeless wishes, raising us but a little above a state of indifference: God, in his word, greatly insists upon it, that we be good in earnest, "fervent in spirit," and our hearts vigorously engaged in religion: Rom. 12:11, "Be ye fervent in spirit, serving the Lord." Deut. 10:12, "And now, Israel, what doth the Lord thy God require of thee, but to fear the Lord thy God, to walk in all his ways, and to love him, and to serve the Lord thy God with all thy heart, and with all thy soul?" and chap. 6:4, 6, "Hear, O Israel, the Lord our God is one Lord: And thou shalt love the Lord thy God with all thy heart, and with all thy might." It is such a fervent vigorous engagedness of the heart in religion, that is the fruit of a real circumcision of the heart, or true regeneration, and that has the promises of life; Deut. 30:6, "And the Lord thy God will circumcise thine heart, and the heart of thy seed, to love the Lord thy God with all thy heart, and with all thy soul, that thou mayest live."[9]

In other words, when we ask what makes a person a Christian, in either of the senses above, we are asking about what a person seeks first. Edwards addresses how this works indirectly in Part 2 of the *Affections,* and then directly in Part 3.

In the course of my teaching career, I have frequently been asked what I think about this or that religious phenomenon. For example, about twenty-five years ago, the following was a regular question:

"How should we view the Toronto Blessing?" I won't try to name more recent such phenomena about which I have been asked, lest I unnecessarily raise red flags with readers. But whenever I have been asked such a question, my response has always been the same: "Go read, or re-read, Part 2 of Edwards's *Treatise on Religious Affections*. See what you think that material has to say to the question, and come back and we will talk specifically." This answer was not entirely intended to give me time to prepare an answer that was helpful rather than hurtful, though it *was* that. This answer also reflected my conviction that no one has ever done a better job than Edwards does in Part 2 of identifying the factors which *are* often used to make such decisions but which *never* should be.

This, of course, has most often been the problem in justification debates and in other debates about the nature of the Christian life and the nature of the church. If Edwards's ultimate goal in the *Affections* was to provide guidelines for detecting "counterfeit Christianity," in Part 2 of the *Affections* Edwards could be said to be discussing "counterfeit counterfeit detectors." Applied to the specific historical context in which he was writing, Part 2 examines many things on which both proponents and opponents of the Awakening were focusing attention, but which really were no signs one way or the other with regard to the genuineness of the Awakening.

That is, in fact, the title of Part 2: "Showing What Are No Certain Signs That Religious Affections Are Truly Gracious, Or That They Are Not." In this material, Edwards lists twelve such "non-signs." Whether the affair in question is the Toronto Blessing, the activities of Anne Hutchinson, or any one of a number of more recent controversial phenomena, the presence or absence of these twelve things does absolutely nothing to help us decide whether the particular phenomenon is, as Edwards would say, "genuinely gracious." The presence or absence of these twelve things reveals absolutely nothing about what is being "sought first" within the phenomena in question.

For example, "It is no sign that affections have the nature of true religion, or that they have not, that they have great effects on the body."[10] And this means, on the one hand, that "Great effects on the body certainly are no sure evidences that affections are spiritual; for we see that such effects oftentimes arise from great affections about temporal things, and when religion is no way concerned in them. And if great affections about secular things, that are purely natural, may have these effects, I know not by what rule we should determine that high affections about religious things, which arise in like manner from nature, cannot have the like effect."[11] But Edwards quickly adds: "Nor, on the other hand, do I know of any rule any have to determine, that gracious and holy affections, when raised as high as any natural affections, and have equally strong and vigorous exercises, cannot have a great effect on the body."[12]

In some ways, this may seem obvious. But the church, both in Edwards's day and ours, still needs the lesson. For example, what one does or doesn't do with one's hands in worship is too often taken as a sure sign of genuine spirituality. Those whose worship is enthusiastic often interpret the stillness of other worshipers as a sure sign of spiritual deadness. Conversely, those whose worship embodies "decency and good order" often interpret the raised hands and clapping of other worshipers as mindless passion. Neither interpretation is necessarily correct. Stillness and quietness in worship may occur in the context of spiritual deadness, but it may also occur in the context of deep and profound reverence. Raised hands and clapping may occur in the context of mindless passion, but it may also occur in the context of fervent worship of the one true God.

But what exactly does this have to do with orthodox belief and moral behavior, let alone missionality? One connection goes back to the twofold question with which we started: what makes a person a Christian? At the very least, the relevance of this non-sign to the second sense of that question is clear. We cannot tell *for certain* whether a person actually is a Christian by the bodily activity (or lack thereof) of that person in worship.

But regarding the first sense of the question, do the non-signs identified by Edwards have any relation to the question of what *causes* a person to become a Christian? It may be difficult to see any relationship between the two with respect to the non-sign discussed immediately above, but other non-signs provide fascinating suggestions about a possible relationship.

For example, non-sign #3 is this: "It is no sign that affections are truly gracious affections, or that they are not, that they cause those who have them to be fluent, fervent, and abundant, in talking of the things of religion."[13] And non-sign #5 is: "It is no sign that religious affections are truly holy and spiritual, or that they are not, that they come with texts of Scripture, remarkably brought to the mind."[14] Without question, these two non-signs apply to the behavior of the "enthusiasts" of the Awakening. The ability to give moving testimonies (perhaps about the powerful bodily effects that had been experienced), or testimonies replete with Scripture references, is no sign one way or the other that the person giving the testimony has genuinely experienced an act of God's justifying grace.

But in light of where Edwards ultimately locates the answer to our question, it perhaps would not be too much to say that Edwards has reference here to more than just the Awakening extremists. It is quite likely, given what he says elsewhere in his writings about "censoriousness" on *both* sides in the Awakening debates, that non-signs #3 and #5 also have relevance to those who are fluent in their theological orthodoxy and in their understanding and utilization of Scripture. To push this point to an extreme—might it be accurate to suggest that, as a matter of fact, Satan himself knows the truth about justification, and everything else? And yet, even if that is accurate, Satan is not himself a Christian; he is not himself justified.

The entire point of Part 2 is that many things often used to define what makes a person a Christian should not be so used—not because these things are themselves bad or unimportant, but because they can be counterfeited by Satan. One of the things that Satan can counterfeit is fluent talk about the things of religion. Fluent and orthodox talk about the things of religion, certainly, is not a sign of the *absence* of justification. But it is not a definite sign of its *presence* either.

All of this brings us to Part 3 of the *Affections*, the most important section of arguably the most important book ever written by a human being. In Section 1, Edwards lays the ontological foundation for the rest of his argument: "Affections that are truly spiritual and gracious, do arise from those influences and operations on the heart, which are spiritual, supernatural and divine."[15] In some ways, this sign that justification has happened is of limited benefit when I am looking at another person. We can never be absolutely certain that another person has experienced "the transition from wrath to grace in history." But this does not make the sign unimportant. Indeed, without this sign, none of the others would be possible. Here is a further statement to this effect:

> From these things it is evident, that those gracious influences of the saints, and the effects of God's spirit which they experience, and entirely above nature, and altogether of a different kind from any thing that men find in themselves by the exercise of natural principles. No improvement of those principles that are natural, no advancing or exalting of them to higher degrees, and no kind of composition, will ever bring men to them: because they not only differ from what is natural, and from everything that natural men experience, in degree and circumstances, but also *in kind*; and are of a nature vastly more excellent. And this is what I mean by supernatural, when I say that, *gracious affections are from those influences that are supernatural.*[16] (emphasis in original)

So Edwards continues to affirm that man can do nothing whatsoever, even to begin to move in the direction of justification. It is God's work, from first to last. Man does nothing whatsoever to cause his justification.

But immediately after the paragraph quoted above, Edwards begins to lay out the distinctive way in which he will connect the internal with the external, the cause with the condition. What are the key elements of what God causes? This is one of the most crucial of all ideas in all of Edwards's theology.

> From hence it follows, that in those gracious exercises and affections which are wrought in the saints, through the saving influences of the Spirit of God, there is a new inward *perception* or *sensation* of their minds, entirely different in its nature and kind from anything that ever their minds were the subjects of before they were sanctified.... There is what some metaphysicians call a new *simple idea*. If grace be, in the sense above described, an entirely new kind of principle, then the *exercises* of it are also new.... Here is, as it were, a new

spiritual sense, or a principle or spiritual sensation, which is in its whole nature different from any former kinds of sensation of the mind, as tasting is diverse from any of the other senses. And something is perceived by a true saint, in the exercise of this new sense of mind in spiritual and divine things, as entirely diverse from anything that is perceived in them by natural men, as the sweet taste of honey is diverse from the ideas men get of honey by only looking on and feeling it.[17] (emphasis in original)

It is precisely here, in this section of Part 3 of the *Affections*, that Edwards directly quotes Thomas Shepard's "Parable of the Ten Virgins."[18] Shepard's response to the antinomian controversy of his day, clearly a dispute over the orthodox understanding of justification and sanctification, helps to shape Edwards's response to the theological issues of his day, which included justification and many other matters as well.

The action that God takes in moving a soul from the kingdom of darkness to the kingdom of light involves this provision of a new spiritual sense, and *this sense is the one thing which Satan cannot counterfeit*. But as important as the existence of this sense is, the exact character or nature of this sense makes all the difference when we ask what makes a person a Christian. Sections 2–4 of Part 3 of the *Affections* provide Edwards's precise and superbly helpful description of this sense. I will provide a couple of appropriate quotations from these sections, and then explore briefly some of the points Edwards makes in the remainder of the treatise.

Section 2 is entitled, "The first objective ground of gracious affections is the transcendentally excellent and amiable nature of divine thing, as they are in themselves, and not any conceived relation they bear to self, or self-interest." After a lengthy examination of the disturbing prevalence of various kinds of "self-interest," even in churches that are theologically sound, Edwards makes this profound claim:

Whereas the exercises of true and holy love in the saints arise in another way. They do not first see that God loves them, and then see that he is lovely, but they first see that God is lovely, and that Christ is excellent and glorious, and their hearts are first captivated with this view, and the exercises of their love are wont from time to time to begin here, and to arise primarily from these views; and then, consequentially, they see God's love, and great favor to them. *The saint's affections begin with God* [emphasis mine]; and self-love has a hand in these affections consequentially, and secondarily only. On the contrary, those false affections begin with self, and an acknowledgment of an excellency in God, and an affectedness with it, is only consequential and dependent. In the love of the true saint God is the lowest foundation; the love of the excellency of his nature is the foundation of all the affections which come afterwards wherein self-love is concerned as a handmaid: on the contrary, the hypocrite lays himself at the bottom of all, as the first foundation, and lays on God as the superstructure; and even his acknowledgment of God's glory itself depends on his regard to his private interest.[19]

Section 4 is entitled, "Gracious affections arise from the mind being enlightened right and spiritually to apprehend divine things." Edwards begins this section with a crucial caution, "*Holy affections are not heat without light*, but evermore arise from some information of the understanding, some spiritual instruction that the mind receives, some light or actual knowledge" (emphasis mine).[20] But, of course, this caution, aimed primarily at those who would downplay the significance of objective truth, must be—and by Edwards is—balanced by his earlier caution: "But yet it is evident, that religion consists so much in the affections, as that without holy affection there is no true religion. *No light in the understanding is good that does not produce holy affection in the heart*" (emphasis mine).[21]

And just exactly what does "holy affection in the heart" produce? That is the focus of Edwards's attention throughout the remainder of Part 3 of the *Affections*. But before we move to a quick consideration of those matters, which might be regarded as answers to the second sense of our question (i.e., how is a person recognized as being a Christian?), a bit more needs to be said about the significance of what Edwards has just argued.

Perhaps this could best be summarized by posing and answering yet another question, one that Edwards posed of himself many times:

why should I exercise faith in Jesus Christ? Or, for the Christian, why *did* I exercise faith in Jesus Christ? Edwards claims that if the answers to those questions are focused *only* on what a person *gets* as a result of exercising faith in Christ, then they are likely to reflect "counterfeit Christianity." The natural person, according to Edwards and according to Scripture, is extraordinarily adept at doing all kinds of things out of self-love. The natural person, therefore, is able to do many "Christian things" that look genuine. But all of those things can be, and often are, counterfeited by Satan. Even faith can be counterfeited—and likely *is* being counterfeited, if the only things about which a professed Christian can talk when asked why she is a Christian are the benefits she receives, or thinks she will receive, as a result of her faith.

On the contrary, "the saint's affections begin with God." But while quoting this part of Edwards's revolutionary sentence, we must not forget the remainder of that sentence, "and self-love has a hand in these affections consequentially, and secondarily only." Self-love *does* play a role in genuine faith. After all, many of the promises made in Scripture are for good things—unimaginably good things—that await the saints of God. These are real blessings, real benefits, and failing to recognize and appreciate them adequately, even in prospect, amounts to a failure to give God the honor and praise that he is due.

And that is the key to the "begin with" language above. The fundamental reason why I, and you, should exercise faith in Jesus Christ is because *he deserves it!* He is worthy of my faith; he is worthy of my worship; he is worthy of my praise. We exercise faith in Christ primarily and fundamentally in order to *give to* God, not to *get from* God. This is the most fundamental answer to our titular question, "What's the Point of Believing and Doing the Right Things?" As we genuinely seek to give glory to God, the blessings roll in, but if we are giving just to get, grave spiritual danger awaits. Jesus, of course, said it best: "But seek first the kingdom of God and his righteousness, and all these things will be added to you" (Matthew 6:33). But Christians in Edwards's day, and in our own, were/are masters at pretending to give in order to get. It was this subtle counterfeiting of Christianity that Edwards wrote the *Affections* to expose.

Something happens in the moment of transition from wrath to

grace in history, something that totally reorients a person's being. It may be called regeneration, or being born again, or the provision of a totally new "relish" for God. Whatever it is called, the new Christian has, for the first time, an ability to love God just for who he is rather than exclusively for what he can do for the Christian—an ability which Satan can never counterfeit.

There are numerous ways in which Scripture gives expression to the multifarious aspects of this transition, justification being one of those. But all of those facets are rooted in the union of the believer with Christ. The Lord, as it were, grafts the individual into Christ. This is the ground on which the believer is justified. Christ's active and passive obedience become the believer's, because the believer is in Christ. Being in Christ also gives to the believer a relish for the beauty of God, a relish which has always described the attitude of the three persons of the Trinity toward one another.

This is Edwards's ultimate, mature answer to the ontological sense of our question, "What makes a person a Christian?" It also leads directly to his ultimate, mature answer to the recognition sense of that question. Observing that others are fundamentally and primarily focused on the glory of God is the best way to tell if they are genuine saints (and should, for example, be admitted to the Lord's Supper). Likewise, and far more often, when we look at our own spiritual lives, what we really are seeking first says a great deal about who we really are.

It is precisely because the WRF sees Edwards's mature answer as profoundly biblical that we have adopted the following as the first two of our official organizational theological affirmations:

- The essence of the true religion (and of Reformed theology) is adoration and worship of the Triune God—Father, Son, and Holy Spirit.
- This Triune God is worthy of the praise and service of all of creation.[22]

The remainder of Part 3 of the *Affections* provide Edwards's detailed understanding of what "seek[ing] first the kingdom of God and his righteousness" actually looks like in real life. All of these sections are extraordinarily important, but I will focus on just a couple of them, the ones which seem most apropos to our question.

In perfect harmony with his statements earlier, Edwards says this in Section 6:

> There is a sort of men, who indeed abundantly cry down works, and cry up faith in opposition to works, and set up themselves very much as evangelical persons in opposition to those that are of a legal spirit, and make a fair show of advancing Christ and the Gospel, and the way of free grace; who are indeed some of the greatest enemies to the gospel-way of free grace and the most dangerous opposers of pure humble Christianity. [At this point, Edwards, in a footnote, cites Thomas Shepard's "Parable of the Ten Virgins."].... Some, who think themselves quite emptied of themselves, confident that they are abased in the dust, are full as they can hold with the glory of their own humility, and lifted up to heaven with a high opinion of their abasement. Their humility is a swelling, self-conceited, confident, showy, noisy, assuming humility .... But he whose heart is under the power of Christian humility, is of a contrary disposition. If the Scriptures are at all to be relied on, such an one is apt to think his attainments in religion to be comparatively mean, and to esteem himself low among the saints, and one of the least of saints. Humility, or true lowliness of mind, disposes persons to think others better than themselves; Philippians 2:3, "In lowliness of mind, let each esteem others better than themselves." Hence they are apt to think the lowest room belongs to them.[23]

He continues in Section 8:

> But here some may be ready to say, Is there no such thing as Christian fortitude, and boldness for Christ, being good soldiers in the Christian warfare, and coming out boldly against the enemies of Christ and his people? To which I answer, There doubtless is such a thing. The whole Christian life is compared to a warfare, and fitly so. And the most eminent Christians are the best soldiers, endued with the greatest degrees of Christian fortitude. And it is the duty of God's people to be steadfast and vigorous in their opposition to

the designs and ways of such as are endeavoring to overthrow the kingdom of Christ, and the interest of religion. But yet many persons seem to be quite mistaken concerning the nature of Christian fortitude. It is an exceeding diverse thing from a brutal fierceness, or the boldness of the beasts of prey. True Christian fortitude consists in strength of mind, through grace, exerted in two things; in ruling and suppressing the evil and unruly passions and affections of the mind; and in steadfastly and freely exerting, and following good affections and dispositions, without being hindered by sinful fear, or the opposition of enemies. But the passions that are restrained and kept under, in the exercise of this Christian strength and fortitude, are those very passions that are vigorously and violently exerted in a false boldness for Christ. And those affections that are vigorously exerted in true fortitude, are those Christian, holy affections that are directly contrary to them. *Though Christian fortitude appears, in withstanding and counteracting the enemies that are without us; yet it much more appears, in resisting and suppressing the enemies that are within us; because they are our worst and strongest enemies, and have greatest advantage against us.* The strength of the good soldier of Jesus Christ appears in nothing more, than in steadfastly maintaining the holy calm, meekness, sweetness, and benevolence of his mind, amidst all the storms, injuries, strange behavior, and surprising acts and events of this evil and unreasonable world. The Scripture seems to intimate that true fortitude consists chiefly in this: Prov. 16:32, "He that is slow to anger, is better than the mighty; and he that ruleth his spirit, than he that taketh a city" ... *There is a pretended boldness for Christ that arises from no better principle than pride* (emphasis mine).[24]

Edwards has not yet finished hammering at this attitudinal point. He concludes Section 8 of Part 3 with this statement:

And that all true saints are of a loving, benevolent, and beneficent temper, the Scripture is very plain and abundant. Without it, the Apostle tells us, though we should speak with the tongues of men and angels, we are as a sounding brass, or a tinkling cymbal, and though we have the gift of all prophecy, and understand all mysteries, and all knowledge; yet without this spirit we are nothing. *There is no one virtue, or disposition of mind, so often and expressly insisted upon, as marks laid down in the New Testament, whereby to know true Christians.... The Scripture knows no true Christians, of a sordid, selfish, cross, and contentious spirit. Nothing can be a greater absurdity, than a morose, hard, close, spiteful true Christian* (emphasis mine).[25]

As Edwards finished Section 8, so he begins Section 9, which is entitled, "Gracious affections soften the heart, and are attended with a Christian tenderness of spirit." He continues:

All gracious affections have a tendency to promote this Christian tenderness of heart.... The less apt [the true saint] is to be afraid of natural evil, having his heart fixed, trusting in God, and so not afraid of evil tidings; the more apt he is to be alarmed, with the appearance of moral evil, or the evil of sin. As he has more holy boldness, so he has less of self-confidence, and a forward assuming boldness, and more modesty. As he is more sure than others of deliverance from hell, so he has more of a sense of the desert of it. He is less apt than others to be shaken in faith; but more apt than others to be moved with solemn warnings, and with God's frowns, and with the calamities of others. *He has the firmest comfort, but the softest heart: richer than others, but the poorest of all in spirit: the tallest and strongest saint, but the least and tenderest child among them* (emphasis mine).[26]

One final point needs to be made about the signs of truly gracious affections—especially the twelfth sign, which Edwards calls "evangelical obedience" and discusses at significantly greater length than he does any other single sign. He begins with this affirmation, "Gracious and holy affections have their exercise and fruit in Christian practice. Not only so, but '*It is necessary* that men should be universally obedient'" (emphasis mine).[27]

When Edwards the theologian uses the word "necessary," one must be sure to give that word the full weight that Edwards the philosopher gives it in such works as *Freedom of the Will* and *Original Sin*. Evangelical obedience is, for Edwards, just as "necessary" as faith in answering the question "What makes a person a Christian?" and that is how he presents it in the conclusion of the *Affections*.

It is just as *necessary* that men be obedient as it is that they exercise faith in Christ. In neither case does human behavior *cause* justification; the Holy Spirit alone is the cause of justification. But a relishing faith and an evangelical obedience are both essential *conditions* of justification—a distinction Edwards makes most prominently in those early sermons on justification. Why? Because the essence of the "transition from wrath to grace in history" is the Spirit's action in grafting an individual into Christ. This truly "non-counterfeitable" action of the Spirit of God literally makes all the difference.

Here it is once again helpful and important to remind ourselves of the essential nature of both faith and obedience. Recall what was said above about the essential nature of faith —*it is an act of giving to God, not an act of getting from God.* At least, that is the case if the faith is genuine. We give ourselves to God in faith because he is worthy, because he deserves all that we have and are. Remember the last verse of that wonderful hymn, "When I Survey the Wondrous Cross":

> Were the whole realm of nature mine,
> That were a present far too small;
> Love so amazing, so divine,
> Demands my soul, my life, my all.

"Demands" and "deserves." If the only reason we exercise faith in Christ is to get something from him, then no matter how wonderful the thing that we are trying to get may be, it is we and not Christ who reigns supreme. And that kind of action can easily be counterfeited by Satan. But actually giving *for his sake, for his glory,* and *for his worship*—that is unquestionably true faith.

So it is with evangelical obedience. When errors regarding justification and sanctification have been made by preachers and theologians, most frequently those errors have resulted from unbiblical substitution of "getting" for "giving" in relation to our Creator and Redeemer. But when "giving to God" has been vigorously maintained as the fundamental motive behind the actions being taken, the truth has usually been preserved.

That is the case because, as Edwards and many others have taught, the law of God is nothing more or less than the objectification of the very nature of God. The Ten Commandments begin with an assertion which is more than a preface; it is the very foundation of all that the Lord is about to say: "I am the Lord your God" (Exodus 20:2). Every one of the following commands—indeed, every single command in the entire Bible—emerges from the fact that the Lord is God, and from the fact of *who* the Lord God is. Contrary to other philosophical traditions, Christianity is rooted in the belief that God is the ultimate reality, and that all other realities, including moral law, emerge from him. In a sense, therefore, God did not have a choice about the law he gave—it was determined by his very nature.

This becomes especially meaningful in the context of this book when we realize, as scholars and ministry leaders are now reminding us, that God Himself is a "missional God." Here, for example, is a most instructive statement from Chris Wright; note especially the flow of his argument and the conclusion to which it brings him (emphasis added):

> The Bible is not just about the solution to our sin problem and how to survive the day of judgment. It begins with creation and it ends with new creation. So our biblical theology of mission needs to take this great beginning and ending seriously.
>
> The creation narrative provides two of the fundamental planks for the foundational world view, for it answers two of the most fundamental questions that all philosophies and religions answer in different ways: *Where* are we? And *Who* are we? That is to say, first, what is this universe in which we find ourselves? Where did it come from and why does it exist and is it even real? Are we gods, or merely animals that have evolved a bit further than the rest? Does human life have any value, meaning and purpose?
>
> *The distinctive answers that the Bible gives to these questions have profound implications for our understanding of mission in God's world in the midst of human beings like ourselves, made in the image of God.*[28]

Later on in this book you're holding, Tim Keller asks and answers the question, "What is God's global urban mission?" In effect, Tim is saying the same thing that Chris Wright is saying—the Lord God himself is a missional God. This is precisely the lesson that Jesus was teaching the scribes and Pharisees (of both first and twenty-first centuries) in what I have called in my introduction to this book, "The Parable of the Running Father." And if the Lord God is himself missional, what does that say about our being missional? At the very least, if Edwards's arguments are correct, it means that those who desire to worship and honor God must themselves reflect the missional character of God.

This lies at the very heart of the way in which Edwards described what makes a person a Christian—relish for the glory of God, the desire to reflect God's glory back to him in both word and deed, in both belief and behavior. Christians want this *even more than* they want personal spiritual blessings. Returning to an earlier point, those who are genuinely regenerated by the Holy Spirit *seek first* his kingdom, his rule, his righteousness, even his "mission." As they seek those things *first*, they are promised by Jesus himself that "all these [other] things" will be added to them as well.

Of course, no one perfectly seeks God's kingdom first. Edwards was not a perfectionist. He knew his Bible and his own heart well enough to avoid that heresy. The sign of a truly gracious Christian is not that he never sins; the sign of a truly gracious Christian is that he truly relishes his God and, therefore, genuinely anguishes over any sin that he does commit.

Any sin! Edwards's understanding of the scope of that phrase can be fully appreciated only by careful examination of his work on *Original Sin*, especially where he discusses the frightening extent of our sins of omission: "The sum of our duty to God, required in his law, is LOVE; taking love in a large sense for the true regard of our hearts to God, implying esteem, honour, benevolence, gratitude, complacence, etc.... It therefore appears from the premises, that *whosoever withholds more of that love or respect of heart from God, which his law requires, than he affords, has more sin than righteousness.*"[29] Obviously, all genuine Christians (including Edwards) experience a lot of anguish! (emphasis in original)

But the anguish is good; it is good in that it reveals what we desire—to relish God more and better, to love him and to obey him more completely. The anguish demonstrates that the Holy Spirit has touched us and has given us a new spiritual sense.

This then may be a guide for us when we deal, as we often must, with others whose theologies or lives (or both) we perceive to be not fully honoring to the Lord, not fully in accord with the teaching of Scripture. It may be a guide for us particularly when we think we see a professing Christian whom we believe doesn't think the right things about justification, or who doesn't live like a justified person.

We begin—or we *should* begin—all such interactions by remembering the anguish we have felt when—not *if*, but *when*—we have discovered our own tendencies to withhold from God the complete love and worship and service that his law requires. We also begin by reminding ourselves of warnings, such as these from Edwards: "All gracious affections have a tendency to promote this Christian tenderness of heart.... [The true saint] has the firmest comfort, but the softest heart: richer than others, but the poorest of all in spirit: the tallest and strongest saint, but the least and tenderest child among them."[30]

Our chief end must always be the same—to maximize glory and honor to our beautiful Savior. That is the ultimate "point" in believing and doing the right things. When we or others think or do anything that fails the maximizing test, our relish of God compels us to speak or to act or to do both. But it is *necessary* that such speaking or acting itself embody *all* of the things which Edwards says characterize genuinely gracious affections.

ONE BRIEF EXAMPLE

So exactly what does this understanding of the relationship between orthodox belief and moral behavior look like, when applied to questions other than that of the very broad relationship between justification and sanctification? The chapters which follow seek to answer this question.

But perhaps it would be helpful here to provide one quick example of how this approach might work when applied to an issue very much before the contemporary conservative Reformed church, especially in the United States right now. That issue is the way in which the meaning of the first three chapters of Genesis should be understood.

Edwards (and the WRF) would certainly say that what one believes about the teaching of Genesis 1–3 is *extremely* important. There is no question whatsoever that denominations and congregations, institutions, and individuals are required to take God at his word in the creation narrative. Whatever God says must be believed and affirmed because that is how, in the realm of belief, we reflect God's glory back to him—we think his thoughts after him. To get even more specific, it is completely appropriate for ordination examinations to probe in detail every candidate's understanding of what Genesis 1–3 teaches.

But, if Edwards is right, Satan could pass such exams—because he knows all too well exactly what happened when God created the world and Adam and Eve. If Edwards is right, the important discussion has just begun when orthodox belief about creation has been affirmed. At least as important is consideration of whether such orthodox belief is, in fact, shaping the affections of the candidate's heart. In other words, is the theologically orthodox candidate actually living as though God is his Creator? How does what the candidate seeks first in his life demonstrate that he relishes the Creator God? How does it shape his attitudes toward, and his uses of, whatever resources he has? How does it shape his actions toward the poor, the sick, the helpless—toward all those whom Jesus mentions in Matthew 11:5? How does it shape his own "missional living?"

Not one of these suggested questions has anything whatsoever to do with getting something from God. Remember that the point in believing and in doing the right things is not to get *from* God but to give *to* God. Whatever one gets from God is absolutely and totally and eternally of grace. But these questions—and all other such questions with respect to all other important theological issues—have everything to do with the way in which Edwards answers the question "What makes a person a Christian?" A Christian is one no longer defined solely by selfish affections. A Christian is one in whose heart the Holy Spirit of God has placed a new sense, a relish for God himself, even for the God who created all things and sustains all things—

and who, therefore, deserves to be honored in the way in which we relate to all those things.

Of course, the details of those relationships are—and, until heaven, will likely always be—complex and subject to discussion and debate among those who love the Creator. But it is critically important that those who believe the right things about how the Creator did his work of creation be able to demonstrate how what they believe actually shapes their lives. In other words, who God is must actually shape the lives of those who claim to believe in him.

SUMMARY AND CONCLUSION

And exactly why is all of this—the nature of our "affections," the things we seek first, a correct relationship between orthodox belief and moral behavior—"missional?" To refer to other contents found elsewhere in this book, it is correct because…

…Andrew McGowan and Thomas Schirrmacher are correct in their descriptions of the overall shape of Reformed theology generally, and of the theology of the book of Romans specifically.

…Tim Keller, Chris Wright, and many others are right in insisting that God himself is "missional" in character.

…the WRF Statement of Faith is right to include a section on "Mission and evangelism."

…the Cape Town Commitment of the Lausanne Movement is right in its description of "the mission of God" and its implications.

> We commit ourselves to the integral and dynamic exercise of all dimensions of mission to which God calls his Church.
>
> God commands us to make known to all nations the truth of God's revelation and the gospel of God's saving grace through Jesus Christ, calling all people to repentance, faith, baptism and obedient discipleship.
>
> God commands us to reflect his own character through compassionate care for the needy, and to demonstrate the values and the power of the kingdom of God in striving for justice and peace and in caring for God's creation.

In response to God's boundless love for us in Christ, and out of our overflowing love for him, we rededicate ourselves, with the help of the Holy Spirit, fully to obey all that God commands, with self-denying humility, joy and courage. We renew this covenant with the Lord—the Lord we love because he first loved us.[31]

All of this is missional because Williams Ames, one of the primary theological influences on Jonathan Edwards, was correct when he gave us that classical definition of theology: "Theology is doctrine or teaching of *living to God*" (emphasis added).

And all of this is missional because living to God in a manner that, in belief and in behavior, reflects God's glory back to him is part of the fulfillment of that wonderful promise that God himself made to his people: "For the earth will be filled with the knowledge of the glory of the LORD as the waters cover the sea" (Habakkuk 2:14; see also Isaiah 11:9).

3.

THE BOOK OF ROMANS AND THE MISSIONAL MANDATE:
Why Mission and Theology *Must* Go Together

THOMAS SCHIRRMACHER

I live in a country where the theology of evangelization has been harmed more than anywhere else. New liberal blueprints have so weakened the proclamation of the gospel that many Christians and churches lack the power of conviction necessary for any type of evangelistic or missions work. Added to that is the paralysis brought on by theological disputes, caused both by liberals as well as devout Christians. Might it not be appropriate, then, to simply make theologizing the main culprit?

However, teaching which is antagonistic to evangelization cannot be answered by an absence of theology. Rather, only through true, healthy, and thoughtful biblical teaching—and through more biblical-reformational theology—will evangelism flourish. I would like to illustrate this point by unpacking the message of Paul's letter to the Romans.

PAUL: THEOLOGIAN AND MISSIONARY

"What is at issue in the letter to the Romans? It all has to do with God's plan for the world and how Paul's mission to the Gentiles belongs in this plan."[1] This close relationship between the letter to the Romans and the practice of missions has been too seldom considered by commentators. Emil Weber, in his important contribution "The Relationship between Romans 1-3 and Paul's Missionary Practice,"[2] did not get beyond Romans 3; and other authors have only sketched out the topic.[3] Nils Alstrup writes in this connection, "Paul is identified as the first Christian theologian and the greatest Christian missionary of all time. However, researchers have not often appreciated how closely these two aspects are related to each other."[4] For that reason Robert L. Reymond calls Paul the "missionary theologian."[5]

At the same time, however, texts from the letter to the Romans have played a major role in the history of missions. For several hundred years, Romans 10:14ff. was one of the favorite texts for missionary sermons.[6] Among Calvinist Puritans in Great Britain and the United States between the fifteenth and eighteenth centuries—to which the great majority of modern Protestant global missions efforts trace themselves back— the concern of missions sermons found a point of entry in the exegesis of the letter to the Romans. Past this point of entry, however, exegesis of Romans remained untouched by what was intense promotion of world missions.

Paul presumably wrote his letter to the Romans in AD 57, at some point during the three months mentioned in Acts 20:2–3 prior to his trip to Jerusalem. His letter was thus written after he had collected funds from all his congregations in order to help the congregation in Jerusalem. From Jerusalem he wanted to travel to Rome, in order to use the church there as his starting point for his additional missions plans, especially the proselytization of Spain (Romans 15:27–31).

ROMANS 1:1–15

Paul does not waste much time in the letter to the Romans before mentioning his missionary plans (Romans 1:8–15). Paul wants to proclaim the gospel to all people without exception, regardless of language, culture, and ethnicity ("Greeks and to barbarians," Romans 1:14) as well as regardless of education or social class ("to the wise and to the foolish," Romans 1:14). Furthermore, it is for that reason that he comes to Rome (Romans 1:15). Paul moves directly from these practical missions concerns to the "real" topic. In the famous verses of Romans 1:16–17, Paul begins his teaching with "For ...". He thus doctrinally justifies what he wants to practically do in Romans 1:8–15. There is no indication that Paul changes the topic at hand between verses 15 and 16.

The first fifteen verses of the letter relate to Paul's concerns. The letter does not begin with the words of Romans 1:16: "I am not ashamed of the gospel...." As early as the greeting in Romans 1:1 Paul describes his mandate to preach God's gospel. His mandate is stated more precisely in Romans 1:5: "to bring about the obedience of faith for the sake of his name among all the nations." He wants to visit the church so that he can also preach in Rome (Romans 1:15). He then explains why he wants to proclaim the gospel to everyone, from Romans 1:16 onward.

Romans 1:16, then, is not a superfluous introduction. Rather, it gives us the actual reason for composing the book of Romans—namely, to demonstrate that the expansion of world missions is God's own plan. Anders Nygren writes in this regard: "While in declaring this Paul is holding firmly to the thought of the introduction and rebuffs suppositions about the cause of the long delay of his trip to Rome, he has already gotten around to his major theme of the gospel as God's saving power. 'It is almost inaudible how he glides from making a personal address to a lecture.'"[7]

ROMANS 5:7–16:27

We find the same thing at the end of the actual teaching portion of Paul's letter. In Romans 15:14 he seamlessly segues from Old Testament quotations about the peoples of the world directly to his practical missional plans, repeating much of what he has already said in the introduction.

At the end of the letter, the reasons for the composition of the letter become even clearer. Beginning in Romans 15:7, Paul demonstrates that Christ has come as much for the Jews as he did for the Gentiles; and in Romans 15:14, after the general verses about the calling of the Gentiles, Paul begins detailing his personal plans. He reports why he can think about nothing other than the mission to the Gentiles. And even here, his central task is to bring the Gentiles to obedience to faith in word and deed (Romans 15:18).

This framework becomes clearer when one contrasts the introduction of Romans 1:1–15 with the complete final section of Romans 15:14–16:27. This framework of the letter to the Romans actually declares the reason for the letter, and states the topic of the letter in its opening and closing verses (Romans 1:1–6; 16:25–27): The "obedience of faith" has to be proclaimed among all peoples and planted, just as the Old Testament foretold (e.g., compare Romans 15:21 to Isaiah 52:15, and the context of Isaiah 52:5–15, from which Paul frequently quotes in the letter to the Romans). The parallels between Romans 1:1–15 and 15:14–16:27 show that Paul keeps the practical missionary considerations of his letter in sight throughout the entire epistle.

On the framework of the letter to the Romans: Parallels between Romans 1:1-15 and 15:14-16:27		
1:1-6	The gospel was foretold in the Old Testament.	16:25-27
1:5	The obedience that comes from faith has to be proclaimed to all nations.	16:26; 15:18
1:7	"Grace and peace to you..."	16:20
1:8	The faith of the Roman Christians is known throughout the whole world.	16:19
1:8-13	Travel plans to Rome via Jerusalem	15:22-29
1:11-12	Paul seeks to be spiritually encouraged by the Christians in Rome.	15:14, 24
1:13	In spite of his wishes, Paul was prevented from traveling to Rome up to this time.	15:22
1:13-15	The gospel has to be proclaimed to all peoples.	15:14-29; comp. 16:26

The letter to the Romans has too often been interpreted as a theological treatise without these points which frame the letter. "Most authors actually ignore the introductory and concluding declarations of his intention and concentrate on the theological interpretation of the core of the letter."[8]

DOCTRINE AND WORLD MISSIONS

Gottlob Schrenk has aptly emphasized, "The letter to the Romans is the most important declaration of the leading missionary of the Christian church."[9] But to what extent is the letter to the Romans a missions document? As is the case with every utterance by Paul, this letter has also grown out of unmitigated missionary activity. However, this letter, much more than Paul's other letters, contains the foundational missionary convictions of the apostle.

This is the reason I, as a missiologist and systematic theologian, wrote a book about the letter to the Romans, a project normally left to exegetes.[10] This most systematic and "most theological" of Paul's letters was written out of the context of concrete missions work. It substantiates, in comprehensive fashion, the justification and necessity of missions in unreached areas through the use of systematic theology and a study of the Old Testament. As a result, we can reach the following conclusions:

- Whoever only pragmatically conducts "missions"—and for that reason, dispenses with "doctrine"—in the end conducts missions in one's own name and does not look after *what God* has said and written about missions.
- Whoever teaches a set of doctrines that does not have missions at the center, and does not lead to practical missions work, teaches in one's own name and disregards *why God* said and wrote particular things.
- Practical missions work always begins with healthy, foundational doctrine and Bible study; healthy, foundational teaching will always lead to practical missions work!

WORLD MISSIONS: THE FULFILLMENT OF THE OLD TESTAMENT

Two special messages that more precisely explain what is at stake in the case of world missions should now be underscored, with the help of Romans 15–16. One message is the meaning of the Old Testament, in order to demonstrate that world missions is desired by God. The other message is that world missions, above all and in the first instance, seek to reach the unreached—the major message of the letter to the Romans.

Let us first turn to the meaning of the Old Testament. Paul reminds the "strong" Gentile Christians "that Christ became a servant to the circumcised"—which is to say, he submitted himself to the Law and in particular to Jewish ceremonial law—"in order to confirm the promises given to the patriarchs" (Romans 15:8). Astonishingly, Paul directly changes from the "promises given to the patriarchs" with reference to the Jewishness of the Messiah to the fact that "the Gentiles might glorify God for his mercy," which relates to non-Jews: "As it is written: 'Therefore I will praise you among the Gentiles; and sing to your name'" (Romans 15:9). He thus reminds Gentile Christians of Romans 9–11, where he has already made it clear that Gentiles have Christ's work and the history of Israel to thank for their salvation.

After Paul has repeatedly made clear that the proclamation of the gospel and world missions do not contradict the Old Testament, there is a last bit of machine gunfire in the form of Old Testament quotations. In Romans 15:9–12, Paul quotes five texts from the Old Testament which demonstrate that the nations will one day glorify God: 2 Samuel 22:50; Psalm 18:49; Deuteronomy 32:43; Psalm 117:1; and Isaiah 11:10. This is because the Old Testament actually underpins and calls for proclamation of the gospel and world missions. Adolf Schlatter wrote about these five quotations:

> The joint prize of God, in which all people participate, is the goal of God which the scriptures proclaimed. In 2 Samuel 22:50, Paul presumably heard Christ, who wants to profess God among the peoples and sing to the praise of his name. It is the work of Christ that the church does this. Deuteronomy 32:43 is quoted because this dictum calls peoples to jointly praise God with Israel. Psalm 117:1 proclaims that indiscriminately and without exception all peoples are invited to praise God. Isaiah 11:10 justifies the worship which people will bring with the fact that they are under the lordship of Christ. ... Paul underpins his intercession with the promises of scripture.[11]

The many Old Testament quotations should not only have convinced (and should convince) the Jews—they were (and are) of significance for Gentile Christians who are not only to rejoice about their personal salvation but who are to bring the gospel to all peoples of the earth in salvific continuity. C.E.B. Cranfield writes in this connection,

> [N]either the continual use of the Old Testament, which is found throughout the entire letter, nor the use of the words "I am speaking to men who know the law" in Romans 7:1 demonstrates that Paul wrote to a predominantly Jewish Christian church. This is due to the fact that the Old Testament was the Bible of the Gentile Christians just as it was for the Jewish Christians, and it is important that Paul presuppose a familiarity and reverence for the Old Testament in his letters to the Galatians and the Corinthians.[12]

The question is often asked as to why Jesus's Great Commission (Matthew 28:18-20; Mark 16:15–16) is not quoted by the apostles after Pentecost, although reference is made to the Great Commission by speaking of Jesus's "command" (e.g., Acts 1:2; 10:42). Was the mission among all peoples never a disputed issue within the New Testament church—and therefore pointing to Jesus's command was superfluous? On the contrary: the mission among the Gentiles was something that only slowly got into gear and was for a long time controversial (e.g., the Council at Jerusalem, the letter to the Galatians). However, if we look at the New Testament discussions about the justification of missions, we are astounded to realize that at that point where we would have quoted the Great Commission it is the Old Testament that is almost always cited. *The Great Commission, then, is the fulfillment of the Old Testament.*

Global missions is not primarily justified by Jesus's Great Commission, but rather by the Old Testament. The Great Commission was, in a certain sense, the starting shot for that which had long been announced and prepared for, and which now was to be finally put into gear. The letter to the Romans, particularly Romans 15, is an obvious example of this, since Paul extensively quotes Old Testament documents in this letter.

The election of the Old Testament covenant people happened with a view to all peoples, such that global missions is already a topic in the Old Testament. The promise to the patriarchs that through them all the peoples of the earth should be blessed (Genesis 12:3; 18:18; 22:17; 26:4; 28:14) is repeatedly drawn upon as a justification for missions work among non-Jews (Luke 1:54–55, 72; Acts 3:25–26; Romans 4:13–25; Galatians 3:7–9, 14; Ephesians 3:3–4; Hebrews 6:13–20; 11:12). In Acts 13:46–49 it is reported that Paul and Barnabas were rejected by the Jews, and for that reason there is justification for their orienting themselves towards the Gentiles in Antioch. In this connection they quote from Isaiah 49:6 (equivalent to Acts 13:47): "It is too light a thing that you should be my servant to raise up the tribes of Jacob and to bring back the preserved of Israel; I will make you as a light for the nations, that my salvation may reach to the end of the earth."

In his concluding address at the council at Jerusalem in Acts 15:13–21, James justifies Paul's right to tell the Gentiles about the gospel by referencing Amos 9:11–12 (similarly expressed in Isaiah 61:4; Psalm 22:27–28; Zechariah 8:22). This is where David's "fallen tent" will be restored—which, for James, is the church—and it brings together the remnant of Jews and the Gentiles who were also coming in ("and all the Gentiles who are called by my name," Acts 15:17). As a justification for the preaching of the gospel to the Gentiles, Peter too connects the Great Commission to the Old Testament: "And he commanded us to preach to the people and to testify that he is the one appointed by God to be judge of the living and the dead. To him all the prophets bear witness that everyone who believes in him receives forgiveness of sins through his name" (Acts 10:42–43).

Accordingly, world missions cannot be presented and practiced independently of the Old Testament, nor can it be presented and practiced independently of Old Testament salvation history and the destiny of the Jewish people. Paul primarily documents this in Romans 9–11. There are two sides that have to be considered in the relationship of Christian missions to the Jewish people: the election of the Jews, and endemic disobedience: "As regards the gospel, they are enemies of God for your sake. But as regards election, they are beloved for the sake of their fore-fathers" (Romans 11:28). Paul also makes it clear that the future turning of the people of Israel to its Messiah Jesus Christ will have unimagined positive repercussions on missionary work relating to all peoples (Romans 11:15, 24–26). There are more than eighty direct quotations from the Old Testament in Romans, and more than seventy additional allusions to the Old Testament. (For the complete list, see http://www.wrf net.org/c/document_library/get_file?folderId=20&name=DLFE-204. pdf.)

The Old Testament justification of New Testament missions, then, shows that global missions is a direct continuation of salvation history—animated by God's action since the fall of mankind into sin and the election of Abraham. Jesus expressly confirmed the Old Testament justification of New Testament missions work in the Great Commission.

> Then he said to them, "these are my words that I spoke to you while I was still with you, that everything written about me in the Law of Moses and the Prophets and the Psalms must be fulfilled." Then he opened their minds to understand the Scriptures, and said to them, "Thus it is written, that the Christ should suffer and on the third day rise from the dead, and that repentance and forgiveness of sins should be proclaimed in his name to all nations, beginning from Jerusalem. You are witnesses of these things." (Luke 24:44–48)

According to these words, there is not only talk of Jesus's coming and the cross in all parts of the Old Testament but also mention of world missions. Forgiveness has to be proclaimed to all the nations.

SYSTEMATIC THEOLOGY AND "THE SCRIPTURES"

Systematic theology is a justifiable and apparently necessary way of bringing God's revelation to humanity and into the heart of the individual. Systematic theology wants nothing other than to be a complete view of things—that is to say, not to invent new theology but rather to see God's entire historical revelation and apply it to the current situation and the world.

In a similar vein, by quoting so extensively from the Old Testament in Romans, Paul does not want to bring about anything new, although as an apostle he was also mandated by God to reveal what up to that time had been a "mystery" (Romans 11:25; 16:25; 1 Corinthians 15:51; et al.). Rather, he was only to convey what God had always revealed and proclaimed.

At the beginning and at the end of his letter, Paul emphasized that his gospel is in accordance with what God revealed through the prophets and in the "scriptures" (Romans 1:2; 16:26). In the entire letter he repeatedly introduces evidence for it, often with express reference to "the Scripture" (Romans 4:3; 9:17; 10:11; 11:2; 15:4; compare "prophets in the Holy Scriptures" in Romans 1:2; "the prophetic writings" in Romans 16:26; and "the Law and the Prophets," Romans 3:21). If Paul had been of the opinion that he could simply place something new atop something old and faded, he would not have so comprehensively discussed the future of Israel. As it was, he had to show that the gospel for the Gentiles was compatible with everything that the Old Testament says about the Jews. It is unthinkable that "the word of God had failed" (Romans 9:6), because "whoever believes in him will not be put to shame" (Romans 9:33). To such "belong the adoption, the glory, the covenants, the giving of the law, the worship… the promises… [and] the patriarchs, and from their race, according to the flesh, is the Christ" (Romans 9:4–5).

NEW TRIBES MISSION AND THE ROLE OF SALVATION HISTORY[13]

Among tribes with whom they worked, missionaries of the New Tribes Mission simply began by building upon topics found within salvation history. They did not begin at the end, with the resurrection, Pentecost, or with the churches started by the apostles. Rather, they started at the beginning, with the creation, the building of the Tower of Babel, the flood, and the patriarchs. The entire history of Israel, and finally, the time which Jesus spent living with his disciples, came later. Only then did they get to the *real* objective.

Additionally, they recounted God's history to both non-Christians as well as the newly converted. Thus, they told about the Christian faith to everyone who wanted to know.

Is that demanding too much? Should it not be the case that one comes to speak of the cross and resurrection as quickly as possible? Is the presentation of salvation history not rather a problem of "post-treatment" than of evangelization?

Now, it would surely be seen as progress if every new convert would receive a good overview of salvation history in post-treatment. However, even given the necessity of post-treatment, the need for pre-paratory work prior to conversion is also not refuted. The cross and resurrection, Pentecost, and the New Testament church can only be rightly understood by someone who already has understood God's history with humanity. How does one expect to explain Jesus's sacrifice on the cross if one does not talk about the sacrifices of Cain and Abel, the patriarchs, and the Israelites? How does a person explain what sin is, if one neither talks about the fall from grace nor the law of Sinai in which God defines what is and is not sin?

One reason, among others, that I am so glad to be a missiologist is that there is an enormous amount to learn from the experiences of missionaries. From early church history onwards, theology has been substantially shaped by the actual situation of evangelizing and conducting apologetics vis-à-vis the non-Christian world. Missionaries from New Tribes Mission have made their program and teaching materials for tribal peoples available for Western churches and audiences. Whoever studies these materials realizes very quickly that what they have in their hands comes *from* practical experience and is written *for* practical experience.

Likewise, it is not by chance that only a small portion of the Bible is systematically written. The larger part of the Bible recounts the events of salvation history and the life histories of men and women with whom God has written his history. Missions should be an important part of basic courses on the faith as well as in theological curriculums, and the orientation toward building a church and world missions should pervade every Christian and theological education.[14] Every subject should contribute to strengthening the church and missions, and be able to convey the fascination of being allowed to participate in the building of God's great work domestically and internationally. "Independent of his special academic discipline, every faculty member of a theological school should give class instruction with a view to the mission of the church."[15]

South African missiologist David Bosch saw his role as missiologist primarily as a critical function for all other subjects, in a way which penetrated them like leaven.[16] However, he also critically observed: "It is a significant problem that the present division of theological subjects was canonized at a time when the church in Europe was completely introverted."[17]

The following illustration should make it clear that the thought of missions should actually provide orientation and motivation to all other disciplines:[18]

Illustration 3-1: Thinking about missions should motivate and determine theological work in other areas of study.

REACHING THE UNREACHED

Having looked at the significance of the Old Testament in the letter to the Romans, let us turn to the second message—and the major objective of the letter: the purpose of world missions, primarily and foremost, is to reach the unreached.

It was not just any type of missions work that prompted Paul to write his letter to the Romans. Paul was referring to his pioneering mission to unreached territories and unreached peoples. Naturally, there were full-time workers on Paul's team who looked after new churches, such as Apollos, Timothy, and Titus—who themselves had to move on (2 Timothy 4:21; Titus 1:5; 3:13). Needless to say, there were also local evangelists. However, the missionary and apostle did not limit himself to local evangelization and to "his" area. Rather, he moved on and continued to plant, as long as there were still areas without Christian churches where work was to be done.

When Paul writes in Romans 15:19 that "from Jerusalem and all the way around to Illyricum, I have fulfilled the ministry of the gospel of Christ," he does not mean that he proclaimed the gospel to every single individual. Rather, he means that he has founded churches in all the strategically important locations he was sent. The same applies to the statement that "I no longer have any room for work in these regions" (Romans 15:23). Paul does not go seeking areas where Christ is known and where preaching is occurring (Romans 15:20). Rather, he is looking for locations where no one has yet proclaimed the gospel and no indigenous church exists. Paul likewise confirms the primacy of missions to unreached areas by reference to the Old Testament: "As it is written, 'Those who have never been told of him will see, and those who have never heard will understand'" (Romans 15:21, from Isaiah 52:15).

Paul calls upon the church in Rome "to strive together with me" (Romans 15:30) and reach the inhabitants of the world who are outside the range of existing churches.

Apparently, the best way of calling upon churches to collaborate is to thoroughly demonstrate from the Old and New Testaments that the expansion of the gospel to the far reaches of the earth belongs to the essence of Jesus Christ's church.

If missions work had more closely considered Paul as a role model, the spiritual map nowadays would doubtless look different. Fortunately, since the International Congress on World Evangelization (Lausanne 1974) and the World Consultation on Frontier Missions (Edinburgh 1980), missions work has more strongly moved into the focus of evangelicalism.[19]

In evangelical missiology, a people group is understood to be an ethnic or sociological unit of individuals that is comprehensive enough to view itself as a group and possesses a sense of belonging on the basis of linguistic, religious, economic, geographic, or other factors. From an evangelical point of view, it is the largest respective group within which the gospel can expand as a movement of church planting without running up against a wall of misunderstanding or lack of acceptance.[20]

I do not want to be heard as saying that Paul had modern missiological or cultural-anthropological definitions in the back of his mind. However, I am convinced that at this point Pauline principles are cast into both modern and manageable forms.

The enormously rapid expansion of Jesus's church at the time of the apostles can only be explained if one takes the described Pauline guidelines into consideration. After all, by AD 65 the known world at that time had been reached by the apostles and other Christians. Had the apostles remained in the churches they planted, or if they had blanketed the province with evangelization, they would never have gotten "to the end of the earth" (Acts 1:8). The churches were rather called on to send workers for missions teams ("messengers of the churches," 2 Corinthians 8:23) and complete the work of the apostles in their surroundings.

This is the manner in which Paul writes to the Thessalonians. It was Paul's missions strategy to start churches mostly in centrally located cities, to install elders trained by him at an early stage, and to soon travel on. The unmitigated penetration of a region with the gospel was something that he left to a metropolitan church. The following is said of the church in Thessalonica: "[Y]ou became an example to all the believers in Macedonia and in Achaia. For not only has the word of the Lord sounded forth from you in Macedonia and Achaia, but your faith in God has gone forth everywhere, so that we need not say anything" (1 Thessalonians 1:7–8).

THE RELATIONSHIP BETWEEN THE CHURCH AND MISSIONS IN THE LETTER TO THE ROMANS[21]

What does the letter to the Romans have to do with the topic of the local church and world missions today? Whoever consults a concordance or conventional commentaries will surely not find an answer immediately. At first glance the letter to the Romans, as an instructional letter, has a lot to do with what the church believes and what message is to be proclaimed—that is, it has to do with the gospel but ostensibly little with the practical relationship between church and missions. This has to do with the one-sided interpretation of the letter to the Romans already mentioned.

Whoever knows Paul's missions strategy knows what we have already seen above with respect to Romans 15–16: Paul wanted to plant churches in strategic locations, and they in turn were to attend to the further tasks of evangelization and planting churches in their regions. While traveling through to Spain, Paul wants to be strengthened by the church in Rome. Paul and his team make missions plans. However, he seeks support from the churches, beginning with evangelization in Rome and extending to the additional missions in new regions. He knows, as a missionary, that he has something to offer the church.

Paul was apparently of the opinion that he could win broad support from the church in Rome for his missions work in Spain—similar to how the church in Antioch was his starting point earlier. He considers doing this by broadly and systematically presenting the gospel, and demonstrating that it was in line with scriptural revelation up to that point.

Even nowadays it has never harmed a church to allow missionaries to bring "some spiritual gift" (Romans 1:11). Missionaries have something to contribute that we do not have—not only firsthand accounts of how they have experienced God when new churches emerge and when impossible situations are forced open, but also the challenges, the uncomfortable situations, and the reminder of persecution.

Paul does not, however, only want to bring the church something spiritual, and he does not only want to receive spiritual care or encouragement from the church (Romans 1:12). Nor, as a missionary, does he only expect logistical backing from the church. His goal is that *the church becomes an ingredient in missions, in that it makes the work of missions its personal issue*. Even if it is unable to geographically or culturally be present where a missionary is active, the church can spiritually stand in the center of missions efforts. It is for this reason that Paul writes the letter to the Romans, and describes to the finest detail that the proclamation of the gospel among all Gentiles is not to be a peripheral matter of faith and of theology. Rather, missions work is to be its center—and indeed, its legitimization.

Section Two

The Church Reaches the World

4.

A MISSIONAL RESPONSE TO POVERTY AND SOCIAL INJUSTICE

P. J. (FLIP) BUYS

I was born and grew up as part of a staunch Calvinistic family. My father was a blue-collar worker, a devout Christian, and a very committed member of the Reformed Churches in South Africa (RCSA). He served as an elder, secretary of the church council, and member of the missions committee as long as I knew him. We had family devotions of Bible reading, prayer, and singing of psalms and hymns every evening, and my father taught us to memorize the Heidelberg Catechism at the age of twelve.

At the same time, I was aware since my early childhood of the segregation, racial hatred, fear, and anger of both white and black people toward each other. I remember how shocked I was at the age of ten, while riding home from school on my bicycle behind a bus for black people, when some blacks spat on me and shouted all kinds of swear words at me. In addition, I often heard white people cursing and using hate speech while interacting with black people.

Those experiences convinced me, at an early age, that our country desperately needed the message of the gospel of God's justice through Christ for sinners, which stirs up a desire in the hearts of Christians to work together for social justice for all.

During my second pastoral charge in Vereeniging (1976–1984), our church became deeply involved with ministry in Sharpeville township.

This township by then was known worldwide, a result of the riots against apartheid legislation that had broken out there. The Sharpeville Massacre, the incident which to that point had resulted in the largest number of South African deaths in a protest against apartheid, also came to symbolize the struggle against apartheid in South Africa.

I never thought that twenty-three years after the riots and deaths that made Sharpeville so notorious as a place of racial tensions and violence, I would become the (white African) pastor of a Reformed church in Sharpeville in 1984, with only black Africans in the flock to which God had called me to be minister and servant. Those years (1984–1989) were the high tide of the revolution by the African National Congress (ANC) against the apartheid system; I often had to drive past burning tires on the streets and through police barricades to minister at church services.

In spite of such tensions we experienced great blessings in the ministry of our church in Sharpeville, and deep Christian fellowship and mutual love developed. I published a little pamphlet in 1985 entitled *Calvinism Does Not Teach Apartheid.*[1] We succeeded in bringing black and white young people from neighboring churches together at retreats to discuss race relations in the light of biblical principles of God's sovereign grace. Several white Reformed church members became involved in small Bible study groups with black church members. Amidst the racial conflicts we truly experienced, in a small way, the truths of Ephesians 2:14–18.

> For he himself is our peace, who has made us both one and has broken down in his flesh the dividing wall of hostility by abolishing the law of commandments expressed in ordinances, that he might create in himself one new man in place of the two, so making peace, and might reconcile us both to God in one body through the cross, thereby killing the hostility. And he came and preached peace to you who were far off and peace to those who were near. For through him we both have access in one Spirit to the Father.

In those years I spent time in the houses (shacks) of the poorest of the poor and realized how the political system in many ways produced devastating poverty and socioeconomic problems for millions in South

Africa. Words like those of Micah 6:8 burnt in my heart: "He has told you, O man, what is good; and what does the LORD require of you but to do justice, and to love kindness, and to walk humbly with your God?"

All these experiences have shaped my thinking. I became a more convinced covenantal theologian/pastor/teacher/ missionary/community development worker, who believes that God has given us the entire Bible that comprises the books of both the Old and New testaments as the supreme revelation of his will. And this is for the extension of his kingdom, in spite of brokenness and sin in our communities.

In my work of the past seventeen years of training pastors, working among the poorest of the poor, and caring for widows, orphans, and terminally ill HIV/AIDS patients, I am constantly reflecting on the gospel of God's transforming grace and its implications for social justice and poverty. I have become more and more convinced that an experiential holistic Reformed theology, focusing on justification by faith as a central aspect of the gospel, should lead to such sanctification, and that a pursuit for social justice is seen and acknowledged as a touchstone of being a true Christian. Over a period of fifty years, it has become my conviction that a church that preaches grace and promotes social justice for all is a church to the heart of God and a custodian of his kingdom. This is one of the many reasons I am supportive of the vision laid out in the World Reformed Fellowship Statement of Faith, especially Section 10, paragraphs 3 ("The Compassion of Christians for the World") and 4 ("The Transformation of Human Community").

A BRIEF HISTORY OF RACIAL DISCRIMINATION AND APARTHEID IN SOUTH AFRICA

It is not possible, and also not within the scope of this chapter, to provide a detailed history of the development of apartheid in South Africa. The basic facts of the developments can just be sketched. Apartheid was a system employed by the dominant white government of South Africa that held the people of the country apart for several decades. The word literally means "apartness."

Discrimination against non-whites was inherent in the South African society from the earliest days. Since the British settled in South Africa in 1795 there had been social, economic, and political exclusion of blacks, and rule by whites, despite the fact that they were only about 10 percent of the population.

When the National Party came into power in 1948, apartheid officially became law. In 1950, the Population Registration Act required that all South Africans be racially classified into one of three categories: white, black (African), or colored (of mixed descent). The colored category included major subgroups of Indians and Asians. Classification into these categories was based on appearance, social acceptance, and descent. For example, a white person was defined as "in appearance obviously a white person or generally accepted as a white person."

Starting in the 1960s a plan of "Grand Apartheid" was executed, emphasizing territorial separation enforced through police repression. All social life was affected, including a legal prohibition of marriage between non-whites and whites, and the sanctioning of "white-only" jobs. Initially, the aim of the apartheid system was presented as a way to maintain white domination in certain parts of the country (those already most developed) while extending racial separation by establishing so-called homelands or "bantustans," with the intent of each tribal group developing a self-governing state.

The National Party rationalized the system by saying it gave blacks an opportunity to participate in a political process within the bantustans. The Christians supporting the National Party government thought it was a fair way for each racial or cultural group to have its own portion of the country where they could govern themselves and maintain their own ethnic cultural traditions and values.

THE OFFICIAL END OF APARTHEID IN 1994

After years of segregation and oppression of blacks, several different chronological events put together led to eventual reform in South Africa. International sanctions, protests, strikes, and demonstrations, as well as decades of turbulent mass action in resistance to the imposition of segregation and oppression, were the order of the day. It stimulated an armed struggle leading to sabotage and bomb blasts that cost the lives of many whites and blacks alike. Black-on-black violence of "kangaroo courts" led to black supporters of the homeland system being brutally killed by burning car tires thrown around them. It led to police and military enforcement of regional and national states of emergency.

In 1976, school riots in Soweto left many children dead. The cause of the riots had been anger about the appalling conditions in black township schools, but also a slogan of "First liberation and then education" that was popularized by black revolutionary and underground Communist leaders. Anger against the Afrikaans language was stirred up by revolutionary leaders, who said that this language was not spoken anywhere else in the world, and that black youth were simply being prepared as slaves for the whites.

Under growing pressure and increasingly international isolation, the government gradually and reluctantly moved towards power-sharing, embarking on a dual strategy of introducing limited reform coupled with intensifying repression and militarization of society.

In 1989, the president of South Africa, P. W. Botha, had a stroke. The party forced him to resign and he was replaced by F.W. de Klerk. Before he became a member of parliament, de Klerk grew up as a committed member of the RCSA and served as an elder leading worship services in the absence of the minister. He was commonly thought to be conservative, in agreement with segregation policies. His first speech as president took the whole world by surprise, as he announced plans to legalize the ANC, Pan Africanist Congress, and South African Communist Party, and to release all political prisoners. He openly said that his biblical convictions of justice obliged him to eventually take this step, and he intended to gain the moral high ground.

Looking back, he said in 2010, "For many years I supported the concept of separate states. I believed it could bring justice for everyone, including the blacks who would determine their own lives inside their own states. But during the 1980s I had concluded this would not work and the system was producing injustice and had to change."[2]

In his historical speech on the second of February, 1990, he said that a totally new and just constitutional dispensation—in which every inhabitant would enjoy equal rights, treatment, and opportunity—would be introduced. He clearly expressed a commitment to equal justice for all under a human rights manifesto, with no discrimination and a free-market economy. The entire edifice of apartheid, so hated around the world, had been finally dismantled in a single speech. Nelson Mandela, who became the next president, had watched the speech on television and later remarked, "It was a breathtaking moment, for in one sweeping action he had virtually normalized the situation in South Africa."[3]

CHANGES SINCE 1994 IN POST-APARTHEID SOUTH AFRICA

Although South Africa has much reason for gratitude over our relatively peaceful transition to a more democratic dispensation and other significant achievements of the past fifteen years, there are also reasons for deep concern remaining—and even new forms of injustice that provide massive challenges.

Encouraging signs include the following:

- International sanctions have been lifted, and free international trade has led to many new international financial investments in the country.
- The country experienced fourteen years of uninterrupted economic growth facilitated by sensible macro-economic policies that the ANC government had implemented, despite its socialist rhetoric.
- The gross domestic product, measured on a purchasing power parity basis, is about $600 billion—about the same size as the Argentine and Polish economies.
- The country has, by far, the largest economy in Africa. With only 6.5 percent of the population of sub-Saharan Africa, South Africa produces a third of the continent's gross economic product and generates two-thirds of the continent's electricity.

- Since 1994, millions of black South Africans have joined the middle class, enlarging the consumer market and contributing to societal stability.
- Since 1994, the government has built more than three million houses for disadvantaged communities. It has also extended water and electricity services to more than 70 percent of all households. Thirteen million children and old-age pensioners receive state allowances.

Areas of great concern are the following:

- South Africa has the highest number of HIV-infected people in the world, and in the wake of the pandemic, two million orphans have been left behind.
- South Africa has become one of the most unequal societies in the world—despite the ANC's commitment to the promotion of equality and that the achievement of equality is one of the founding values in our Constitution.
- Almost 50 percent of South Africans live in poverty.
- A Human Science Research Council study has shown that poor households have sunk deeper into poverty since 1996.
- The way that affirmative action has been implemented has led to millions of highly skilled young people leaving the country to find employment in other countries. People who are not qualified and competent have been put in management positions they cannot handle. This has resulted in a total collapse of public services, corruption and bankruptcy of many municipalities. Since 2009, the country is experiencing more strikes and demonstrations of people in townships—including rioting against the deterioration of roads, sanitation, water supply, and medical and civil services—than ever before.
- The education system has also deteriorated, leading to a lesser number of students graduating from grade 12. Thus, doors for employment or continued tertiary education are closed for many young people.

- An emerging new phenomenon is that an increasing number of white families are falling into extreme poverty. Research pointed out that poverty in the white community has increased 400 percent since 1994. It is no longer unusual to see white people begging on the streets. According to the latest official statistics from 2006, there were nine hundred thousand unemployed white people in South Africa—all living in total destitution. This phenomenon is seen by many people as the result of reverse apartheid and unjust labor legislation that has led to new forms of poverty and destitution.

- However, there is still more poverty in the non-white community and more unemployment of unskilled people, than in white communities. The so-called Black Economic Empowerment (BEE) legislation has produced quite a few black millionaires but has not succeeded in reducing poverty and unemployment at large in black communities.

- South Africa suffers from rampant violent crime. Since 1994, more than three thousand farmers have been murdered in tens of thousands of farm attacks, and many brutally tortured and /or raped. It is estimated that fifty people die every day due to violent crime and robbery in South Africa.

LEGACIES OF THE PAST AND NEW CHALLENGES

Although apartheid died, its effects and legacies linger on because the issues of unjust power that haunted the apartheid era are still with us in many ways. The many decades of isolation and fear, the pain and hatred of centuries, will need generations to heal. We as South Africans still have a long way to go to move beyond racial hegemony to a real unified national identity. Racial tensions continue to manifest themselves in various ways. Irresponsible politicians address mass meetings and open their meetings by chanting a song with the following words:

> *Ayasaba amagwala* ("They are scared, the cowards")
> *Awudubule (i)bhunu* ("Do shoot the [or "a"] farmer")
> *Ziyarobha le zintsha* ("They rob us, these dogs")

The word "farmer," in this context, is used as an expletive to refer to whites—or more specifically, to Afrikaners. A supreme court ruled the song was tantamount to "hate speech." But the ruling party and its allies came out in defense of the song's violent lyrics, saying it reflected their heritage and struggle for freedom against the white apartheid government.[4]

The brutal slaying on April 3, 2010, of prominent extreme right white Afrikaner leader Eugene Terre'Blanche, at the hands of his black farmhands, could not have occurred with more sinister timing. Terre'Blanche, 69, was first beaten to a pulp with a *knopkierie* (an African club with a large knob on one end used to smash the skulls of animals and men) and then hacked to pieces by a machete while he was lying in bed, taking a nap. There is little doubt that his murder will continue to reverberate politically across the country, and especially within the embattled white Afrikaner farming community, where it will shine a stark light on their grievances and growing schism with the ruling ANC and the state.

In light of all this, South Africa desperately needs Christians in all spheres of society who deliberately seek to be instruments of reconciliation and peace, speaking of and showing the gospel's transforming grace. Christians ought to be on the forefront in the pursuit of peace (Proverbs 16:7; Hebrews 12:14), and doing of justice (Micah 6:8), in a country still bleeding from so many wounds of the past.

KEY BIBLICAL TERMS

In seeking to understand the biblical foundations of social justice, it is necessary to see how the goal of doing justice is to reach a condition of peace. At the same time, establishing peace with God and neighbors results in doing justice. Therefore, as it is put in Psalm 85:10, "righteousness and peace kiss each other." Part and parcel of doing justice to achieve peace is to care for the poor, hungry, and deprived. It is appropriate to consider briefly the meaning of key terms from a biblical perspective.

Peace

The word *shalom* (שׁלוֹם) is the most prominent Old Testament term for peace. It has a wide range of connotations—wholeness, health, security, well-being, and salvation—and could apply to an equally wide range of contexts. It can apply to the state of the individual (Psalm 37:37; Proverbs 3:2; Isaiah 32:17), the relationship between people (Genesis 34:21; Joshua 9:15) or nations (e.g., absence of conflict—Deuteronomy 2:26; Joshua 10:21; 1 Kings 5:12; Psalm 122:6–7), and the relationship between God and his people (Psalm 85:8; Jeremiah 16:5).

Peace as a sign of God's blessing is most often associated with the grace by which God establishes or reestablishes his covenant (Exodus 34:25; 37:26; Isaiah 54:10); hence it becomes a synonym of reconciliation. It is also sometimes synonymous with tranquillity and rest, as opposed to a state of war between individuals or peoples. Man has to seek peace, ask for it, and "make" it (2 Chronicles 13:11; Proverbs 17:1; Matthew 5:9; Mark 9:50; Romans 12:18; 1 Timothy 2:2, etc.). The presence of peace signified God's blessing in the covenant relationship (Malachi 2:5; cf. Numbers 25:12), and its absence signified the breakdown of that relationship due to the disobedience and unrighteousness of God's people (Jeremiah 16:5, 10–13; cf. Psalm 85:9–11; Isaiah 32:17).

There is no separation between internal (or spiritual) and external peace; the latter is symptomatic of the former and the first proclaims the conditions for the latter (e.g. Psalm 122:6–7). In general, peace is a gift of God (Numbers 6:26). The announcement and proclamation of peace is accompanied by the declaration of its conditions, of which the principal one is the observation and fulfillment of the righteousness of God—no peace without righteousness (Psalm 72:3-7; 85:9–11; Isaiah 32:17)! There is no peace for the wicked (Isaiah 8:22; 57:21). It is for this reason that, at a time when the final defense of Jerusalem is being contested, the prophets denounce the false hope held out by words of peace spoken by false prophets (Jeremiah 6:14; 8:11, 15; Ezekiel 13:10; Micah 3:5). Jesus likewise denounces the false security of men in view of the imminence of judgment (Luke 17: 26–36; 19:42–44; cf. 1 Thessalonians 5:3).

Christ Himself is offered as God's gracious gift of peace—"he himself is our peace" (Ephesians 2:14); "since we have been justified by faith, we have peace with God through our Lord Jesus Christ" (Romans 5:1). He has made "peace by the blood of his cross" (Colossians 1:20). The redeeming work of Christ, which is to reconcile "all things" to God, to justify sinners freely by the mediation of the new covenant, is entirely contained in this word: *peace*. By Christ and in Christ we know that God is a "God of peace" (Philippians 4:9; Colossians 3:15; 2 Thessalonians 3:16).

This peace of God, which is received by faith in Jesus Christ, is a peace which we have to manifest in our lives just as the love that God has for us produces in us love for our brethren; like love, peace is a fruit of the Spirit (Galatians 5:22). That is why the preaching of the gospel of peace carries with it also the exhortation to "live in peace," to "be in peace," to "seek peace with all" (Romans 12:18; 14:19; 2 Corinthians 13:11; 2 Timothy 2:22–26; Hebrews 12:14; 1 Peter 3:11; 2 Peter 3:14). Jesus taught that those who make peace are blessed and will be called children of God (Matthew 5:9).

The eschatological implications of *shalom* make it clear that our English word "peace" is much too weak to convey the full rich meaning of the Hebrew word. The prophets pointed beyond the crises of exile and subsequent setbacks to a time when *shalom*, characterized by prosperity and well-being (Isaiah 45:7; Ezekiel 34:25–26), absence of conflict (Isaiah 2:2–4; 32:15–20; Ezekiel 34:28–31), right relations (Isaiah 11:1–5; Micah 4:1–4; Zechariah 8:9–13), restoration of harmony in nature (Isaiah 11:6–9; Ezekiel 47:1–12), and salvation (Isaiah 52:7; 60:17; Ezekiel 34:30–31; 37:26–28) would again return. Often this eschatological (or end-time) expectation of peace in the Old Testament was associated with the coming of the Messiah, as in Isaiah 9:6, where the future Messiah is termed the "Prince of Peace." His reign would be one of "peace"—not only for Israel but throughout the whole earth (Zechariah 9:9–10).

Cornelius Plantinga summarizes all of the above well.

The webbing together of God, humans and all creation in justice fulfillment and delight is what the Hebrew prophets call *shalom*. We call it peace, but it means far more than peace of mind or a cease-fire between enemies. In the Bible shalom means *universal flourishing wholeness, delight*—a rich state of affairs in which natural needs are satisfied and natural gifts fruitfully employed, a state of affairs that inspires joyful wonder at its Creator and Saviour, opens doors and welcomes the creatures in whom He delights.[5]

Justice

Only justice can produce *shalom*. Justice is rooted in the character of God. "For the LORD is righteous, he loves justice" (Psalm 11:7, NIV 1984). Justice is the establishment of a right relationship—primarily between God and people, secondarily between people themselves, and thirdly between people and the whole of creation.

The quality of a person's relationship with God is reflected in his relationship with his fellow humans and the whole of creation. Justice is applicable at all levels of society, and is relevant in every area of life. The opposite of righteous is "evil," "wicked," or "wrong" (cf. Psalm 1:6; Zephaniah 3:5). The worship of Yahweh entails a respect for the rights of others (cf. Exodus 20:2ff; Isaiah 1:1; 6:6ff; Amos 5:14ff, etc.).

Biblical legislation was designed to help especially those in danger of being the victims of injustice—namely widows, orphans, and foreigners (cf. Exodus 22:2; Leviticus 19:15,33; Deuteronomy 24:1, etc.). In the royal psalms, the role of the human ruler as representative of God emphasizes that in legal matters, decisions must be made that create right and just order, especially for the poor (Psalm 72:2). Peace is not possible in a land and system where justice is not nurtured. The primary responsibility of the national leader to secure the well-being of all the citizens is not a matter that is settled by "securing" the borders from without. It depends also on the flourishing of justice within. It is characteristic of the biblical understanding of peace as *shalom* that it cannot be seen to exist where the cause of the poor is undefended, and where oppressive conditions and acts are allowed to exist. Where the poor are defended, and oppression and exploitation stopped, peace and righteousness are as natural and *consistent* as the seasons, the fall of rain, and the waxing and waning of the moon.

A central activity of the monarchy is to secure help for the weak and needy. Psalm 72:12–14 repeatedly declares this function as the task of the king. Indeed, there is no other specific activity ascribed to, or hoped for, from the human ruler than justice for the weak and the poor. That is the function of the king in the kingdom of peace. The way to peace and well-being is found only where power assumes responsibility for justice and is clothed in compassion, regarding as precious and valuable the life of every citizen in the land.

The hope for an era characterized by righteousness was rooted in the prophetic revelation of the messianic rule and the establishment of God's kingdom on earth (Isaiah 11:1–9), whose rule will extend to the nations (vv. 10–16) and will last forever (9:7). The fullness of righteousness will be manifest at the return of the Lord Jesus, when all those who have been justified will also be glorified (Romans 8:30). The goal of salvation history moves toward the final glorious manifestation of God's kingdom, where justice and peace shall reign and all creation will be renewed in "righteousness"—that is, all creation will be right with God (2 Peter 3:13).

After a lifetime study of the Old Testament and Semitic languages, generally and specifically of the terms "righteous" and "justice," Bruce Waltke concludes with the following observation:

> The church will put the proverb, "The wicked advantage themselves by disadvantaging others, but the righteous disadvantage themselves to advantage others," within her commitment to the Lord Jesus Christ. He is the supreme example of righteousness as conceptualized in Proverbs. He became poor that we might become rich; he gave up his life that we might have eternal life. Moreover, the church's catechism teaches that our Lord gave his church his Spirit to empower her to live his sort of life. Her best resolutions to live righteously will fail. Apart from God's grace, her best social efforts are splendid vices, for they are all tarnished by self-interests.

Let the church look to the Triune God from whom every good and perfect gift comes, including the gift to give one's life to serve others.[6]

The Poor and Poverty

The many Hebrew words translated "poor" in the Bible emphasize not only the material destitution of those involved but their weakness, dependence, or low status in society, and hence their being easily oppressed. Overlapping with terms like "widow," "orphan," or "needy," the poor are described as those who are weak with respect to the rest of the community. The responsibility of the community is stated as "you shall support him" so he can continue to take his place in the community (Leviticus 25:35). One of the dilemmas of the poor is their loss of community (Job 22:5; Psalm 107:4–9, 33–36). Indeed, their various needs include systems and people who prevent the poor from being secure and becoming contributing members of society.[7]

The Pentateuch emphasizes equitable treatment for the poor. Justice was neither to be withheld from the poor (Exodus 23:6) nor distorted because a person was poor (Exodus 23:3; Leviticus 19:15). Such equity is illustrated by the collection of ransom money from rich and poor alike (Exodus 30:15). As part of the covenant community, the poor person was to be treated with respect (Deuteronomy 24:10–11) and supported, even economically, by other Israelites, since they were not to charge interest to the poor (Exodus 22:25; Leviticus 25:35–38).

Beyond direct legislation a number of special provisions (social security systems) were put in place to provide opportunities for the poor. Gleaning laws focused on the widow, fatherless, stranger, and poor (Leviticus 19:9–10; 23:22; Deuteronomy 24:19–22). During the sabbatical year debts were to be cancelled (Deuteronomy 15:1–9), and the year of Jubilee provided release for Hebrews who had become slaves through poverty (Leviticus 25:39–41, 54). During these festivals the poor could eat freely of the produce of all of the fields (Exodus 23:11; Leviticus 25:6–7, 12).

Further stipulations to aid the poor included the right of redemption from slavery by a blood relative (Leviticus 25:47–49), support from the third-year tithe (Deuteronomy 14:28–29), and special provisions regarding the guilt offerings. This latter law illustrates the relative nature of the concept of poverty. If someone could afford the normal atonement lamb she could bring two pigeons (Leviticus 5:7), but further consideration (substituting one-tenth ephah of flour) is made for one who cannot afford even two pigeons (Leviticus 5:11). Clearly, the Law emphasized that poverty was no reason for exclusion from atonement and worship! In general, the responsibility of the poor to work and where possible earn their income was always maintained as a way to assist them to retain their dignity.

Motivation for such legislation was God's concern for the poor. God listened to the cry of the needy (Exodus 22:27), blessed those who considered them (Deuteronomy 24:13, 19), and held accountable those who oppressed them (Deuteronomy 24:15). The Lord based this position on his relationship with his people; he was their God (Leviticus 23:22) and had redeemed them from slavery (Deuteronomy 24:18).

The highest concentration of terms for the poor in the Old Testament is found in the poetic books. The Psalms dramatically portray the difficulties of physical poverty. Helping the poor is identified with righteousness (Psalm 112:9) while oppression of the afflicted is one of the crimes of the wicked (109:16). The Psalms also move beyond the sphere of social poverty to speak of spiritual humility (25:9). The poor are paralleled to the godly (12:1, 5), the upright (37:14), and those who love the Lord's salvation (40:17; 70:5); and they are contrasted to evil men (Psalm 140:1, 12), the wicked (37:14; 109:2, 22), and fools (14:1, 6; 74:21–22).

Frequently in the Psalms, especially lament psalms, the poor called to the Lord for help (Psalm 34:6; 70:5; 86:1; 109:21–22), knowing that he heard their cry (69:33). The psalmist understood that God was the just judge of the poor. The Lord was seen as their refuge (14:6), deliverer (40:17), and provider (68:10). He rescued (35:10), raised (113:7), and satisfied them (132:15); it was the Lord who secured justice for the poor and the needy (140:12).

More than any other book, Proverbs gives visibility to the causes of poverty. Because of the book's didactic nature, the emphasis is upon controllable circumstances, but other reasons are included. Poverty is a result of laziness (Proverbs 6:10–11; 10:4; 20:13; 24:33–34), lack of discipline (13:18), idleness (14:23; 28:19), haste (21:5), excess (21:17; 23:20–21), and injustice (13:23).

The Wisdom Literature paints a realistic picture of poverty in the ancient world. The poor are vulnerable (Proverbs 18:23), shunned by friends (Proverbs 14:20; 19:4, 7), and become servants to the rich (Proverbs 22:7). Poverty brings sorrow (Proverbs 31:7) and can lead to crime (Proverbs 30:8–9). Poverty is quite realistically presented in Job 24, where the poor are portrayed as hungry, thirsty, naked, and suffering from various kinds of injustice and oppression including the loss of property, family, and life. Yet obedience to the Lord is more important than riches. This priority is evidenced in the comparison of poverty with other areas of life. It is better than foolishness (Proverbs 19:1; Ecclesiastes 4:13), lying (Proverbs 19:22), even being a rich liar (Proverbs 28:6), or having rich pride (Psalm 28:11).

The Wisdom Literature is emphatic in its encouragement to help those who are poor. Giving to the poor is encouraged (Proverbs 11:24; 28:8, 22, 27) while oppression of the poor is against one's maker (Proverbs 14:31; 17:5). Rulers are taught not to oppress the poor (Proverbs 28:3; 29:14; 31:9). Those who help the poor are the righteous (Job 29:12–17; Proverbs 29:7; 31:20), while the wicked do not care for the poor (Job 20:19; Proverbs 29:7; 30:14).

Certainly the most grievous examples of poverty and the severest rebukes come from the prophets. It should be noted, however, that the prophets were not primarily spokespersons for the poor or the oppressed peoples; they were spokespersons for God. Amos is quite graphic in his portrayal of the oppression of the poor. The poor are bought and sold, trampled, crushed, oppressed, forced, and denied justice by those who are in a position to do otherwise. Their treatment is a striking example of the waywardness of God's people from the covenant obligations and their unique relationship with the Lord. "[T]hey sell the righteous for silver, and the needy for a pair of sandals—those who trample the head of the poor into the dust of the earth and turn aside the way of the afflicted" (Amos 2:6–7).

The emphasis of prophetic invective fell upon the leaders. Instead of defending the poor and upholding the Law of God, they took bribes and gifts to pervert justice (Isaiah 1:23). Neglecting the clear call of Scripture to provide for the poor, they passed unjust laws and deprived the poor of their rights (Isaiah 10:1–2; Jeremiah 5:27–28), taking their goods and their land (Isaiah 3:13–15; 5:8). Isaiah accents their abuse: "'What do you mean by crushing my people, by grinding the face of the poor?'" (Isaiah 3:15). Yet the people were held accountable for their actions as well. Ezekiel, for example, reminded the people that they had joined with the leaders in such oppression (Ezekiel 22:26–29) and pointed out the primary responsibility of the individual was to obey God (Ezekiel 18:16–17).

Jesus stressed the need to give to the poor (Matthew 19:21; Luke 12:33) and to provide for them (Luke 14:13, 21). He identified with poor people and, like many poor persons, he did not have a home (Luke 9:58). He taught how difficult it was to be rich (Matthew 19:23–24) and the necessity of spiritual poverty for a relationship with God (Matthew 5:3).

Paul's sensitivity to the poor is consistent with the teaching of Jesus and the agenda of the early church. He understood that the word of Christ cut across sociological boundaries and that the church was made up of poor and rich alike (Galatians 3:28; Colossians 3:11; cf. 1 Corinthians 1:27–29). His stress on the collection for the Jerusalem church exhibits this concern in a practical way (Romans 15:26; 1 Corinthians 16:3; 2 Corinthians 8–9; Galatians 2:10) and was a test whether Christians had real love for Christ (2 Corinthians 8:8–9).

James emphasizes that true religion is to care for widows and orphans (James 1:27), and highlights God's sensitivity to the poor and their faith (2:5). He notes that discriminating between the rich and the poor is both a sin against God (2:9) and an insult to the poor (2:6). The very nature of God himself, James insists, is that he has care for the poor and hungry.

To summarize: The Bible teaches that God provides for the poor, delivers the poor, secures justice for the poor, hears the poor, shows no partiality against the poor, protects the poor, will not forsake the poor, and gives food to the poor. This, then, is the kingdom to which we belong. We are called to be ambassadors of God, and as such we are called to stand up on behalf of the poor. To do less is to rebel against God. Worse, to do less is to falsely represent the character of God to the world, to slander his name among the nations—and therefore, by God's own definition, to be wicked.

Love

Christianity's teaching on love is unparalleled in the history of religion and provides the energy for doing justice and caring for the poor. God's eternal love motivated him to send Jesus Christ to redeem this world (John 3:16; 16:27; 17:23).

In the Old Testament the unshakable, steadfast love of God is contrasted with the unpredictable, capricious moods of heathen deities. The Hebrew word for love, *hesed*, does not indicate an emotional response to beauty, merit, or kindness. Rather, it refers to undeserved love—whether or not the object of God's love is lovable, worthy, or responsive (see Deuteronomy 7:7–9). God's love does not change. In the Old Testament it is pictured through exile and failure as persisting with infinite patience, neither condoning evil nor abandoning the evildoers. It has within it kindness, tenderness, and compassion (Psalm 86:15; 103:1–18; 136; Hosea 11:1–4).

The Law enjoined wholehearted love and gratitude for God's choosing and redeeming of his people (Deuteronomy 6:20–25). This was to be shown in worship, but also especially in humane treatment of the poor, the defenseless, the resident alien, slaves, widows, and all suffering oppression and cruelty (cf. also Hosea 6:6; 7:1–7; 10:12–13). Love for God and for "your neighbor as yourself" (Leviticus 19:18) are thus linked in Israel's Law and prophecy. While much love of another kind lies within the Old Testament, the major points are God's loving initiative, the moral quality of love, and the close relationship between love for God with love for others.

In the New Testament, Christian love reveals the fulfillment of all the promises of God's love in and through Jesus Christ. The new commandment—to love one another with the same ardent, self-giving love as Christ loved—colors the whole New Testament. The Greek word group for love—ἀγάπη, ἀγαπάω (*agapē, agapaō*), and the adjective ἀγαπητός (*agapētos*, beloved)—appears approximately 320 times in the New Testament. Love is to be the mark of the Christian.[8]

The greatness of Jesus's love moved him to "lay down his life for his friends" (John 15:13). He laid down his life for us (1 John 3:16). The mutual love of Father, Son, and disciples must be the fundamental fact in Christianity because God himself is love (1 John 4:8, 16). We know God's love by the Incarnation and the cross. Thus we know and believe the love God has for us, and that love itself is divine ("of God"). It follows that "whoever loves has been born of God and knows God. Anyone who does not love does not know God….No one has ever seen God; [nevertheless] if we love one another, God abides in us" and we in God (1 John 4:7–8, 12).

Our love is directed first toward God. But our love for him demands that we do not love the world, but that we love God's Word and his commandments and our Christian brothers and sisters. This commandment we received, "whoever loves God must also love his brother" (1 John 4:21) is prefaced by "if God so loved us, we also ought to love one another" (1 John 4:11). Indeed, if one closes his heart against his brother or sister, "how does God's love abide in him?" (1 John 3:17).

Love for one's fellow Christians does not exclude, but instead leads on to, a wider love (2 Peter 1:7) obeying the command of Jesus to love one's enemies (Luke 6:27–37; cf. also Romans 12:20–21). If love fails within Christian fellowship, it certainly will not flourish beyond it, but evaporate in mere words (1 John 3:18). Jesus's demand that the disciples love each other "as I have loved you" (John 13:34) was, by every human standard, new and astonishing. No human had ever loved perfectly like Jesus ("to the end," John 13:1). When John drew the conclusion that "we ought to lay down our lives for the brothers," the implication follows that love means never shutting one's heart against another Christian in need (1 John 3:16–17), but rather rejoicing to sacrifice one's temporal good for another's blessing.

One of the key factors that helps explain the rapid expansion of early Christianity is the love displayed among the first Christians.

This love did not go unnoticed at the time. The third-century African writer and apologist Tertullian tells us that the pagans of his day had to acknowledge the extraordinary love of the Christians. The pagans were forced to say, "See... how they love one another... and how ready they are to die for each other." In an ancient Latin Christian dialogue entitled *Octavius,* the pagan Caecilius criticizes the Christians because "hardly have they met when they love each other.... Indiscriminately they call each other brother and sister."

Contemporary writers have also noted the supreme importance of love to the Christian faith. Summarizing the Christian life, the distinguished Presbyterian theologian B. B. Warfield states, "Self-sacrificing love is thus made the essence of the Christian life."[9] Reviewing the virtues of power, knowledge, religious experience, doctrinal orthodoxy, and service, John Stott concludes from Galatians 5:22 that "love is the pre-eminent Christian grace."[10]

In his remarkable book *The Rise of Christianity*, Rodney Stark not only reveals historical facts, but also brings a sociologist's perspective to bear on the puzzle behind the success of early Christianity. He says that there were three ways in which the early Christians were remarkably different from their pagan neighbors:

1. When the great epidemics hit the urban centers, while others just fled, Christians stayed to care for the sick; and several died in the process of doing so.
2. When Christians were persecuted, they did not respond with retaliation or guerrilla warfare, but died while praying for their persecutors.
3. When Rome conquered all the nations, all national borders were opened. The cities became fiercely multiethnic, which lead to a great deal of ethnic tension. The Christian church was the first institution in the history of the world that brought people together across those ethnic barriers and said race means nothing.[11]

Why were the Christians so much more compassionate to the sick? Why were they so much more forgiving to their persecutors? Why were they so much more ethnically inclusive than anyone else had ever seen?

Tim Keller, in a 2004 series of sermons on Christian hope, suggested that there is one main answer—their attitudes and lifestyle were dependent on what they believed the ultimate future to be. Christians had hope! They were shaped by a joyful certainty of God's future: eternal glory and love. Therefore they could stay in the cities—because they were not afraid of death since they knew that after death comes God's love. The reason they did not retaliate against their persecutors with violence and terrorism is because they knew that at the end of time God would judge everything and put everything right. They were ethnically inclusive because they believed that there is one God, who is busy gathering his new people from every tribe, tongue, and nation.

Mercy

Mercy is a divine quality by which God faithfully keeps his promises and maintains his covenant relationship with his chosen people, despite their unworthiness and unfaithfulness (Deuteronomy 30:1–6; Isaiah 14:1; Ezekiel 39:25–29; Romans 9:15–16, 23; 11:32; Ephesians 2:4). The biblical meaning of mercy is exceedingly rich and complex, as evidenced by the fact that several Hebrew and Greek words were used to express the concept. Consequently, there are many synonyms used in translation to express the dimensions of meaning involved— "kindness," "lovingkindness," "goodness," "grace," "favor," "pity," "compassion," and "steadfast love." Prominent in the concept of mercy is the compassionate disposition to forgive offenders or adversaries and to help or spare them in their sorry plight.

At the heart of the concept of mercy is the love of God, which is freely manifested in his gracious saving acts on behalf of those to whom he has pledged himself in covenant relationship. In the Old Testament, it was his chosen people Israel whom he elected to be his own and to whom he showed mercy (Exodus 33:19; Isaiah 54:10; 63:9). God persistently put up with his disobedient and wayward people, and continuously sought them out to draw them back to himself.

Hosea pictures God as a loving father who looks down from heaven with a yearning heart of compassion upon his rebellious and wayward people (Hosea 11; cf. Jeremiah 31:20). He also regards Israel as an unfaithful and adulterous wife whom God loves as a faithful husband in spite of her apostate and sinful condition (Hosea 1–3; cf. Isaiah 54:4–8). Isaiah depicts God as a mother who has compassion on the son of her womb (Isaiah 49:15). These pictures reveal God's mercy in rich and different ways. The remembrance of God's mercy gives a repentant person the hope and assurance of divine favor and of reconciliation with the offended Lord.

In the New Testament a very descriptive Greek word is used for Jesus's mercy toward the needy (Matthew 9:36; 14:14; 20:34). It expresses his pity and compassion by means of an intense verb, literally translated "to be moved in one's bowels." The Hebrews regarded the bowels as the center of the affections, especially those of the most tender kindness. Jesus was described as being deeply moved toward the needy and spontaneously acting to relieve their suffering—to heal (Matthew 20:34; Mark 1:41), to raise the dead (Luke 7:13), and to feed the hungry (Matthew 15:32).

The most characteristic use of mercy in the New Testament is that of God's provision of salvation for mankind in Jesus Christ (Romans 11:30–32; Ephesians 2:4). God is "the Father of mercies" (2 Corinthians 1:3), bestowed on those who believe in his Son. It is because he is "rich in mercy" that he saved those who are spiritually dead and doomed by their sins (Ephesians 2:4–6). It is out of God's mercy that one is forgiven and granted eternal life (1 Timothy 1:13–16).

Because God has freely extended his mercy irrespective of worthiness or faithfulness, people are to respond by showing mercy to others, even though they do not deserve it or seek it. Indeed, people are commanded to be merciful, especially to the poor, the needy, widows, and orphans (Proverbs 14:31; 19:17; Micah 6:8; Zechariah 7:9–10; Colossians 3:12). God regards mercy more than the ritual sacrifice (Matthew 9:13). God's mercy in Christ actually puts people under obligation to act toward others as God himself has acted toward them.

Members of the Christian church are to show compassion and practical concern for each other. They are to give aid and relief, love and comfort to one another, as Christ freely gave to them in their need. The apostle James teaches the essential nature of such good works as being of the very essence of genuine faith (James 1:27; 2:14–26). It was the mercy that the good Samaritan had toward the man who was beaten and robbed that was singled out by the Lord for special commendation (Luke 10:36–37). To be full of mercy is a distinguishing virtue of our citizenship in the kingdom of heaven (Matthew 5:7).

IMPLICATIONS OF THE RELATEDNESS OF TERMS

It is clear that the biblical concepts of *peace*, *justice*, *mercy* and *love* combine in a Christian response to poverty and care for the needy. Each of these terms (and especially all of them together) reflects the character of God. The poor often live lives that break God's heart and should break ours as well. A God-centered approach to alleviating poverty should reflect a pursuit for social justice, with lovingkindness and merciful compassion. Only in the context of pursuing peace will the poor really be helped to become responsible stewards in God's creation themselves.

The pursuit of reconciliation as the heart of the Christian story — both vertical (with God) and horizontal (with our fellow human beings)—has to respond to the barriers of race, ethnicity, and class that leads to injustice and poverty. A central task of the church is to learn how to build relationships of reconciliation that express the newness of the kingdom in social, economic, political, and gender relationships. Churches also have to fulfil their prophetic calling to testify to governments against systems and policies and political actions that provoke hatred and racial tensions and lead to poverty for sections of a community.

One humble example is the testimony that the committee of the Synod of the RCSA has recently sent to the president of South Africa to stop the politicians in his party from uttering hate speech in lyrics they sing at public meetings, and at the same time to plead with the white right-wing section of the Afrikaner Weerstandsbeweging not to take revenge into their own hands as response to the murder of a prominent leader. A conducive atmosphere for reconciliation is also created where churches reach out across racial and cultural boundaries with loving and compassionate care for widows, orphans, and people living with HIV and AIDS in destitute poverty.

COMPREHENSIVE UNDERSTANDING AND APPLICATION

Service to God and others should not be compartmentalized into spiritual versus social, or task versus relational. It should radiate a total way of life sharing. Community transformation through a holistic response to poverty takes seriously the effects of sin over all of life and the earth—the sin of Genesis 3 that alienated men and women from God, from self, from others, and from the environment. Community transformation is the reversal of this sin, the restoration of God's order in creation, and God's intent for humans to be full image-bearers of God. Such transformation will make people more fully human, worshipers of God by the power of the gospel in word and deed. The completion of this task will only occur at the culmination of this age, when Christ returns.

Community development is more than projects and new programs. As we submit more to the lordship of Christ, our lives are changing to reflect the image of Christ (2 Corinthians 3:18) and our service is taking new forms.

THEOLOGICAL AND ECUMENICAL TRENDS IN COMPREHENSIVE HOLISTIC UNDERSTANDING

Since the 1900s, social issues have divided the church into two basic camps: conservative and liberal. Fundamental and conservative churches tend to neglect social issues and place their focus on evangelism and the teaching and preaching of the Word. At the same time, churches that fall in the liberal category have social issues as their primary concern and tend to neglect the teaching of sound doctrine, preaching the gospel, and calling unbelievers to repentance and faith in Christ. If you value teaching, knowledge, and believing the right doctrine, you probably fall on the conservative side of the issue. If mercy, social justice, and action drive how you envision your faith working itself out, you may easily be identified with the more liberal side of the above options.

There is broad consensus amongst theologians that the social gospel has been perhaps most clearly defined by its most famous protagonist, Walter Rauschenbusch. Writing in 1907, he spoke of the "immense latent perfectibility in human nature." He said that we are now at the point in history when all things can come together and produce a race of happy, prosperous, peaceful people, working together harmoniously and in love. This will be the kingdom of God, now coming into fruition. All that is necessary is that we set ourselves free from the false doctrines and ideas that have held us back in the past. "Religious faith and moral strength must be directed toward these last great social tasks."[12]

The social gospel concentrates not so much on individual salvation of one's own soul, but rather on the "evangelization" and "conversion" of social structures and institutions to a "Christian" form, culminating in the promised kingdom of God. Since many of the social gospel leaders were socialistic or progressive in their economic and political outlook, they considered activities that led to this type of society as being "evangelistic"—evangelizing the social structures.

Conversely, the responsibility that the visible church has in the social and economic spheres is denied, in general, by mysticism, pietism, certain types of eschatologism, and to some extent by Barthianism or the theology of crisis. Some churches believe that social issues hinder the real work of evangelism and preaching. They argue that evangelism is the only historical aim of mission. They argue for the centrality of gospel proclamation and then argue that social involvement is a distraction from this central aim. Such people may accept that individual Christians should have compassion on those they meet who are in need, but believe that the organized, corporate mission of the church is evangelism alone.

Beginning in 1974, the Lausanne Movement, led by the Lausanne Committee for World Evangelization (LCWE), became a major expression of evangelical concern for evangelism and, increasingly, social responsibility. This congress established social involvement as a dimension of the evangelical understanding of mission. In the opening plenary session, John Stott argued that mission should not simply be equated with evangelism but that instead, we should speak of the total mission of the church, which includes both evangelism and social concern.

The resulting covenant said "we affirm that both evangelism and socio-political involvement are part of our Christian duty." But not everyone was happy with this emphasis. A number of evangelical Christians feared that in the inclusion of socio-political involvement, evangelism would inevitably be edged out.

In June 1982 the Lausanne Committee for World Evangelization brought together both sides of the debate for the Consultation on the Relationship between Evangelism and Social Responsibility in Grand Rapids, Michigan. In 1984 the Lausanne Committee and the World Evangelical Fellowship (now the World Evangelical Alliance) arranged an international consultation in Wheaton, Illinois, to continue discussion of the relation of church and mission, as well as the problems of social justice that had not at that stage been aired by evangelicals.

This idea of an integral relationship was affirmed more recently when evangelical development agencies from around the world met in 2001 in Oxford to form the Micah Network. They produced a statement called "The Micah Declaration on Integral Mission." The term "integral mission" comes from the Spanish "misión integral," the term commonly used in Latin America for what others describe as "holistic ministry," "Christian development," or "'transformation." The declaration defines integral mission as follows:

> Integral mission or holistic transformation is the proclamation and demonstration of the gospel. It is not simply that evangelism and social involvement are to be done alongside each other. Rather, in integral mission our proclamation has social consequences as we call

people to love and repentance in all areas of life. And our social involvement has evangelistic consequences as we bear witness to the transforming grace of Jesus Christ.

If we ignore the word of God we have nothing to bring to the world. Justice and justification by faith, worship and political action, the spiritual and the material, personal change and structural change belong together. As in the life of Jesus, being, doing and saying are at the heart of our integral task.[13]

A BIRD'S-EYE VIEW OF POVERTY WORLDWIDE, AND SPECIFICALLY IN AFRICA

Jeffrey Sachs, in his book *The End of Poverty*, divides the current population of the world into the following four categories:

- *The poorest of the poor* (who have to try and survive on less than one US dollar per day) are approximately one billion, or one-sixth of the world population.
- *The poor* who can—just—succeed in surviving, since they are able to provide for their basic needs. These constitute about 1.5 billion.
- *The middle income group*, which consists of about 2.5 billion.
- *The high-income group* who (like the poorest of the poor) count about one billion (about one-sixth of the total population).[14]

Those who live in extreme poverty do not have enough to provide for their basic needs. Therefore, they are hungry and sick most of the time; do not have clean drinking water, sanitation, or proper housing at their disposal; nor can they afford education for their children. According to Sachs, neither can they by themselves—without outside help— escape from the poverty trap in which they are caught. It is estimated that eight million people of this group die annually of hunger and malnourishment. The situation becomes still more critical if the following is kept in mind:

1. After an initial decrease in poverty, since 1996, the number of people in the poorest category has increased again to 1.2 billion.[15]
2. Secondly, the gap between rich and poor is widening steadily. Gina Buijs demonstrates that the 600 million poorest people together earn only one-eighth annually of the income of the 200 richest people in the world.[16]
3. Sachs points out that since about 1980, development aid to the poorest has not increased but decreased.[17]

Africa, especially south of the Sahara, is the very poorest part of the world. Sachs classifies 50 percent of the population of sub-Saharan Africa in his category of "the extreme poor."[18]

Although extreme poverty in South and East Asia has decreased since 1980, it has increased in Africa. According to Sachs, Africa today is poorer than when most of its countries became independent fifty or so years ago.[19] Since the huge development organizations like the World Bank and the International Monetary Fund appeared on the scene in the 1960s, the economic development in Asia and Latin America has passed Africa. Here are a few shocking statistics:

- Ten to fifteen thousand African people die *daily* of diseases like malaria, tuberculosis, and AIDS.
- Between one and three million children die annually in Africa.
- In 2000 the average life expectancy of people in Africa was only forty-seven years—thirty-one years less than those in developed countries. In some countries the average is a mere twenty years, as a result of the AIDS pandemic.

Sachs rightly criticizes the still-prevalent view that the blame lies only with the Africans and especially the African governments, and that therefore Africans alone should take the blame for their problems. This is too restricted a view, he says, as already proven by the failure of structural adaptation programs and the still greater poverty in Africa.

MISSIONAL MINISTRY: POINTING TOWARD THE COMING OF THE KINGDOM OF GOD

Wherever Calvinism has been professed in a really pure and consistent form, it has always manifested a genuine concern that the truth of special revelation be brought to bear on all realms and aspects of human life. Calvinism is the antithesis of the anabaptistic position that would virtually limit the relationships of Christianity to the realm of special grace and isolate that realm from all significant connection with "the world." Not world flight, but world conquest, has been the watchword of real Calvinism.

Every aspect of all human life—including the body, mind, will, and emotions and all of life and all the earth—has been tainted and damaged by sin. This has alienated men and women from God, from self, from others, and from the environment. Therefore, since the fall of Adam and Eve in sin, futility is built into the universe and sin is a universal trait of humanity, both rich and poor. Sin also penetrates our cultures and societies, affecting our social, economic and political systems. HIV/AIDS and its consequences is just another revelation of total depravity, as the suffering caused by it is sometimes experienced as consequences of personal sins and sometimes caused by the sins of others.

Our understanding of the universal effects of sin should lead us to seek community transformation as the reversal of sin and its consequences; and to seek the restoration of God's order in creation, including God's intent for humans to be his image-bearers in all aspects of their lives. Doing our work from the presupposition of the reality of total depravity leads us to understand that transformation of individuals and communities must go much deeper than merely changing conditions of poor socialization, releasing untapped potential in people and communities, or changing environmental conditions. In obedience to the commission of our God, we have to integrate words as well as deeds of God's love in Christ through the power of the Holy Spirit to all people crossing our way. We must present the gospel; call people to repentance, faith, and eternal reconciliation with God through Christ;

and manifest deeds of mercy and compassion, extending the goodness of God's kingdom on earth in the name of Christ.

Christians working in community transformation must take a good look inside before thinking about looking outside. Do we really have and radiate the attitude of John the Baptist—that Christ must increase and we must decrease as we walk with the poor? Christians should have such a quality of spiritual life that it allows us to enter a suffering community not as saviors, but as servants of *the* Savior.

Pride, perfectionism, and good management skills will not wear well in God's work, unless they are seasoned with love and compassion. Growing in humility will not only find favor with the Lord, but will also find favor with the people God has called us to serve.

THE WORLD REFORMED FELLOWSHIP AS A POSSIBLE FACILITATOR FOR ECUMENICAL COOPERATION IN INTEGRAL MISSION

It is my firm belief that biblical and Reformed faith, through God's grace, can be conducive to holistic integral ministry. The biblical mandate to care for the poor, widows, and orphans is not only a mandate of the church in Africa but also to the worldwide church. It is the stated goal of World Reformed Fellowship to be a network of relationships, developing mutually beneficial partnerships to assist local believers with network for communication and sharing of ministry resources. The WRF challenges Reformed Christians to weep with those who weep (Romans 12:15) and share the burden of the afflicted portion of Christ's body (1 Corinthians 12:26) in Africa. Ministry partnerships to serve the suffering poor in Africa seek not only to relieve the misery of countless thousands of people, but are also a powerful testimony to the holistic transformational thrust of a Reformed world- and life-view.

5.

WHAT IS GOD'S GLOBAL URBAN MISSION?

TIMOTHY KELLER

What is a city?

Today, a city is defined almost exclusively in terms of population size. Larger population centers are called "cities," smaller ones "towns," and the smallest are "villages." But we must not impose our current usage on the biblical term. The main Hebrew word for city, *iyr*, means any human settlement surrounded by some fortification or wall. Most ancient cities numbered only about one to three thousand in population. "City" in the Bible meant not so much population size as density. Psalm 122:3 refers to this density: "Jerusalem, built as a city should be, closely compact."[1]

The word translated "compact" meant to be closely intertwined and joined. In a fortified city, the people lived close to one another in tightly compacted houses and streets. In fact, most ancient cities were estimated to be five to ten acres, with 240 residents per acre. By comparison, contemporary Manhattan in New York City houses only 105 residents per acre.[2]

In ancient times, then, a city was what would today be called a "mixed use" walkable human settlement. Because of the population's density, there were places to live and work, to buy and sell, to pursue and enjoy art, to worship and to seek justice—all within an easy walk. In ancient times, rural areas and villages could not provide all these elements, and in our modern time, the "suburb" deliberately avoids this settlement pattern. Suburbs are definitively dedicated to single-use zones—so places to live, work, play, and learn are separated from one another and are reachable only by car, usually through pedestrian-hostile zones.

What makes a city a city is proximity. It brings people—and therefore residences, workplaces, and cultural institutions—together. It creates street life and marketplaces, bringing about more person-to-person interactions and exchanges in a day than are possible anywhere else. This is what the biblical writers meant when they talked about a "city."

URBAN MISSION IN THE BIBLE

Jerusalem

Earlier in the Old Testament the redemptive importance of the city lay in Jerusalem itself being a model urban society—"the joy of the whole earth" (Psalm 48:2, NIV)—demonstrating to the world what human life under God's lordship could be. Many have spoken of the "centripetal" flow of mission during this era. God called the nations to believe in him by drawing them in to see his glory embodied in Israel, the holy nation he had created, whose corporate life showed the world the character of God (Deuteronomy 4:5–8).

However, the book of Jonah stunningly foreshadows a major change, the "centrifugal" New Testament mission of sending believers out into the world. Jonah is the only Old Testament prophet sent to a pagan city to call it to repentance. God's final statement is striking: the Lord calls Jonah to love the great pagan city of Nineveh because of the vast number of its spiritually blind inhabitants (Jonah 4:10–11).

Babylon

This movement from centripetal to centrifugal reaches another stage when Israel is taken into exile. The Jews are taken to live in the wicked, pagan, bloodthirsty city of Babylon. What is the relationship of believers to such a place? Jeremiah 28 and 29 hold out a remarkable outline for a believer's stance toward the city. God tells his people to "increase… do not decrease" (Jeremiah 29:6, NIV), to keep their distinct community identity and to grow. But he also tells them to settle down and engage in the life of the great city. They are to build homes and plant gardens. Most striking of all, God commands them to serve the city, to "seek the peace and prosperity of the city" and "Pray to the Lord for it" (Jeremiah 29:7, NIV). They are not simply to increase their tribe in a ghetto within the city but are to use their resources to benefit the common good.

This is quite a balance! The values of an earthly city contrast sharply with those of the city of God, yet citizens of the city of God must be the best citizens of their earthly cities. God calls the Jewish exiles to serve the common good of the pagan city. He also has a very practical goal: serving the good of the pagan city is the best possible way for the people of God to thrive and flourish. "…if it prospers, you too will prosper" (Jeremiah 29:7, NIV).

God is still concerned with his plan of salvation, the establishment of his people—and that is exactly what happened. Because the Jews moved in and sought the peace of the great pagan city, they accumulated the influence and leverage needed to eventually return and restore their homeland. In addition, Jews remained somewhat dispersed throughout the cities of the world as a cosmopolitan, international ethnic group that became a crucial base for the spread of the Christian message after Jesus.

Resident Aliens

Is there any reason to believe that the model for Israel in Babylon should serve as the model for the church? Yes.

In exile, Israel no longer existed in the form of a nation-state with its own government and laws. Instead, it existed as an international community and counterculture within other nations. This is also now the form of the church, as Peter and James acknowledge when addressing believers as "the Dispersion" (James 1:1) and "exiles" (1 Peter 1:1). Twice Peter uses *parapidemois* as a word for exiles—"resident aliens"—people who live in a country neither as natives nor as tourists passing through. Peter calls Christians to live in the midst of pagan society in such a way that others see their "good deeds and glorify God" but warns them to expect persecution, nonetheless (1 Peter 2:11–12).

The echoes of Jeremiah 29 are evident in Peter's epistle. Like the Jewish exiles, Christian exiles are to engage in their cities, serving the common good rather than conquering or ignoring them. They should expect that the society around them will be both hostile and attracted by believers' lives and service in the city. Peter indicates that believers' good deeds will lead at least some pagans to glorify God.

In "Soft Difference," his article on 1 Peter, Miroslav Volf shows how the tension Peter envisioned (between persecution and attraction, and between evangelism and service) does not fit neatly into any of the historic models of relating Christ to culture.[3] Unlike models that call for a transformation of culture or a Christendom-like alliance of church and state, Peter expects the gospel to always be highly offensive, never completely embraced or accepted by the world. This is a caution to those evangelicals and mainline Christians who hope to bring about an essentially Christian culture. And unlike models that call solely for evangelism and are highly pessimistic about influencing culture, both Peter in 1 Peter 2:12 and Jesus in Matthew 5:16 expects some aspects of Christian faith and practice to be highly attractive in any pagan culture, influencing people to praise and glorify God.[4]

Samaria and the Uttermost Parts of the Earth

The church lives as an international, dispersed fellowship of congregations, as Israel did under the exile. In Acts 8, we see God forcibly dispersing the Christians from Jerusalem, thus boosting Christian mission enormously. They immediately went to Samaria, a city that Jewish people would have been taught to despise as much as Jonah despised Nineveh or the Jews despised Babylon. But unlike the reluctant prophet or exiles, the gospel-changed Christians were immediately effective in urban mission in Samaria (Acts 8:1).

When we finally come to the early church, we see that God's redemptive mission no longer centers on any particular city, such as Jerusalem or Babylon. All the cities of the world become crucial. In

Acts 17, Paul goes to Athens, the intellectual center of the Greco-Roman world. In Acts 18, he travels to Corinth, one of the commercial centers of the empire. In Acts 19, he arrives in Ephesus, perhaps the Roman world's religious center—the hub of many pagan cults and particularly of the imperial cult, with three temples for emperor worship. By the end of Acts, Paul makes it to Rome, the empire's power capital, the military and political center of that world. John Stott concludes: "It seems to have been Paul's deliberate policy to move purposefully from one strategic city-centre to the next."[5] By reaching the city, Paul reached the whole society, as evidenced in the letter to the Colossians. In this epistle, Paul follows up disciples in cities along the Lycus Valley—Laodicea, Hierapolis, Colossae (Colossians 4:13–16)—even though he had never visited those places personally. They were likely converted through the Ephesian ministry. If the gospel is unfolded at the urban center, you reach the region and the society.

The reasons urban ministry was so effective can be summarized as follows:

- Cities are culturally crucial. In the village, someone might win its one or two lawyers to Christ, but winning the legal profession requires going to the city with the law schools, the law journal publishers, and so on.
- Cities are globally crucial. In the village, someone can win only the single people group living there, but spreading the gospel to ten or twenty new national groups/languages at once requires going to the city, where they can all be reached through the one lingua franca of the place.
- Cities are personally crucial. By this I mean that cities are disturbing places. The countryside and the village are marked by stability and residents are more set in their ways. Because of the diversity and intensity of the cities, urbanites are much more open to new ideas—such as the gospel! Because they are surrounded by so many people like and unlike themselves, and because they are so much more mobile, urbanites are far more open to change/conversion than any other kind of resident. Regardless

of why they may have moved to the city, once they arrive there the pressure and diversity make even the most traditional and hostile people open to the gospel.

The early church was largely an urban movement that won the people of the Roman cities to Christ, while most of the countryside remained pagan. Because the Christian faith captured the cities, however, it eventually captured the society, as must always be the case. Rodney Stark develops this idea in *The Rise of Christianity*.

> To cities filled with the homeless and impoverished, Christianity offered charity as well as hope. To cities filled with newcomers and strangers, Christianity offered an immediate basis for attachments. To cities filled with widows and orphans, Christianity provided a new and expanded sense of family. To cities torn by violent ethnic strife, Christianity offered a new basis for social solidarity....People had been enduring catastrophes for centuries without the aid of Christian theology or social structures. Hence I am by no means suggesting that the misery of the ancient world caused the advent of Christianity. What I am going to argue is that once Christianity did appear, its superior capacity for meeting these chronic problems soon became evident and played a major role in its ultimate triumph...[for what Christians] brought was not simply an urban movement, but a new culture.[6]

Christian mission won the ancient Greco-Roman world because it won the cities. The elites were of course important, but the Christian church did not focus on them alone. Then, as now, cities were filled with the poor, and the urban Christians' commitment to the poor was visible and striking. Through the cities, Christians changed history and culture by winning the elites as well as identifying deeply with the poor. Richard Fletcher, in *The Barbarian Conversion*, shows the same thing occurred during the Christian mission to Europe from AD 500-1500.[7]

URBAN MISSION TODAY

The Growing Importance of Cities

In 1950, New York and London were the only world cities with metro-area populations of more than ten million people. Today, however, there are more than twenty such cities—twelve of which achieved that ranking in the last two decades—with many more to come. World cities are becoming more and more economically and culturally powerful. Cities are the seats of multinational corporations and international economic, social, and technological networks. The technology/communication revolution means that the culture and values of global cities are now being transmitted around the globe to every tongue, tribe, people, and nation. Kids in Iowa or even Mexico are becoming more like young adults in Los Angeles and New York City than they are like adults in their own locales. The coming world order will be a global, multicultural, urban order. World cities are increasingly crucial in setting the course of culture and life as a whole, even in areas of the world, such as Europe and North America, where cities are not literally growing in size.

There is a second reason that world cities are so important to the Christian mission. The millions of newcomers in burgeoning cities have characteristics that make them far more open to the Christian faith than they were before arriving. First, they are more open to new ideas, and to change in general, after being uprooted from traditional settings. Second, they greatly need help and support to face the moral, economic, emotional, and spiritual pressures of city life. The old kinship support networks of the rural areas are weak or absent, while in the developing world often have "next to nothing in working government services."[8]

On the other hand, churches offer supportive community, a new spiritual family, and a liberating gospel message. "Rich pickings await any groups who can meet these needs of these new urbanites, anyone who can at once feed the body and nourish the soul."[9]

The Need for Contextual Churches

However, there is a great barrier to urban mission that is not in the cities themselves nor in urban residents, but in the church. The sensibilities of most evangelical churches and leaders are often non- or even anti-urban. Many ministry methods have been forged outside of urban areas and then simply imported, with little thought to the unnecessary barriers this erects between urban dwellers and the gospel. When such ministers go into a city and set up ministry, they find it hard to evangelize and win urban people. They also find it difficult to prepare Christians for life in a pluralistic, secular, culturally engaged setting. Just as the Bible needs to be translated into readers' vernacular, so the gospel needs to be embodied and communicated in ways that are understandable to the residents of a city.

What are some of the characteristics of a church that are contextualized and indigenous to a city? People in urban ministry are aware of the sharp cultural differences between racial/ethnic groups and socioeconomic classes, while people living in more homogeneous places (and every place is more culturally homogeneous than a big city) are often blind to how many of their attitudes and customs are very particular to their race and class. In short, effective urban church leaders must be far more educated and aware of the views and sensitivities of different ethnic groups, classes, races, and religions. Urbanites know how often members of two different racial groups can use the identical word to mean very different things. Consequently, they are circumspect and careful when approaching issues that racial groups see differently.

Second, traditional evangelical ministries tend to give believers relatively little help in understanding how they can maintain their Christian practice outside the walls of the church while still participating in the world of the arts and theatre, business and finance, scholarship and learning, and government and public policy. Away from big cities, it may be more possible to live one's life in compartments, with Christian discipleship largely consisting of activities done in the evenings or on the weekend.

That doesn't work in cities, where people live most of their lives in the careers or the long work hours of their jobs.

Third, most evangelical churches are middle-class in their corporate culture. People value privacy, safety, homogeneity, sentimentality, space, order, and control. In contrast, the city is filled with ironic, edgy, diversity-loving people who have a much higher tolerance for ambiguity and disorder. If a church's ministers cannot function in an urban culture, but instead create a kind of non-urban "missionary compound" within it, they will discover they cannot reach out, convert, or incorporate many people in their neighborhoods.

Fourth, the non-urban church is ordinarily situated in a fairly functional neighborhood, where social systems are strong or at least intact. Urban neighborhoods are vastly more complex than other kinds, however, so effective urban ministers learn how to exegete these neighborhoods. Also, urban churches do not exegete their neighborhoods simply to target people groups for evangelism, though that is one of their goals. They look for ways to strengthen the health of their neighborhoods, making them safer and more humane places for people to live. This is seeking the welfare of the city, in the spirit of Jeremiah 29.

Traditional liberal churches often perceive mission strictly in terms of social improvement. Their goal is to make the city a more just and humane society, by working for economic and social justice and for the common good. This is partly right. Traditional conservative churches often perceive mission strictly in terms of church growth. Their goal is to grow and increase the church of God within the city, by increasing the number of conversions and thus the power of the churches. This is partly right.

These two things, however, must be combined because either of them alone will wither. You can't really serve the city without a constant stream of new converts, changed and empowered by an experience of grace, the new birth. On the other hand, church growth will come to a screeching halt if churches are filled with people who ignore or are hostile to the common good of their neighbors.

A church that only "does good" to the household of faith, and not to "all" (Galatians 6:10) will be (rightly!) seen as tribal and sectarian. If pagans don't "see your good deeds" they won't "glorify God," or at least not in the same proportions. Ironically, if urban churches put all their energy into evangelism and none into serving the needs of the city, their evangelism will be much less effective. An experience of grace inevitably leads to a life poured out in deeds of service to the needy (Isaiah 1:10–18; 58:1–10; James 2:14–17). God tells the Israelites that they should serve the needs of the poor "alien"—a foreigner who may be a non-believer— because they were once aliens in Egypt, but he delivered them (Deuteronomy 10:19). An experience of grace should always lead you to love, especially your poor, unbelieving neighbor.

Biblically, an experience of saving grace, through evangelism, leads to radical sharing of wealth and helping the needy. When the world sees this sharing, that there is "not a needy person among them" (Acts 4:34), a more powerful evangelistic witness results (Acts 4:33). Thus "doing justice and preaching grace" go hand in hand, not only in the experience of the individual Christian, but also in the ministry and effectiveness of the urban church.[10]

It takes a movement to reach a city. Reaching an entire city takes more than having some effective churches in it, or even having a burst of revival energy and new converts. To change a city with the gospel takes a self-sustaining, naturally growing movement of ministries and networks around a core of new church multiplication.

What does that look like? Here are a few suggestions:

- Christians live in the city in a posture of service.
- New businesses and nonprofits renew their slices of culture in large and small ways.
- Believers integrate their faith with their work so that every vocation becomes a kingdom activity.
- Campus ministries and other evangelistic agencies organically produce new Christian leaders who stay in the city and move into the churches and networks.

- People use their power, wealth, and influence for the good of others on the margins of society, to advance ministry, and to plant new churches.
- Churches and individual Christians support and commission the arts.

Let's break this down a bit further.

New churches form the heart of these gospel ecosystems. They provide spiritual oxygen to the communities and networks of Christians who do the heavy lifting, over decades, to renew and redeem cities. They are the primary venue for discipleship and the multiplication of believers, as well as being the financial engine for all the ministry initiatives. This ecosystem is, therefore, a critical mass of new churches. They must be gospel-centered, urban, missional /evangelistic, balanced, growing, and self-replicating in diverse forms, across traditions, integrating races/classes. This is the most basic core of the ecosystem.

The ecosystem also fosters networks and systems of evangelism that reach specific populations. In addition to campus ministries, which are especially important as a new leader development engine, other very effective, specialized evangelistic agencies are usually necessary to reach the elites, reach the poor, and reach Muslim, Hindu, and other particular cultural/religious groupings. Networks and organizations of cultural leaders within professional fields, such as business, government, academia, and the arts and media, are part of this ecosystem as well. It is crucial that these individuals be active in churches that thoughtfully disciple and support them for public life. These leaders must also network and support each other within their own fields, spawning new cultural institutions and schools of thought.

The ecosystem is also marked by agencies and initiatives produced by Christians to serve the peace of the city, and especially the poor. Hundreds and thousands of new non-profit and for-profit companies must be spawned to serve every neighborhood and every population in need. United and coordinated church alliances and institutions also serve Christian families and individuals and support their long-term life in the city (e.g., schools, theological colleges, and other institutions that make city living sustainable for Christians over the generations).

Additionally, this ecosystem has overlapping networks of city leaders. Church movement leaders, theologians/teachers, heads of institutions, and cultural leaders and patrons with influence and resources know one another and provide vision and direction for the whole city.

Isolated events or individual entities that crystallize into a growing, self-sustaining movement become "tipping points." Here are a couple possible "tipping points":

The gospel movement tipping point. A church planting project becomes a movement when the ecosystem elements are all in place and most of the churches have the vitality, leaders, and mind-set to plant another church within five to six years of their own beginnings. When the tipping point is reached, a self-sustaining movement begins. Enough new believers, leaders, congregations, and ministries are being naturally produced for the movement to grow without any single command-and-control center. The body of Christ in the city funds itself, produces its own leaders, and conducts its own training. A sufficient number of dynamic leaders is always rising up. The number of Christians and churches doubles every seven to ten years. How many churches must be reached for this to occur? While it is impossible to give a number that would hold for every city and culture, all the elements in the ecosystem must be in place and strong.

The whole-city tipping point. A gospel movement tipping point is an important goal. But there is another. When a gospel movement tipping point is reached, it may be that the eco-system grows the Body of Christ to the point that whole-city tipping point is reached. That is the moment when the number of gospel-shaped Christians in a city becomes so large that Christian influence on the civic and social life of the city—and on the very culture—is recognizable and acknowledged. For example, neighborhoods stay largely the same if new types of residents (richer, poorer, or culturally different from the rest) comprise less than

5 percent of the population. Some prison ministers report that if more than 10 percent of the inmates become Christians, it changes the corporate culture of the prison. The relationships between prisoners and those between prisoners and guards all change. Likewise, when the number of new residents reaches somewhere between five and 20 percent, depending on the culture, the whole neighborhood ethos shifts. In New York City, some groups have a palpable effect on the way life is lived, when their numbers reach at least 5 to 15 percent and when the members are active in public life.

How likely is it that an urban gospel movement could grow so strong that it reaches a "city-changing tipping point," at which time the gospel begins having a visible impact on the city life and culture produced there? We know this can happen through God's grace. The history books give us examples. However, only rare Christian leaders, like John Wesley, will live to see the movements they have begun grow to such a level of effectiveness. So urban ministers should make this their goal, and give their whole lives to it, but not expect to see it in their own lifetimes. That's the right balance between expectation and patience that we need to strike if we are going to see our cities loved and reached for Christ.

6.

A MISSIONAL APPROACH
TO THE HEALTH OF THE CITY

SUSAN M. POST

My professional background began in health care. I spent more than a dozen years working for a New York City hospital, managing various aspects of hospital services and ambulatory care. I saw my professional vocation as an avenue for expressing my Christian faith. I was a Christian who worked in a helping field, hoping to express God's grace in my life to others. It seemed to be a good calling.

My life took a turn, and I found myself in seminary. I did not enroll in seminary for vocational reasons; I simply wanted to know God's Word and to understand more of who God is. In those years God's Word was opened to me in new and exciting ways. I was astounded at how rich and deep the Word is. During this time, I began to see and to gain a better understanding of the Bible as a whole, rather than in its various parts. God's grand story of redemption, God's own *mission* became clearer to me. As I gained a redemptive historical perspective, I began to see more clearly this aspect of God's character—this God who is working in people and creation to move everything toward restoration. Not only was God working in history in this way, but God continues to work like this in our world today. He is redeeming all aspects of life—including my own professional field of health-care delivery. This transformational restoration of health—*shalom* health—is part of his new creation. It is not enough for me simply to provide health care as a Christian. Rather, health-care delivery itself needs to reflect the character and the heart of God and the restoration that he is bringing.

Poverty affects many aspects of a person's life, including one's health. By the same token, health is not only a physical matter. We are created as integrated beings, with our physical, emotional, spiritual, and relational components affecting one other. People living in at-risk communities have a variety of health needs that are closely related to complex factors in their lives. I see how far short the health-care system falls in bringing about complete health. Poverty and culture both affect people's health—not only what one eats, or can afford to eat, but also a lack of hope for the future affects one's lifestyle and health significantly. Communities of poverty need the church, and the church needs its community. The presence of God's people can play a powerful role in ushering neighborhoods toward God's redemption.

I was first introduced to Esperanza Health Center in North Philadelphia in 1999, when I volunteered there during my first year of seminary. *Esperanza* is the Spanish word for hope. I was struck immediately by Esperanza's holistic emphasis and Christ-centered approach to patient care. This model was something I had not seen before; nonetheless, it was something I had longed for throughout my career in health care. These were not simply Christians delivering health care. This was *Christ-centered* health care—compassionate, holistic, incarnational, with movement toward holistic health for its patients.

Five years later, I found myself accepting the position of executive director at Esperanza. I was completely unprepared for this task, and I see now that God was probably as interested in transforming me as he was in any transforming work to which he had called me. God has a way of using ministry to refine us as we participate in his work.

THEOLOGICAL FOUNDATIONS: GOD'S CONCERN FOR HEALTH AND WELL-BEING

Scripture needs to be our starting point as we seek to understand God's mind and heart for health care among the urban poor. The many challenges people in our cities face and the struggles of those who live in poverty are complicated and can only be understood within the context of the gospel. Ministry must be based on more than observed needs. Esperanza's goal is to be an expression of God's salvific work in North Philadelphia. As we examine Scripture in search of a context in which to offer an urban health-care ministry, we quickly discover that the Bible has much to say about this. Scripture shows us the character of God, his desires for the inner city, and his concern for people.

GOD IS A REDEMPTIVE GOD

We have a redemptive, missional God. In fact, the Bible is one grand story of redemption, from start to finish. This redemptive work continues in this era, between Christ's inauguration of the kingdom of God here on earth and its complete fruition at the time of Christ's return. Understanding the redemptive character of God displayed throughout Scripture is foundational to discovering God's purposes in health-care ministry among the urban poor. We see God's particular concern toward the vulnerable who live in our cities—the modern-day widow, orphan, and alien. God's consistent, redemptive character shows us that God is always moving toward this sin-broken world to bring about restorative *shalom*. God is bringing about a new creation—transforming personally and corporately—and he is using his people, the church, in his restorative work. The WRF Statement of Faith describes this restorative work as follows:

> We affirm the great need for Christians to be clothed with compassion in the name of Christ, in the midst of poverty, disease, injustice, and all forms of human misery.... We understand the transformation of community to be the comprehensive reversal of the effects of sin over all of life and all the earth that alienated men and women from God, from self, from others, and from the environment and the restoration of God's order in creation.[1]

Creation "Shalom"

We see in the book of Genesis that God is the creator of the world. He created the heavens, the earth, and all that is in them and on them. God created people to be in relation with one another and with himself; he created humans in his image and gave them work to do. God gave people responsibility to care for one another, for all living things, and for the earth. He gave them the cultural mandate to be fruitful and multiply, and to rule over creation (Genesis 1:28). As image-bearers, they were to take up his work in this world by taking care of it.

God also gave the gift of his presence. By design, God would be with his people, and they would share their lives with him, communicate intimately with him, and enjoy him in everyday life. The created world consisted of beauty, whole relationships, intimacy with God, good work, and peace (*shalom*)—a world where everything fit, where all was as it was meant to be. All that is created points to the glory of God (Psalm 19:1–4). And God looked at all he created and declared that it was good. Unfortunately, the world did not stay in this beautifully created state.

"Vandalized Shalom": Our Fallen and Broken World

The beauty and *shalom* of creation was broken in Genesis 3 with the rebellion of Adam and Eve. Cornelius Plantinga, in his book *Not the Way It's Supposed to Be*, describes this brokenness as "vandalized *shalom*."[2] Even here, however, God demonstrates his redemptive character. Almost immediately after disobedience breaks their perfect relationship with God, his disobedient children Adam and Eve are given the promise of future redemption (Genesis 3:14–15). The promise is indeed there, but the curse of the fall now permeates all of life.

The fall orients everything away from God, including all of life and human behavior. The effects of sin show up in broken relationships, difficulty in working the land, lies, selfishness, injustice, and slavery. Since the fall, it has been difficult for people to know or understand God. Descriptions of this brokenness can be seen in almost every story in Scripture, and its effects continue even today. The effects of personal and systemic sin can be clearly seen in all areas of life in our urban communities—family brokenness, poverty, oppression, addiction, and hopelessness. Redemption in Christ is the only ultimate and decisive antidote.

Restoration—New Creation

The theme of the New Testament is the revelation of God, the rightful King, establishing his rule over all creation. Through Jesus Christ, God reveals himself to his people and restores all of creation. God is reconciling all things to himself (Colossians 1:19–20). This reconciling and restoration are not limited to the relationship between God and his people but extend to all that sin has taken away. Social order will be restored, captives will be released, and those in darkness will be free (Luke 4:16–21). The promise of *shalom* is fulfilled in Christ. We see this today in our urban communities. Inner-city churches naturally are engaged in this new creation—often ministering to children whose fathers are incarcerated, offering GED classes so that people can obtain employment, and preaching a real hope that breaks into the circumstances of life to bring reconciliation with God and restoration of soul, mind, and body.

While the kingdom of God is a sure and promised reality, we only have to look around our world and inside our hearts to understand that redemption is not completely present. We still see brokenness, but redemption has come. As Herman Ridderbos notes, "The great framework of redemptive history has arrived at its turning point in Jesus's coming. And it will reach its final turning point in his coming again."[3] The kingdom of God is no longer a distant hope—it is a promised reality that has been set in motion by Jesus Christ.

This salvation brings new creation. This new creation is not throwing out what is broken, but restoring—a salvaging of that which was broken. This is practical, tangible, and extends as far as the curse is found. This restoration process is the work of the church today, realized in partnership with the Holy Spirit. This is the essence of urban mission, and indeed of all missional activity. To participate in this new creation, or salvaging of vandalized *shalom*, is the calling of Esperanza Health Center.

We are not left to wonder what this re-creation will look like, especially for poor urban communities. Scripture gives us several clear pictures, including Psalm 48, Isaiah 65, and Revelation 21. These restoration pictures are characterized by joy and delight because of God's presence and sense of *shalom*—flourishing, purposeful life, characterized by right relations with God, with one another, and even with creation itself. These pictures describe peoples who will be rejoiced over and whom are a delight to the Lord. Children will play, thrive, and have a future; adults will live long, healthy lives; they will all have good places to live and adequate food to eat; they will enjoy the work of their hands; there will be no more tears, no death, no mourning; they will be blessed. New-creation communities will enjoy safety, justice, reconciled relationships, blessings and hopeful futures (Isaiah 65:17–25; Zechariah 8:3–13, Revelation 21:1–4).

It is hard to imagine this as we look at our broken-down communities. But God is at work, even now, restoring and transforming all of creation. God is a redeeming God.

GOD IS A COMPASSIONATE GOD

God reveals himself to be compassionate throughout Scripture, in both his words and actions. As God's image-bearers, we are called to be people of compassion in God's world. At Esperanza Health Center, God's character of compassion provides a framework for ministry.

In the book of Exodus, when Moses asks God to show himself, God responds,

> Then the LORD came down in the cloud and stood there with him and proclaimed his name, the LORD. And he passed in front of Moses, proclaiming, "The LORD, the LORD, the compassionate and gracious God, slow to anger, abounding in love and faithfulness, maintaining

love to thousands and forgiving wickedness, rebellion and sin." (Exodus 34:5–7, NIV)

It is as if God is telling Moses that his very name—his very character—is compassion, grace, love, and forgiveness.

God describes himself as compassionate—but even more, he *shows* himself to be compassionate. Early in the book of Exodus the people cried out to God, and God responded with compassion.

> During that long period, the king of Egypt died. The Israelites groaned in their slavery and cried out, and their cry for help because of their slavery went up to God. God heard their groaning and he remembered his covenant with Abraham, with Isaac and with Jacob. So God looked on the Israelites and was concerned about them. (Exodus 2:23–25, NIV)

This pattern of God's compassion can be seen throughout Scripture. God's people cry out in their misery; God *hears* their groaning, *remembers* his covenant promises, *is concerned*, *has compassion* on the people, and then *delivers* his people. Compassion for people is at the center of the heart of God. God's compassion is restorative (Deuteronomy 30:1–20). God's compassion gathers, restores, comforts (Isaiah 49:10, 51:3); it forgives (Psalm 51:1). It brings back the banished one, it spares (Malachi 3:17). God's compassion protects, especially the widow and the fatherless (Zechariah 7:9–10), and compels him to bring back the wayward one (Exodus 3:7–10; 2 Kings 13:23; Isaiah 54:6–10; Nehemiah 9:27–28). This pattern of compassion is further developed in the ministry of Jesus Christ and often is seen in the context of healing.

> Jesus went through all the towns and villages, teaching in their synagogues, preaching the good news of the kingdom and healing every disease and sickness. When he saw the crowds, he had compassion on them, because they were harassed and helpless, like sheep without a shepherd. Then he said to his disciples, "The harvest is plentiful but the workers are few. Ask the Lord of the harvest, therefore, to send out workers into his harvest field."

He called his twelve disciples to him and gave them authority to drive out evil spirits and to heal every disease and sickness. (Matthew 9:35–10:1, NIV 1984)

This compassion—God graciously having concern and acting on behalf of undeserving people—is key to the ministry of those he calls to serve him in health care. Understanding God as a deliverer from bondage is a key component in a vision for health-care ministry. God not only sees and is concerned, but he delivers people from oppression and brokenness.

GOD IS AN INCARNATIONAL GOD

A third characteristic of God that is helpful to consider in health-care ministry is that God is incarnational—he comes near to his people. Our God is not distant. The beautiful intimacy of God and people at creation was severed by the fall, but throughout biblical history we see God moving toward his people. He progressively establishes his presence among his people by way of a tabernacle in the desert, then a temple, and eventually through his own Incarnation walking on this earth as a man. In giving us the gift of his Holy Spirit, he now lives in those who are united with him in Christ. Eventually, he will make his dwelling completely present with his people, and God himself will be their God (Revelation 21:3). God pursues and comes near to people. He is the Holy of Holies, and yet he draws near us in intimate relationship.

The incarnational character of God extends to the church, and to healing ministry. There is a healing power in the presence of a loved one. My own father suffered a massive stroke years ago, taking away his ability to speak and understand language. My only way of connecting with him was to physically go to where he lived and sit with him—incarnationally. I saw how my presence with him during his final years—my wordless presence, with touches and smiles—were a real factor in his healing and sustaining process.

This healing and incarnational presence of the church is described in the book of James.

Is anyone among you in trouble? Let them pray. Is anyone happy? Let them sing songs of praise. Is anyone among you sick? Let them call the elders of the church to pray over them and anoint them with oil in the name of the Lord. And the prayer offered in faith will make the sick person well; the Lord will raise them up. If they have sinned, they will be forgiven. Therefore confess your sins to each other and pray for each other so that you may be healed. The prayer of a righteous person is powerful and effective (James 5:13–16, NIV).

The church is called to be present with the sick and suffering one, to pray with and anoint the one who is in need of healing. We are to help each other confess and receive forgiveness, to pray for one another. God uses the community of the church for healing.

GOD IS A HEALING GOD

God is concerned about our health, in all its forms. This concern, demonstrated by God in Scripture, looks very different from the American health-care system. The modern Western world has incorporated a dualistic, materialistic worldview. This results in a view that separates the physical body from the spiritual and emotional aspects of the person, and it affects our approaches to health-care delivery. God doesn't do this. We see throughout Scripture a consistent picture of God's concern for the health of the whole person. We often see God at work in this way at Esperanza.

One of our employees tells of her first visit as an Esperanza patient years ago. She had stomach problems. After several visits with her doctor, including diagnostic testing, her doctor asked her, "Maria, is there anyone in your life you are holding back forgiving, or anyone who has not forgiven you? Could this stomach problem have to do with this?" The answer was yes—Maria had been experiencing a conflict in her family whereby she was wronged, and Maria had not been able to move past this. She talked with her doctor about it; they prayed together about it; and soon Maria, with God's help, was able to forgive her family member. The result was that Maria's stomach problem disappeared, her relationships were reconciled, and her trust in

God was strengthened. Maria's problem was not simply physical; it was emotional, relational, and spiritual. Our health care needs to treat the whole person.

When God called his people out of Egypt, he set up systems to lead the people toward healthy living. He instructed them what to eat and what not to eat and defined good hygiene and ways to keep from spreading diseases. He set up relational and sexual guidelines, systems for seeking and obtaining forgiveness, ways to approach and worship him, and many other laws to govern their daily living. It can be seen that may of the laws God set in place were to ensure the complete health of the people. He did not separate physical, emotional, spiritual and re-lational—they all are components of individual and community health.

Jesus shows himself to be the healing Savior. Many of his miracu-lous signs were healings. And, consistent with the Old Testament view of whole health, Jesus's healing did not separate the physical from the emotional or spiritual. Jesus saw people as they had been created—as integrated beings. He healed and touched the leper (Luke 5:13); he healed and stopped to speak peace to the woman who touched his gar-ment (Luke 8:48); he healed and forgave the paralytic (Luke 5:20); he healed and fed the little girl (Luke 8:55); he healed and brought sanity to the demon-possessed man (Luke 8:26–39).

Healing was a tangible demonstration of Jesus's messiahship. When a discouraged John the Baptist sent word to Jesus from prison asking him, "'Are you the one who is to come, or should we expect someone else?'" Jesus's response to John was telling. He said, "'Go back and re-port to John what you have seen and heard: The blind receive sight, the lame walk, those who have leprosy are cleansed, the deaf hear, the dead are raised, and good news is proclaimed to the poor'" (Luke 7:20–23, NIV). In other words, Jesus was saying, "Look at my healing, and you will know I am the Messiah." Jesus's healing and his salvation are not to be separated.

The relationship between salvation and healing is further seen as Jesus starts to send out his disciples. When Jesus sent his disciples out in ministry, he sent them to preach the gospel and to heal people (Luke 9:1–4, 6). Jesus engages his disciples in healing as Jesus healed—in concert with the good news. It is a demonstration of the kingdom of God itself. The physical and the spiritual are not separated. Healing appears to be somehow a reflection of redemption and salvation. Healing was both the manifestation of the kingdom of God and a sign to point others to God so that they could know Christ. Jesus is a healing Savior.

GOD IS A CALLING GOD

God calls people to participate in his work. In creation, God gave humans the responsibility to care for his creation. In God's new creation after the fall, he calls his people to participate in this new creation—in God's kingdom-building here on earth. In health-care ministry, this calling can be well described by the words of the prophet Micah, who reminds God's people what God truly calls them to: "To act justly and to love mercy and to walk humbly with your God" (Micah 6:8, NIV).

This calling to justice and mercy is repeated throughout Scripture in a variety of ways, and is consistent with the redemptive and compassionate character of our God. This calling is given by the incarnational God who comes close and leads his people to do the same. This is the calling of our healing God—not just for those in health care, but also for his church. Responding to this calling requires the church to be concerned for the modern-day widows, orphans, and aliens—the single mother raising her family without a husband, the kids on the street who are essentially alone with uninvolved parents, the family who has just arrived in the United States and doesn't speak English. Each is vulnerable, and God calls his people to care for them.

God's people in health-care ministry need to find practical ways to live out this calling. There are many injustices that go unchallenged in the U.S. health-care system. Systemic injustices have contributed to the forming of communities of poverty, as well as areas of personal irresponsibility that have caused the difficult circumstances patients face. God calls his people to always do justly, always love mercy, and always walk humbly with those we serve.

It is a mystery that God calls us to participate in his work—he could do so much better without us. The church often chooses a form of religion without this type of engagement. But throughout Scripture we see God's strong unequivocal call to all his people. When the Israelites complained that God did not hear their cries when they had prayed and fasted, God challenged them in their sin (Isaiah 58). The type of fasting, or religious activity, he calls them to is very different from what they have been doing. His call is to loose the bonds of wickedness and let the oppressed go free (v. 6), to share bread with the hungry one and bring the poor into their house (v. 7), to cover the naked one (v. 7), to stop pointing the finger and speaking about others, and to satisfy the desire of the afflicted (v. 10). This is how we participate with God in his work.

Jesus also describes this calling to justice and mercy when he speaks about the final judgment. At that time the Lord will separate his people based on their response to his call. To those who fed the hungry, gave drink to the thirsty, welcomed the stranger, clothed the naked, and visited the sick and in prison, he will say, "'Come, you who are blessed by my Father, inherit the kingdom prepared for you from the foundation of the world'" (Matthew 25:34).

This is our calling as people of God. We are to engage with the Lord in his redeeming work of bringing justice to our communities with his compassionate mercy.

ESPERANZA HEALTH CENTER'S MISSIONAL APPROACH TO HEALTH-CARE DELIVERY

Esperanza Health Center was founded in the late 1980s. It was founded by Dr. Carolyn Klaus, whose husband was a pastor. Their church was learning about the kingdom of God, and Dr. Klaus decided to serve God with her medical gifts by focusing on the poorest people in Philadelphia—the Spanish-speaking Puerto Rican population in North Philadelphia. Lacking resources, she asked her church small group to become involved with some of her patients whose needs far exceeded the time or resources available to help them. As her church became involved, those patients who were connected to church people became healthier faster—they were being helped and cared for more holistically by the members of her church. And her small group became healthier as well, as they participated in God's calling to justice and mercy. Dr. Klaus saw the importance of this connection between health-care delivery and the church, and so she formed Esperanza Health Center.

Today Esperanza Health Center receives fifty thousand visits from members of our community annually. More than twenty medical providers serve at three locations, including a health and wellness center. The community continues to be the poorest in the city, its residents primarily Latinos or African Americans. Esperanza's missional foundation has not diminished; rather, it is the basis for all decisions and what leads us into the future. However, keeping this missional focus requires developing tangible strategies for health-care delivery that are biblical, allowing us to participate in God's work through his church as a vehicle for bringing healing, restoration, wholeness, and transformation to individuals and our community.

God's People Gathered for Ministry

It is vital that participants in this ministry be committed believers in Jesus Christ. It might go without saying that a mission organization expects every missionary to be believers in Christ, but this is an area in which many Christian health-care ministries are tempted to compromise. Throughout the years we have found that this is foundational to our ministry. Missional hiring is essential. We pray for every candidate for every position; we describe our ministry and discuss with them their calling and commitments to God's work. Discerning God's will is not always easy, but we have found that if the candidate is praying and the leaders of the ministry are praying, together we are more likely to understand God's calling for the candidate.

Hiring in this way allows us to be equally yoked together in ministry. This helps as we make decisions together, as we grow relationally and spiritually with one another, and as we try to encourage others. This unity allows us to submit ourselves to God's Word as we make decisions together—and when we have differences of opinion to move in the future together. We are united in Christ, each contributing our unique gifts with Christ as the head of our health center.

FEARFULLY AND WONDERFULLY MADE: HOLISTIC CARE

In practical ways we see the importance of health care that functions from an integrated view of body, mind, and spirit. Many patients bring physical symptoms that originate from non-physical problems. At times the symptoms of stomach problems or back pain are a result of stress and worry. Exposure to violence causes many physical symptoms. Fear of domestic violence also presents a variety of physical symptoms. If we simply respond to the physical symptoms a patient presents, we miss the root cause of the person's need for healing. As healing professionals, we need to follow Christ's example of talking with the hurting one, asking about their bodies, their emotions, and their relationships—with God, with one another, with themselves. We need to seek *shalom* for each person we have the privilege of meeting.

Our calling to integrated health care influences the care we provide, as well as the services we offer. Throughout the years as we've provided medical care, we've seen that many patients suffer from mental health afflictions. Stress, anxiety, depression, post-traumatic stress, or drug and alcohol addiction are present in some form in the majority of our patients. Seeing our patients in light of Christ's care for them, we have developed a strong team of mental-health professionals and make counseling available to patients at any primary-care visit. Additionally, we equip each employee to respond to patients on a spiritual level. Spiritual issues may surface at any time during a patient's visit. Praying with patients is so common at Esperanza Health Center that almost any employee has the opportunity daily.

Coming Near: An Incarnational Health-Care Model

How does a health-care ministry serve incarnationally? We see from Scripture the incarnational character of God—always pursuing people, meeting them in the context of their lives, and drawing them to himself. This coming near—or incarnation in health care—is important to understand and to incorporate into our model of health care. Incarnation begins with identification with our patient, as Christ identified with us in our humanness. At times it also means taking the first step toward our patients, initiating a deeper relationship and a deeper partnership for *shalom* for the patients.

Locating near our patients. We have found that one way to come closer to our patients is to locate our health centers in the neighborhoods where they live. In some ways it would be easier to have patients come to one large health center located in a community that is not so dangerous, or one with more resources. However, locating within communities allows our patients to see that we desire to be accessible to them, and that we want to know them, come to them, and partner with them in their health and overall *shalom*. As Christ broke into our world to show us the Father, we hope that moving toward our patients in this way demonstrates the love God has for them.

Hablamos Español y Inglés. Jesus Christ entered into our world and he spoke to us, showing us the Father, using human language and actions. He used language to share with us what God is like. At Esperanza, each of our medical providers and staff members speak both Spanish and English. This is very important in bridging the gap between the medical provider and the patient; it is difficult enough to describe things to a medical clinician in our own language, but much more difficult to do so in a non-native language. As Christ demonstrated his love for us by reaching into our worlds through language, we want to demonstrate God's love to our patients in our commitment to come to them in their language, even if it isn't native to us.

We have a high commitment to this, at times sending staff to immersion language study in Spanish-speaking countries for up to three months. Additionally, we try to hire people within their community. Not only do they often speak both Spanish and English, but they know and understand the culture and ways of the community better than an outsider.

Incarnational presence. More than half of our staff live within our service area. This is one of the most effective ways to identify with our patients. Living within the context of ministry allows each of us to gain an understanding of our community, to see the needs of our patients, and to share in the struggles of daily living. While living within our service area is not a requirement for employment, we ask each new employee to consider and pray about this. This is not an easy step for many to take—intentionally moving into an under-resourced and often unsafe neighborhood—but it is important to prayerfully consider and seek God's direction. After all, most missionaries typically move to the country and live among the God has called them to serve.

Often in urban ministry we try to serve from a distance, but God wants us to come close to the ones we serve. My own experience with this has been a great joy. I've received far more from experiencing community with my patients than I have given. Living among our patients gives me a better view of the health care we need to provide, and my neighbors are my best consultants in helping determine what may or may not work. More important than that, the gift of developing relationships with neighbors, learning about other cultures, and seeing how God is at work here encourages me and adds to the joy in my ministry.

Partnering with the community. Health care in the United States is often offered by a physician who has all the knowledge and the power to prescribe or deliver health care. It is often a one-way transaction. Health care is best delivered within the context of partnership with patients, whereby patients take responsibility for improving their own health. Ministry within communities of poverty is often conducted like health care in given in the United States; the missionary delivers, or *prescribes*, what's best for the community—without sharing power or bringing liberating help. Health-care ministry will always work best within the context of partnership.

Esperanza is increasingly moving in this direction. Our first major initiative has been to train and disciple community health promoters. Community members from local churches participate in a fifty-hour training covering basic health topics from taking blood pressures to understanding hypertension, diabetes, obesity, newborn care, HIV, etc., as well as sharing one's faith. These health promoters are then supported by Esperanza as they carry out health initiatives in their churches or neighborhoods. In some ways, these community members are far more capable of affecting health than our trained medical providers. This is real partnership—helping the community raise its own health status.

Strong Foundations: Prayer and Worship

In addition to the strategies of incarnational ministry and holistic care, growing in our spiritual foundation is vital. One of the most important characteristics of the people of God is that they worship, and for those serving the Lord in ministry, *all* work should be an act of worship. It is easy for us to stand on our own merit and work with human energy to serve God, and this is especially true in the difficult work of health care among the poor. In the healing of people and communities, God's Spirit must reign, and service must be a response of worship for the God who is our great healer. It is important for health-care ministers (such as those working with Esperanza) to grow and maintain spiritual maturity in order to glorify the God to whom we owe everything.

Experiences of worship and prayer need to be woven into the fabric of all health care. The most powerful aspect of this at Esperanza is gathering daily for devotions. Each workday at each site begins with all employees gathering to focus on the mission and ministry, and to approach the Lord together. This half hour is voluntarily led by a different person at each site each day, and is part of the paid workday. It is a time filled by personal testimony, Bible study, prayer, or worship—a reminder to us of God's character and greatness, and of our need for him. This time grows us, binds us together, and refocuses us on our work and ministry. There is great power in worshiping the Lord as a community.

Once every few months we also close the health center for a day to have extended times of spiritual retreat together. These disciplines of daily devotions and quarterly retreats have been our tradition since Esperanza began, and we have found them to be life-bringing to us, helping us remember the Lord in all that we do.

Prayer is our most important foundational resource, and it undergirds our life together. The teams pray together for each patient on the schedule. By praying for our patients consistently, we are reminded of God's good work in their lives —leading us to worship him more and also helping us to see the patient as a creation of God. In the midst of hectic, long days it can be tempting to cut our time of prayer short, but we realize that when things are hectic we need prayer even more. God truly has blessed us in prayer and worship.

Having prayed for one another and for our patients routinely, it is natural to pray during a patient's visit. It is especially helpful when a patient tells us of a difficulty in her life, or if she is worried about a health concern. We are privileged to walk alongside our patients, praying for them and for our neighborhoods as well. God challenges us to care beyond the walls of our health centers and to intercede for our communities. This binds us even more to our patients and to God's redemptive work.

Compassion: Suffering with Our Community

The longer I serve God in North Philadelphia, the more I relate to the prophets of the Old Testament. Usually the prophet was placed in a position to see the brokenness and effects of sin in the lives of the people. Generally, God used the prophet to show the people this "vandalized *shalom*"—this living as orphans, this brokenness—was *not* as it was meant to be. In many cases, as God gave the prophet eyes to see this brokenness, the prophet was overwhelmed with grief. Prophets were often called to weep over the difficulties of the people. Reading the prophetic books can be difficult—seeing how far God's people stray and the pronounced effects of the fall. And yet, those weeping prophets usually had enough vision to announce the redeeming character of God, to express hope that God would not abandon his people, and to show that God would act and respond to the calamity that surrounded them. They wept with unwavering hope.

Henri Nouwen describes well this compassion of Christ.

Here we see what compassion means. It is not a bending toward the underprivileged from a privileged position; it is not a reaching out from on high to those who are less fortunate below; it is not a gesture of sympathy or pity for those who fail to make it in the upward pull. On the contrary, compassion means going directly to those people and places where suffering is most acute and building a home there. God's compassion is total, absolute, unconditional, without reservation. It is the compassion of the one who keeps going to the most forgotten corners of the world, and who cannot rest as long as he knows that there are still human beings with tears in their eyes. It is the compassion of a God who does not merely act as a servant, but whose servanthood is a direct expression of his divinity.[4]

This type of compassion is only possible because of the power of the resurrection, and it becomes more of a reality in our ministry as we share in Jesus's sufferings in this world. Looking straight into the brokenness in our patients' lives—at times sensing that we are looking right into the face of death—and then remembering the character of God, we gain confidence that God does redeem, and that his grace is utterly sufficient for our patients, our community, and for us. God lets us experience this fellowship of suffering with him, and as we participate, our hope in him grows.

Reflection, and Serving as a Prophetic Voice

We have a responsibility to continuously reflect on our work and ministry. We cannot be content to settle on one way of doing things because missions work is dynamic. We are constantly learning and evaluating in light of our mission and God's purpose for us. Additionally, we have a responsibility to share what we've experienced and learned with others—to be a prophetic voice in our field, and in particular, health and the church, in the context of God's concern for the poor.

What does it mean to be a prophetic voice? Practically, it means using every avenue and platform available to share the things God is teaching us as we serve him. We need to speak to churches and student groups, attend conferences, and engage those who are interested. We need to engage in political speaking and writing on behalf of the underserved or uninsured. We must communicate to a variety of audiences, using existing forums or creating new ones. Being a prophetic voice means speaking to the church and the world, influencing our city, fellow believers in the churches, and the health-care community.

We have something to speak to the church: the church is called to participate in holistic healing. We can encourage the church to study and consider God's call to healing ministry within the church. We can also speak out more to our churches about God's concern for the poor—particularly churches in the United States who distance themselves from the poor and God's message about our role in compassion.

To our communities of poverty we are ambassadors, bringing the message that God makes all things new. To the medical field in general, we have a message that God has created us as physical, spiritual, and emotional beings, and that health care needs to acknowledge and address patients in these terms. To Christ-following medical providers, we have a responsibility to encourage and help these brothers and sisters follow Christ faithfully in their own practices and work.

Esperanza Health Center, and other ministries engaged in health care delivery for the urban poor, have much to learn. But the opportunities to participate in God's restorative work in hurting communities are great. The Lord himself has promised to be in this redemptive work. Ultimately, the great healer will heal our land.

7.

A MISSIONAL RESPONSE TO GLOBAL VIOLENCE AGAINST WOMEN

DIANE LANGBERG

I swore never to be silent wherever and whenever human beings
endure suffering and humiliation. We must always take sides.
Neutrality helps the oppressor, never the victim.
Silence encourages the tormentor, never the tormented.[1]

—*Elie Wiesel, 1986 Nobel Prize acceptance speech*

I grew up the daughter of an Air Force colonel. My father was usually in uniform—or sometimes a flight suit because he was a pilot. However, no matter where we lived and no matter what he was doing, it was clear that he was a colonel in the United States Air Force. Not only did my father's outward appearance indicate who he was, but because he was a man of integrity, he was a man of his uniform all the way through. His carriage, his manners, his speech, his time use, and his respect toward those over or under him—in uniform or out—always demonstrated who he was.

He taught us the importance of reflecting who we were as well. My brother and I were the colonel's kids. We, along with our father, represented the government of the United States. We were expected to act accordingly. We responded with "Yes, sir," and "Yes, ma'am." We learned how to greet officers who came to the house. We learned how to answer the phone. We learned how to stand at attention when the flag was lowered for the day, no matter where we were on the base. My father went out in the name of the US. Since we went with him, we too went out under that massive name.

I write *this* chapter as a representative of a different name. I do not write as a representative of the US; instead, I write in the name of the Lord Jesus Christ—a far more massive and serious responsibility. Although I learned at an early age a little of what it means to come in the name of another, I am now far more aware of the enormity of such a calling, and of the name that I bear.

You are, I anticipate, reading this in the name of Jesus—the name in which you live and move and have your being. Living out your life in the name of Jesus means you are bearing *his* character out into this world. There is much we could say about our world—much that calls for the attention of the people of God. We are going to consider only one sliver: violence against females.

Sadly, this has not been a topic of central interest to the church of Jesus Christ. How that must grieve the One in whose name we live, for to ignore the issues we will consider is, frankly, to ignore the heart of God and to fail to live in his name. So let us look together at this world our God *so loved*, and see the plight of females created in his image and loved by him.

According to Amnesty International, one in three females world-wide—nearly one billion—are beaten, coerced into sex, or otherwise abused in their lifetime.[2] One in three—think about that statistic the next time you sit in an airport or walk through a crowded marketplace or sit in a conference or in the pews of your own church. In fact, make a point of *visualizing* one in three females. When you do, you will understand that you are constantly in contact with women who know all too well what it means to be beaten, coerced into sex, or otherwise abused. They are here.

If we think specifically about the United States, most studies suggest that one in four females is sexually abused by the age of eighteen.[3] This is not just an "out there" problem. If you browse the web for sites related to sexual abuse among Christian women, you will quickly discover that little girls in Christian homes have been abused by so-called Christian fathers, uncles, teachers, and pastors. Rape, one of the most underreported of all crimes, is believed to happen to one in five women in the US. About five million domestic-abuse victimizations occur each year among US women eighteen and older. Estimates indicate that a woman is battered every fifteen seconds. More than three women are murdered daily by their husbands or boyfriends. Pregnant women, the most vulnerable of women, are more likely to be victims of homicide than die of any other cause.

Battering is the leading cause of injury in women ages 15–44, more than rape, mugging, and car accidents combined. Statistically, it is far more dangerous for women to go home than to walk city streets alone at night. These numbers do not change when you survey the Body of Christ. Chuck Colson stated that "about 25% of Christian homes witness abuse of some kind."[4] In the United States, where there are many laws protecting women on the books, being born female is still something of a risk.

Moving back out into the wider world, the most brutal and destructive manifestation of an anti-female bias is female infanticide. There are countries today where baby girls are left in the jungles to die, given poison at birth, or buried facedown in the ground immediately after birth. There are no overall statistics, but a minimum estimate would place the casualties in the hundreds of thousands. They are killed because they had the audacity to be born female. Sex-selective abortions count for an even higher number of missing girls. It is estimated that as many as a million baby girls are aborted by parents determined not to raise a daughter. A recent article in *The Economist* stated that demographics worldwide suggest that one hundred million females are simply missing—aborted or left to die at birth.[5]

Giving birth itself is the most dangerous labor in the world. Some six hundred thousand mothers die in agony every year. Child marriage, female genital mutilation, and other traditional practices cause physical and psychological harm to countless females. Girls have acid thrown in their faces for attending school; they are stoned to death for being raped; and, in a vain attempt to protect them, have their breasts ironed or disfigured by their own mothers in a country where they are usually raped by age thirteen. Violence is a major health and development issue for girls worldwide. Domestic violence, incest, dowry violence, acid killings (40 percent of victims under age eighteen), "honor killings," and mutilation all destroy lives. Young girls are especially susceptible to HIV, and in some countries the infection rates for girls are three to six times higher than for boys.[6] Women now represent 50 percent of the thirty-three million people living with HIV/AIDS.[7]

Women are also the vast majority of the poorest of the poor. And finally, there is the sex trafficking of girls and women that is utterly destroying close to a million females annually, as they are moved across national boundaries and sold into virtual slavery. A woman or girl is sold somewhere in the developing world every ten minutes in order to supply this global sex trade. Sex trafficking is a brutal and large-scale destructive force of girls and women today. We will consider this in more detail later.

Several years ago I took my first trip to Rwanda, and while there I visited the genocide memorial in Kigali. There is a plaque in that memorial that gives the definition of genocide, as defined by the United Nations. Genocide means *any* of the following acts committed with intent to destroy, in whole or in part, a national, ethnical, racial, or religious group:

1. Killing members of the group
2. Causing bodily or mental harm to members of the group
3. Deliberately inflicting on the group conditions of life calculated to bring about its physical destruction, in whole or in part
4. Imposing measures to prevent births within the group
5. Forcibly transferring children of the group to another group

As such, the following acts are considered punishable: genocide; conspiracy to commit genocide; direct and public incitement to genocide; attempt to commit genocide; and complicity in genocide.

I have worked for the past thirty-seven years with women who have been victims of incest, rape, domestic violence, and trafficking.

I have listened to their stories here in the US and around the world. It was a stunning moment to stand in front of that plaque in Kigali and realize its hideous applicability to females around this world. Consider with me each of the acts of genocide, and how they apply to women worldwide.

Killing members of a group. Are you familiar with the term "honor killing"? There is an old saying in China: "for a woman to starve to death is a small matter; for her to lose her chastity is a calamity." A young Kurdish girl falls in love with an Iraqi boy and spends unsupervised time with him. Her family is enraged, assumes she is no longer a virgin, and says she must die. She is dragged to the street, thrown to the ground, kicked, her skirt ripped; after all this, she is stoned to death with rocks and concrete blocks. Once dead, men would cover her body—for, you see, the obscenity is in viewing bare flesh, not in her murder. There are probably five to six thousand such "honor killings" a year around the world.[8]

Causing bodily or mental harm to a group *and* deliberately inflicting on the group conditions of life calculated to bring about its physical destruction in whole or in part. Thirty-nine thousand baby girls die annually in China because parents do not give them the same physical and medical care they give to sons. In India, bride-burning (immolating a female for an inadequate dowry) occurs every two hours. Two million girls disappear worldwide because of gender discrimination. Girls and women around the world face beatings and violence every day. More girls have been killed in the last fifty years, *because they were girls*, than men were killed in all the battles of the twentieth century. Females have food withheld, medicines withheld, education withheld. Females are forced into prostitution, and many die of AIDS by their late twenties. And do not forget: one hundred million females are simply missing from the global population.

Imposing measures to prevent births within the group or forcibly transferring children of the group to another group. This leads us to the catastrophic problem of rape around the world. Rape has become endemic in the country of South Africa. In Kenya, female political candidates carry knives and wear several layers of clothing to deter rape—which is used to humiliate and discredit them, hence keeping them from holding office. Rape is an honored tradition in Ethiopia. If you want a particular girl and think your chances are slim, you rape her. She is shamed and ruined, and the rapist is granted the girl, who then has to marry her rapist. Gender violence is epidemic in Zambia, and there are billboards all over the country in an attempt to stem the tide of rape.

Rape is also used to terrorize and undermine tribal structures, and to dilute an ethnic strain. In Darfur, the Janjaweed militias gang-raped women of three different tribes and mutilated them to mark them as rape victims. Half the women in Sierra Leone have been raped, and the UN says 90 percent of girls and women over the age of three were raped during that country's civil war. Currently, eastern Congo is the capital of rape worldwide. A recent UN human rights panel says that hundreds of thousands have been raped during the conflict there. Rape in Congo is pervasive; one-third of the victims are children, and 13 percent are children under the age of ten.

In 2008, the United Nations declared rape as a weapon of war for the first time; a UN commander stated that it is becoming more dangerous to be female than to be a soldier in an armed conflict. According to UN accounts, in some areas three-quarters of females have been raped.[9] They have been disfigured and tortured in order to terrorize the general population. It is also used to impregnate, as it then dilutes the genetic strain of a particular tribe. Genocide.

It is mind- and soul-numbing to hear such things, is it not? It feels so overwhelming that it ceases to feel like it matters. Who can do anything with such a tsunami of figures? As Joseph Stalin noted (and he of all people should know)—one death is a tragedy; one million is a statistic. Now of course it is not true that one million deaths is only a statistic—it consists of one million individuals, each created in the image of God and gifted for life and impact on their world. However, Stalin's maxim captures what happens to us when we try to absorb the true level of evil and destruction in our world: precious, individual lives full of horrific suffering become mind-numbing statistics.

Were we to sit, listen to, and talk with each of the females in these alarming statistics, our hearts would break and the impact would be profound. Therefore, I would like to take you into a story—a true one.

This was a real female, one I knew for many years. She was my client, and she gave me a gut-wrenching front-row seat to violence against females. She has given permission for her story to be told. She taught me many things, and I am her debtor. She died not all that long ago, and I would like to use part—and believe me, it is *only* part—of her anguished story to take you by the hand into a world many of us know little about. I do this so that you, who live bearing the name of Jesus, might see, hear, and feel the devastation of a female life—and weep as your God weeps over such things.

She was brought to me by her pastor's wife. She came terrified; she had been incubated and raised in evil, horror, and incomprehensible suffering. I was young, compassionate, idealistic, and naïve in the ways of evil. She was mute; I talked. She sat in my tiny office on an uncomfortable chair, curled up in a fetal position and visibly shaking. Every sound and movement panicked her. I did not understand. I was twenty-six years old and knew next to nothing about trauma and abuse. Little did I know that I was sitting with my one of my most significant teachers, from whom I would learn much over the coming years.

It was six months before she spoke one word. She came faithfully every week. I realized much later what a bold step that was. I took it lightly then, for I assumed it was simply what clients do. Over time I learned to talk less and just sit with her. I learned to acknowledge her fear, and told her I did not understand it but wanted to. I told her I was safe. I didn't know that the word "safe" had no meaning for her, as she had never known safety.

One day I asked her a question and wondered if she might be willing to write out the answer for me during the week. I had little hope of success. She returned, having written the answer beginning at the center of the page and writing outward in concentric circles. I had to keep turning the pages in order to read it. Later, I learned that she had hoped such a presentation would annoy me and that I would not read it, or perhaps even throw her out.

I did read every word. It was a telling of a tragic incident, a gang rape—just one small peek into a life full of trauma. I followed my reading with a question, and she answered! I got excited and slapped my hand on the arm of the chair—which scared her to death, causing her to "leave" again for several weeks, going way back inside her head and becoming mute once more. I learned later that any sudden movement was terrifying because in her world it meant pain and damage. Fast-moving hands were weapons.

I went to a supervisor about the incident. I had been hearing about sexual abuse from other clients, but had never heard about it in graduate school; such things were not taught in the 1970s. I was told not to believe the stories. I went back to my client and told her I knew nothing of such things, either by personal experience or by training. I wanted to help, but she would have to first be my teacher and I her student, while I struggled to comprehend such evil and suffering—and tried to figure out what might help and heal in some capacity. Graciously (and perhaps out of desperation) she agreed to do so, and we began a journey that would span many years.

Jesus told us, "'Do not fear those who kill the body but cannot kill the soul'" (Matthew 10:28). But we *do* fear those who can kill the body. They are frightening, murderous, abusive and damaging. They come in the night; they toy with us. They are big, and when they leave we are torn up and in excruciating pain. Sometimes we wish they *would* just kill the body so it would end. They grow fear in us until we reach the point of being afraid of all human beings, certain they too will hurt us. What else would you expect when you learn that the first event of your life upon coming home from the hospital was the extinguishing of cigarettes on the bottom of your little feet because you had the audacity to be born a girl?

Wonder of wonders—they cannot kill the soul. "The LORD will protect you from all evil; He will keep your soul" (Psalm 121:7, NASB).

How we want that to mean our bodies and our lives are safe. It does not. Bodies can be battered, chained, raped, sold, and kicked. Bodies can be tossed aside, not fed, and laughed at. The mind becomes fractured. The mind cannot bear what the body must. It divides up the memories and stores them in compartments, each away from the other because the whole cannot be born. This is not me, we think; this is actually happening to another.

But somehow the soul is protected from all evil. It is hungry, when the body no longer feels hunger due to deprivation. The soul longs for light, when all else is darkness. The soul searches out love, when hatred and evil are everywhere. What keeps the soul alive? How could anything live in such an environment? Mystery, who can understand—the soul lives and seeks and finds the God who loves children, even female ones. The evil is not allowed to own the soul.

"[T]he wicked…sits in the lurking places of the villages; in the hiding places he kills the innocent…. He lurks to catch the afflicted; he catches the afflicted when he draws him [or her] into his net" (Psalm 10:3, 8–9, NASB). As time went by, I listened and heard things I had never imagined. I learned that men who are called fathers can hate, mutilate, and rape little girls; they can be so given over to evil that they treat their daughters like chattel. In fact, they can treat daughters as less than that, for many treat their furniture with more care than she got. She was used to teach her brothers and cousins about sex. She was sold to neighborhood men to help pay the rent. She was used to clean a house that should have been condemned by the health department. I saw pictures of trash and waste hip-high throughout the rooms. She was made to eat with the dogs. Eventually she was tied, blindfolded, and taken by van across state lines to be trafficked for weeks at a time. "Trafficked" was not a word back then. "Abuse" was barely in the common vocabulary of this country. The only word she heard for it was "whore." That, she was told, was what she was and always would be.

I struggled. How can such things be? How can they go on for years without anyone speaking? Where was her mother? I learned that mothers can be so hardened they "do not see" and "do not hear." I learned that mothers who finally cannot avoid seeing decide that the child must have done something to deserve such treatment—even as she tends a broken body, washes the blood off, and keeps her home from school for weeks at a time so others will not ask questions. As Isaac Watts wrote: "Can a woman e'er forget the infant of her womb… Yes, says the Lord, but should nature change and mothers' monsters prove, Zion still dwells upon the heart of everlasting love." Some mothers are indeed monsters.

Unlike the woman before me, my body was untouched, but my mind—like hers—struggled to absorb the full reality of her life. Where was the God that I love? Where was the Jesus who wept? Where was he who opened his arms for the children and rebuked those who tried to turn them away? Why did he bring her to me? What did he expect *me* to do? No skill or theory would heal such evil and pain. She believed in him, but oh how she struggled to trust that he loved her. No wonder: There was no love here on earth to even give her a glimpse of that wonderful, boundless love. She could not imagine what she had never known.

I pleaded with God, "Teach her; show her how much you love her. It would alter her; it would comfort her; it would bless her." There was much pleading and much silence. Then, one day, it was as if the Spirit of God himself had spoken, "Do you want her to know my love?"

"Yes, Lord, I do."

"Then go back in that room and love her the way I do. Carry her pain with her; hear her cries and absorb her story; walk with her no matter how great the darkness; demonstrate my love in the flesh. Live before her in my name. Then she will know."

In that little room I began to learn something of the love of God that far exceeded my previous knowledge and experience. I later realized it was one of the gifts she gave me. I learned that the love of God bent down, way down into the muck and mire of this world, into the darkest corners running with rats. "[H]e was despised…he was pierced…he was crushed…He was oppressed, and he was afflicted" (Isaiah 53:3, 5, 7). I saw that his love led him to become like us *so that* we might actually become something like him. I understood more of what it means when it says, "Surely he has borne our griefs and carried our sorrows;... and with his stripes we are healed" (Isaiah 53:4–5). I saw that love, a beautiful thing, becomes utterly filthy for the one who is loved, in order to make the filthy clean. I learned something of the waiting of love—waiting for a thought to be spoken, waiting for a heart to hear, waiting for a life to step toward the One who loves.

Years later, she sent me a card that said, "I knew nothing of love when I met you. The word meant as little to me as a description of the color green to a blind person. Having sat with you, now I know something of love and God's love for me. Thank you." However, that is not the way it was when we started. It was I who learned the love of God, through the school of her great suffering.

"When sin is accomplished, it brings forth death" (James 1:15, NASB). Comprehending the depth of evil was overwhelming. It is frightening to think that we can look at another human being and not know that he or she is full of great evil and darkness. We see with our eyes and hear with our ears, and so judge one acceptable and another not. God sees and hears inside the heart. The acceptable is devoured in his holiness, and the unacceptable, odd-looking one with strange behaviors is fully accepted and loved in his sight. Over time, God gave me something of his eyes. He sees and loves the leper, the outcast, the tormented, and the unwashed. He notes self-righteousness, pride, and religiosity and calls it dead men's bones. How unlike us he is.

Sitting with her gave me the gift of the eyes of God. The world he has shown me through her is not the one I used to see. Now I see a world that breaks his heart. Now I see that the worst thing in this world is sin. It is what holds us in bondage, distorts us, makes us subhuman, and drives us from the face of the lover of our souls. We think "little" toxins are not so bad; we fool ourselves about our own sins even while we sit in judgment on the sins of others. The great evils perpetrated on her taught me the great evil of the smallest sin. One cancerous cell can end up swallowing up an entire life, rendering the person unrecognizable.

Her body began to fail. Year after year, more things were wrong. No human body can endure such trauma and not be weakened by it. I saw her less as she got frail. She became a faithful intercessor for me.

During her last years she had me write down my travels and speaking and writing, so that she could pray daily, multiple times per day, from a pain-wracked body in a small bed. In her weakness she was a warrior. She knew her Redeemer; she knew of his great love for the world; she knew he too had been broken for the broken of this world; and she believed he still had healing to do and prayed he would do some through me.

And again, I learned. I learned about strength in weakness. I saw faithfulness carried out through gritted teeth. She wanted to go home to Jesus, but she knew she was here for a reason and believed one of those reasons was intercession for the saints. Only eternity will tell the fruit of that labor. It is not fruit measured by this world. By the world's standards she was not known; she had not accomplished great things, and many would have seen her as useless or even perhaps a drain on the system. But unknown to most she was a warrior doing battle in the hidden places for the servants of God. I was blessed by her fight, and I learned yet again that value is not measured as this world measures things—including the Christian world. It is in the hidden places of the heart, where the God who sees weighs what he sees. When what is hidden honors his great name and brings him glory, the weight is immeasurable.

She died last year. She heard the welcome home, "Well done, good and faithful servant," she longed to hear. She, who knew hell, now knows heaven. She who lived darkness is basking in the Light of the World. She who saw the evil of men's hearts and the diabolical work of the enemy of our souls has now seen glory. And again, I am learning. She has given me a glimpse into eternity where she now sits in the heavenlies. She resides near the Great Intercessor who sits at the right hand of the Father. I think she is very close to his heart.

* * *

Now listen: on the plaque in the memorial in Kigali, Rwanda, following the definition of genocide, is the list of those things that are punishable as genocide. One of them, number five, is complicity. The word literally refers to "folding together." It means to be an accomplice, a partner in wrongdoing. To be silent about the global violence against females is to be folded together with those who carry out such violence. (Basyle Tchividjian has an excellent discussion of this phenomenon in the next chapter in this volume. He calls it "robbery through omission by silence.")

As the church of Jesus Christ, we are witnesses to the truth. Yes, that means speaking boldly about the God who came in the flesh to redeem broken humanity, but it also means speaking the truth about that brokenness and calling evil by its right name. A truth teller disturbs, alerts, wakens, and warns against indifference to injustice and complacency about the needs of human beings. The world knew what was happening in Germany in the 1930s—and remained silent. The world knew about the Warsaw ghetto and Auschwitz and remained silent. The world knew about the genocide in Rwanda and remained silent. Silence is not a virtue; it is a vice two times compounded, for it contains both indifference to the victims and complicity with the destroyers.

There is precedent for the care of females in the life of the One whose name we bear. He arrived as the seeming illegitimate son of a virgin in a culture that should have stoned her because she was very much outside the parameters. In other words, she was deemed worthy of an honor killing. His genealogy has several trashed women in it—Tamar, Rahab, Ruth, and Bathsheba. That list brings into his history such things as incest, prostitution, interracial marriage (which was forbidden in that culture), and adultery. He went from there to swim upstream, by saying things like looking on a female as a sex object is the equivalent of adultery (worthy of stoning in that culture).

He began his ministry by blessing an unnamed bride in Cana. Women publicly traveled with him—a stunning and offensive situation in that culture. He treated one woman as a male disciple when he affirmed her presence at his feet, and treated another as an apostle when he gave to her the privilege of first telling others of his resurrection. He paused in his work of saving the world to raise a girl child from the dead, return a son to a widow, and a brother to two grieving women. He accorded women dignity, honor, safety, education, and privilege.

If he did these things for women and girls, should not his body do the same? Should not the mission of God in Christ be the mission of God's people?

Christ's teaching calls us to the mission field of women and girls as much as his life. To the woman caught in adultery, something he condemned, he said, "'Neither do I condemn you; go, and from now on sin no more'" (John 8:11). Do you suppose such a Savior would rain down condemnation on the girls and women of this world who are dying of AIDS? He taught us that what we have done (or not) to the "least of these" we have done *to him*. Would we leave him to die, allow him to be trafficked and brutally raped, and turn blind eyes to violence against his person?

Do you suppose the Savior who touched lepers would ignore the girls and women of this world who are considered unclean and untouchable? He calls us, through his brother James, to note that pure religion in the sight of God our Father is to visit the widows and orphans in their distress (James 1:27). Do you think such a Savior would say that trafficked girls, abandoned girls, mutilated girls, prostituted girls, and violated girls might qualify as orphans? Might he suggest to us that women who are sold across a nation's borders, threatened by honor killings, infected by AIDS, abandoned, or relentlessly battered by their husbands could possibly qualify as widows? Do you not hear the voice of our Savior calling us to crawl all over this world searching for the abandoned, neglected, dying, abused, and trafficked? We who carry the name of Jesus have often failed to look anything like him in relation to the females of this world—even those in our own home and pews.

I am keenly aware that I am writing primarily to those who actively carry the name of Jesus—to people who seek to go out into this world in his name and his character, who seek to be missional, who intend to follow Jesus into the world. I am also aware that many of my readers are working in jobs where these topics are relevant, and are reading this particular chapter because they are interested or invested in these topics. For that, I am grateful. But what do you think might happen if the Spirit of God got hold of every single reader of this chapter, of this book? What might he accomplish for the girls and women of our fallen world?

The first thing—always the first thing in God's work—would be repentance. God's kingdom is the kingdom of the heart. If he does not rule there, in all the corners hidden away in us, then our external work will not bear his character no matter how successful or big it looks. Some of you reading this material are part of the statistics I have quoted —male and female alike. Some grew up with domestic abuse; some have been sexually abused, and others raped. I urge you to deal with it in truth. Seek out help; learn how those events still hold you and deceive you. If you want to minister in this world in the name and image of Jesus, then courageously face what has been done to you so that the Spirit of God can work deeply to set you free.

Others of you might feed the beast I have described, or tolerate it mutely in the life of someone you love. The way you think about females, treat them, or speak to them is demeaning, degrading, and perhaps humiliating. Perhaps you are feeding on the toxic waste of pornography in your computer or in your mind (see John Freeman's excellent chapter later in this section). You may be successful and praised by all, but you are *not* living in the name of Jesus. You are bearing the stench of fallenness in your mind and life rather than the fragrance and likeness of Jesus Christ. Seek help; speak the truth about yourself so that Jesus has rule over the kingdom of your heart. If you do not, you will continue to feed on death and become its slave, even as you verbally speak the name of Jesus.

Some—perhaps even many—of us are uncomfortable with the things I have written. We do not like these topics and do not want to see. We judge those who are suffering. Since we are at heart nothing like our God, he generally makes us very uncomfortable. To be made over into the image of One so utterly unlike us *requires* becoming uncomfortable! I pray we will not harden our hearts.

We also need to recognize that the plight of females is also about the plight of males. Men cannot traffic females, abuse them, mutilate them, rape them, or throw acid on them without also destroying themselves. Males cannot degrade, humiliate, objectify, or lust after females without destroying themselves. And males are not the only perpetrators. Females also traffic, abuse, and cause great pain to boys, girls, and women. *This* is the world we live in. These devastations are not just done by them, but by us. They are not just "over there," but they are here, wherever "here" is for you—in your country, your town, your churches, and your homes.

Twenty centuries ago baby girls were considered a liability. Demographics in the first century, in certain parts of the world, were stunningly imbalanced between male and female. Female infanticide was not uncommon; infant girls were often considered the equivalent of deformed, and were killed by exposure. In essence, it was permitted by law to leave them outside the city on the dung heap to die. That is about as clear a judgment of "worthless" on a human life as can be made.

There was, however, a growing group of people who seemed to think this judgment was in error. Rather than accepting the culture's assessment regarding the value of females, they went outside the city to the dung heaps to find and rescue the abandoned baby girls. Their decision was both risky and sacrificial. It required standing against the mainstream and making a judgment that ran counter to the culture of that time. It meant the giving of life, time, and goods to someone else's discarded baby girl. It meant extending the circle of one's responsibility. It meant being devalued and disdained, for stooping so low as to treat that which was deemed worthless as precious.

Who were these people? They were the first-century church, traveling outside the gates to the garbage heaps of those days to rescue baby girls. They went to the dung heaps in the name of Christ—the one who sought us out when we were in the mire, as if we were precious gold in the sewer. We were sought out, and no darkness could hide us nor filth conceal us—we who had prostituted ourselves to another. The church of the first century did for others what had been done for them by God himself.

And so I end where I began. The missional call that was answered by our first-century brethren is not unlike the call before us in the twenty-first century church and community. The question that remains to be answered is whether or not we too will go outside the city gates to pursue and rescue those found worthless in the eyes of this world, and to sacrificially work among them.

"'Our Father in heaven, hallowed be your name. Your kingdom come, your will be done, *on earth as it is in heaven.'*" (Matthew 6:9–10, emphasis mine). To hallow the name of God is to reverence his character, to defend his honor, and to obey his authority. One of the major tests of hallowing the divine name is our attitude toward our fellow humans. The injustice of humans toward other humans profanes the name of God—it wounds, wears away, and renders the name of God common.

One of the supreme opportunities before the church today is created by the suffering of females around the globe. May our response be one that honors the name of the God who created them.

8.

WORSHIP AND CHILDREN:
A Missional Response
to Child Sexual Abuse

BASYLE TCHIVIDJIAN[1]

There is a story about the late American evangelist, D.L. Moody who arrived home late one evening from preaching a revival service. As the tired Moody climbed into bed, his wife rolled over and asked, "So how did it go tonight?" Moody replied, "Pretty well, two and a half converts."

His wife smiled and said, "That's sweet. How old was the child?"

"No, no, no," Moody answered. "It was two children and one adult! The children have their whole lives in front of them. The adult's life is already half-gone."[2]

Too often, society views children in the same manner as Moody's wife. Instead of treasuring little ones as God does, we often consider their value as secondary to that of adults. This is completely contrary to how Jesus views and values children. "'Truly, I say to you, unless you turn and become like children, you will never enter the kingdom of heaven'" (Matthew 18:3).

And yet, our culture often finds itself overlooking the most basic needs of its children, while adults are busy tending and caring for themselves. This devaluing of children often leaves them exposed to indescribable harm that results in physical, emotional, and spiritual consequences. Wess Stafford, president of Compassion International, puts it all too accurately, "Small, weak, helpless, innocent, vulnerable, and trusting, they are waiting victims for our simple neglect and most evil abuse. No matter what goes wrong, the little ones pay the greatest price."[3]

To a significant degree, what I have to say in this chapter follows directly and builds substantially on what Diane Langberg has said in the previous chapter. Indeed, Diane and I have worked together on numerous projects that both of our chapters address, some of which are referenced in her chapter and/or mine.

In 2009, the United States government substantiated that 10.1 out of every 1,000 children were abused or neglected. An additional 16,676 children died from abuse and neglect.[4] Another study found that 38 percent of women in the United States were molested as children under age 18, and that between 9 and 16 percent of males in the United States were molested before their 18th birthday.[5] With 75 million children in the United States, this translates to almost 15 million children who will be sexually victimized over the next 18 years.

This crisis is not limited to the United States, but is international in scope, especially with the rise of computer child trafficking and computer crimes. A 2009 study concluded that an estimated 7.9 percent of men and 19.7 percent of women globally experienced sexual abuse prior to the age of eighteen.[6]

It is time for the church to confront this deadly epidemic! God demands nothing less.

Perhaps most tragically, the evils of child sexual abuse are quite prevalent within the Christian community.[7] News reports of children being sexually abused within the faith community are almost a daily occurrence. An older survey conducted by Christian Ministry Resources found that child abuse allegations made against American churches averaged approximately seventy per week. The actual number is likely much higher, since the report only included churches that are insured, and only took into account abuse allegations that were actually reported.[8]

Sadly, we in the evangelical community have largely ignored the sin of child sexual abuse. As a result, Christians have often unwittingly contributed to the suffering of victims because of failure to protect children and adequately respond to disclosures of abuse. Additionally, the church has too often overlooked the many needs of those within the congregation who are adult survivors of sexual abuse. The response of the Christian community to the sexual abuse of children all too often pushes these precious souls away from the arms of Jesus and hinders them from experiencing the glorious gospel.

It is time for the Christian community to demonstrate love and adoration of our God, by loving and protecting precious little ones and sending them into the arms of Jesus, regardless of the effort required or the difficult consequences we may face. And it all begins with worship.

WORSHIP IS OUR PURPOSE

As children, many of us were taught that foundational first question of the Westminster Shorter Catechism—that our chief purpose is to glorify God and to enjoy him forever. In other words, the very purpose for which God has breathed life into each one of us is to give him glory, which finds its apex in worship. If worship is the culmination of our God-given purpose, then logic dictates that it is also a God-given command. Jesus makes this clear in Luke 4:8 when he cites Deuteronomy 6:13, "'You shall worship the Lord your God, and him only shall you serve.'"

Not only are we commanded to worship, but our worship must be acceptable to the object of our worship—God. Worship is not acceptable when its heart focus is on anyone or anything other than God. This was most vividly depicted in the Acts account of Ananias and Sapphira in Acts 5. Though they demonstrated an outward appearance of worship through the donation of their property proceeds, the true object of their worship was exposed by their dishonesty in holding back some of the proceeds for themselves. Outward "worship" with an inward focus on anything but God is not authentic and is unacceptable to a holy God.

Finally, and perhaps most importantly, the author of Hebrews tells us that it is impossible to offer acceptable worship without the finished work of Christ: "Therefore let us be grateful for receiving a kingdom that cannot be shaken, and thus let us offer to God acceptable worship, with reverence and awe" (Hebrews 12:28). In explaining this passage, John Calvin writes, "We, in embracing the Gospel, have the gift of the Spirit of Christ, that we may reverently and devoutly worship God."[9] John Frame adds, in his book *Worship in Spirit and Truth*, "[W]orship is not about God's thanking us; it is about our thanking him."[10] By and through the work of Christ, we are equipped to worship God for the purpose of demonstrating authentic thanksgiving to and for him.

WORSHIP IS OUR PRACTICE

Since we are designed to be God-worshipers, it is imperative for us to be reminded that we are to worship God in all that we think, say, and do. Paul writes, "So, whether you eat or drink, or whatever you do, do all to the glory of God" (1 Corinthians 10:31). And as John Frame again articulates, this command "covers all human activities, including buying of cabbage. If we buy cabbage to the glory of God, he is pleased; if we do not, he is not."[11] If buying cabbage to the glory of God pleases the Triune God, then certainly loving children into the arms of Jesus pleases God as well!

Christ said, "'Whoever receives one such child in my name receives me'" (Mark 9:37). Were not all his children created to glorify and worship him? Are not all these precious little ones paramount beings of evangelistic concern in his Great Commission, as well as to his incarnate human heart? In this one powerful statement, Christ communicates the incredible value he and his Father place upon all children, in that our love for God is demonstrated by how we love and "receive" children. The truly missional church can do no less!

In short, we express our love for God through our love for children. One pastor once remarked, "Something is deeply amiss in the soul that does not descent (or is it really ascent) to love and hold a child."[12] In other words, it is impossible to authentically love God and not love his little ones. The *Merriam-Webster Dictionary* defines "welcome" as to "accept with pleasure the presence of." In essence, Jesus is saying that we worship him through accepting with pleasure the presence of children—who are also designed to be worshipers of our great God! Loving, protecting, and advocating for children is an essential component of our overall worship of God, and an important tool God uses to raise up little worshipers.

THE ROBBERY OF WORSHIP—SATAN'S AGENDA

"'Whoever causes one of these little ones who believe in me to sin, it would be better for him if a great millstone were hung around his neck and he were thrown into the sea'" (Mark 9:42). The term "cause" is defined as "something that brings about an effect or result." Thus, not only does God impose a heavy judgment upon those who hurt children within the church, but he also places an awesome responsibility upon Christians to protect little ones and not to be a stumbling block in their relationship with him. As man's chief end is to glorify God, Satan's chief objective is to rob God of that glory and worship by and through the physical and spiritual destruction of his worshipers. This dark agenda often begins with Satan's attempt to destroy the most vulnerable of worshipers, children!

A 2004 study by The Barna Group found that two-thirds of professing Christians made a profession for Christ before their eighteenth birthday.[13] Thus, it should come as a no surprise that Satan is tirelessly working to hurt children, in order to prevent them from spending a lifetime and eternity worshiping God. The hurt experienced as a result of childhood abuse is often severe, far-reaching, and lifelong.

Researchers at the Centers for Disease Control and Prevention found that individuals who suffered one or more "adverse childhood experiences" were at higher risk for alcoholism and alcohol abuse, depression, illicit drug use, intimate partner violence, multiple sexual partners, sexually transmitted diseases (STDs), smoking, suicide attempts, early initiation of sexual activity, and adolescent pregnancies.[14] Not only does child abuse impact an individual's physical and emotional well-being, it also negatively shapes a person's spiritual perspectives. There are a number of studies documenting the impact of abuse on spirituality. One study of 527 victims of child abuse (physical, sexual, or emotional) found a significant "spiritual injury," such as feelings of guilt, anger, grief, despair, doubt, fear of death, and belief that God is unfair.[15] All of these issues can rob a survivor's ability to know and relate to his Heavenly Father.

Perhaps this tragedy was summarized best by a survivor of child sexual abuse who told me, "Because of my abuse [within a Christian community], I absolutely despise anybody who calls themselves a Christian." Isn't it clear that Satan's dark agenda is to rob God of worship through harming children? This is the ultimate in spiritual warfare!

Christians must begin working toward welcoming little ones into the arms of Jesus by gaining a greater understanding of how those who victimize children operate within the Christian environment (robberies of commission). Then they must understand how the Christian community all too often falls short in effectively responding to abuse disclosures (robberies of omission). It is only after we have grasped these two forms of robbery that we will be in a position to understand how the gospel empowers us to be used by God to restore worship to those who have been ravaged by child sexual abuse.

ROBBERY THROUGH COMMISSION— CHILD SEXUAL ABUSE

"Child molesters are very professional at what they do and they do a good job at it." This is the testimony of a convicted child molester.[16] If child molesters are so "good" at what they do, it is imperative that we learn the methods of operation that offenders use within the Christian community. After being asked how he selected children in a church to abuse, an offender responded,

> First of all you start the grooming process from day one...the children that you're interested in...You find a child you might be attracted to...For me, it might be nobody fat. It had to be a you know, a nice looking child...You maybe look at a kid that doesn't have a father image at home, or a father that cares about them...if you've got a group of 25 kids, you might find 9 that are appealing...then you start looking at their family backgrounds. You find out all you

can…which ones are the most accessible…you get it down to one that is the easiest target, and that's the one you do.[17]

Though each offender is unique in how he goes about intentionally targeting and perpetrating children, there are some common methods used within religious environments. These methods often focus on exploiting the very characteristics that make the faith community so unique. An ability to identify and possess a general knowledge of five common avenues for exploitation will better prepare Christians to protect our younger worshipers. The abuse is often hidden in the following:

1. The exploitation of "religious cover"
2. The exploitation of faith issues
3. The exploitation of authority
4. The exploitation of needs
5. The exploitation of trust

The Exploitation of "Religious Cover"

I want to describe a child molester I know very well. This man was raised by devout Christian parents and as a child he rarely missed church. Even after he became an adult he was faithful as a church member. He was a straight-A student in high school and college. He has been married and has a child of his own. He coached little league baseball and was a choir director at his church. He never used illegal drugs and never had a drink of alcohol. He was considered the clean-cut, all-American boy. Everyone seemed to like him, and he often volunteered in numerous civic community functions. He had a well-paying career and was considered "well to do" in society. But from the age of 13 years old, this boy sexually molested little boys. He never victimized a stranger; all of his victims were "friends." I know this child molester very well because he is me![18]

The above is the testimony of a convicted child molester. "Religious cover" is the outward demonstration of religious practices or doctrine that covers over more sinister intentions and behaviors. Our churches and Christian communities often attract those who abuse children because they have little fear of being detected or caught there. These individuals use "religious cover" to gain the access and trust of children and their families.

In a highly publicized case, Father Lawrence Murphy sexually abused as many as two hundred deaf or hard-of-hearing boys and often used spiritual language or religious concepts in the abuse. For example, he told one victim, "God wanted him to teach the boy about sex but that he had to keep it quiet because it was under the sacrament of confession."[19]

Oftentimes, abusers within the church are the ones who appear to be the most "put together," spiritual, generous, and kind. This behavior is intentional and is designed to deceive a community that is used to judging others by outward deeds and appearances. A recent study found that hard-core offenders who maintain a significant involvement with religious institutions "had more sexual offense convictions, more victims, and younger victims."[20] These findings are consistent with a community that is least suspecting of those who exploit "religious cover" to sexually victimize children.

The Exploitation of Faith Issues

Experienced abusers within the church understand the power that issues of faith wield upon children. These issues are often distorted and manipulated by offenders in order to coerce victims to submit to abuse and remain silent. The distortion of biblical truths is a common method used by offenders to exploit faith issues and perpetrate abuse. For example, sometimes abuse will be justified as an act of "love." The offender may say, "Don't feel bad; this is the expression of God-ordained love." Other times offenders will shame children by confusing them that their "participation" in the abuse is "sinful." Comments such as "You should be ashamed of your sin" go a long way in keeping a little one silent about ongoing abuse. An abuse survivor once told me that her abuser captured her silence and submission by repeatedly telling her, "Because of your sin, God doesn't care about you, but I do."

The spiritual impact that such faith exploitation has upon a child victim is both complex and, oftentimes, lifelong. Perhaps the greatest damage is the inability of many abuse survivors to distinguish these biblical truths and terms from their experience. Not surprisingly, many of these abuse survivors want nothing to do with matters related to faith.

The church must take practical steps to educate its members on the true meanings of basic religious terms and doctrine, and it must also make members aware of how people inside the church can twist and distort these truths for sinful purposes. Furthermore, the Christian community must also understand the impact of such exploitation and be sensitive to abuse survivors who find certain biblical truths to be deeply destructive because of the harm they have suffered. The Christian community must strive to find ways of speaking the gospel to abuse survivors that will not hurt or confuse.

The Exploitation of Authority

Those who hurt children within the church are aware that these children are often taught to obey authority without question. In a fallen world, such authority will often be exploited and misused by abusers who have worked themselves into leadership positions. When leaders are given unbiblical absolute authority, abusers can create an environment whereby behaviors and activities will seldom be questioned or challenged by adults, let alone by children. What is most harmful is that such total power and control is usually justified as being sanctioned by God. The resulting culture is one in which the offender has almost unlimited access to and control over the child. Then the child is open to ongoing abuse and a great deal of confusion.

In her book *This Little Light*, Christa Brown recounts how her youth pastor exploited his authority in order to gain her submission. She writes: "Eddie [the pastor] always said that God had chosen me for something special. I guess I really wanted to believe that. Doesn't every kid want to think they're special? Besides, who was I to question a man of God? It wasn't my place. My role was to be submissive."[21]

The Exploitation of Needs

How many churches can you think of that are *not* in need of volunteers to help with our children and young people (e.g., nursery, youth group, vacation Bible school, etc.)? Many offenders have grown up in the faith community and are well aware of this constant need for assistance. Those who abuse children will go to great lengths in exploiting the needs of the church for the purpose of gaining access to our children.

Upon being released from prison, a sexual offender approached a pastor and asked, "Does your church take ex-cons?" The pastor replied, "Well son, if they are truly repentant we do." The offender followed up with, "Oh, I am, pastor. I was in prison for passing a bad check. You can check on me if you don't believe me. And while I was there, I found the Lord, and there was this hymn I dearly loved. And I knew it would be a sign from God, whatever church was playing that hymn, that was the church for me. Pastor, when I walked by your church this morning, you were playing that hymn." Had the pastor checked on this person, he would have learned that he had just served time in prison for sexually abusing children. Instead, he was eventually allowed to fill an ongoing church need—director of the youth choir—where he was able to victimize more children.[22] The faith community must carefully screen those who have access to children and put up accountability and monitoring safeguards.

The Exploitation of Trust

Another convicted child molester said, "I consider church people easy to fool…they have a trust that comes from being Christians. They tend to be better folks all around and seem to want to believe in the good that exists in people. I think they want to believe in people. Because of that, you can easily convince, with or without convincing words."[23] For a variety of reasons, we naively tend to automatically lower our guard when we are amongst professing Christians. This same naivete is why offenders flock to the faith community; no other environment provides them such quick and easy access to children without the fear of raising concerns.

A number of years ago, our family had just moved to an area and was looking for a church. At that time our eldest child was an infant, and at each visiting church we dropped her off at the church nursery. Yes, I entrusted my child to the care of a complete stranger at a strange new place. Could you imagine walking into Walmart and handing your child into the care of the greeter while you shopped? Though I don't think I would be so careless today, the reason I did not think much about it then was that it was a church; I automatically trusted those within a new church environment.

It is common for many of us to refer to those in our church as our "church family." Missionaries often tell me that they were instructed as children to refer to every adult on the mission field as "uncle" or "aunt." However, it is common knowledge that most children are not sexually victimized by strangers. In fact, one study found that only 10 percent of child molesters victimize children they do not know.[24] The Christian community must come to terms with the heartbreaking reality that those who pose the greatest risk to our children are within our families, churches, and circles of friends.

Understanding these five avenues of exploitation is the first step that the Christian community must take to minimize the opportunities for those who wish to rob God of his worship by harming little worshipers.

ROBBERY THROUGH OMISSION

> And they were bringing children to him that he might touch them, and the disciples rebuked them. But when Jesus saw it, he was indignant and said to them, "Let the children come to me; do not hinder them, for to such belongs the kingdom of God." (Mark 10:13–14)

This passage is perhaps one of the most powerful biblical illustrations of how all too often it is those who walk closest to Jesus who prevent children from approaching him. It is not that the disciples did not care about these children, but like Moody's wife, it almost seems as if they believed that the children were distracting Jesus from his work.

Our Lord could not have been clearer that children are his pressing priority, and that he takes great pleasure in their presence. Our reluctance to acknowledge and embrace the reality that God treasures little ones with no less love than adults can discourage children from approaching Jesus. A common way this plays out in the church is when we fail to respond to child sexual abuse disclosures in a manner that demonstrates love and value of those who have been victimized. All too often, the Christian response is rebuke and silence.

Omission by Rebuke

The most obvious manner used by the disciples to keep children away from Jesus was through open rebuke. God is robbed of worship when Christians criticize those who come forward to disclose abuse, or simply "keep down" children and their families by failing to address allegations in a manner that draws them closer to the arms of Christ. Though such rebuke takes various forms, it is often "justified" using the rationale that such disclosures "distract" the church from carrying out its work.

Not long ago, I met with an individual who had been abused years earlier at a missionary boarding school. He told me that when he approached the school staff about the abuse and requested to contact his parents who were hundreds of miles away, he was told "Africans will end up in hell" if his parents had to leave the field to address his abuse situation. Needless to say, this young man remained silent. In my work, I often hear about church leaders who openly rebuke abuse survivors for coming forward because their disclosure "hurts the cause of the gospel."

Sometimes such rebukes are more subtle, but no less damaging. For example, it is not uncommon for church members to rally around alleged perpetrators within the church who claim innocence and are perceived by the congregation as the actual "victim." Inevitably, the family of the alleged victim will be ostracized and will sometimes even be openly criticized for being the "cause of such pain." At a recent conference, prosecutors were asked about their observations regarding the supportive role pastors play in child sexual abuse cases. More than two-thirds indicated that they had observed pastors in a supportive role only for the accused perpetrator, not the alleged victim. What a devastating message of rebuke communicated to a child when her church leader so openly supports the one who has been the source of so much deep pain.

Rebuke can also come from a church that does not understand the complex emotional and spiritual dynamics of child sexual abuse and of those who offend. Experienced offenders who get caught will sometimes tearfully confess to some form of "inappropriate" behavior and beg for forgiveness and mercy, knowing that such a response will often result in the immediate embrace of the church body. This is often followed by a concerted effort by church leadership to bring about "healing" through reconciliation. If the abuse survivor or their family resists such a push, they are often rebuked for being unforgiving, and sometimes even formally disciplined.

A similar form of rebuke takes place when church leaders express impatience with the long road of recovery experienced by most abuse survivors. I have heard stories of victims being asked by their pastor, "Why can't you just forgive and move on?" Such an expression communicates that the church has grown weary with this matter and that *it* is the party that wants to "move on."

When the Christian community rebukes abuse survivors or their families, it inevitably will silence their pain or send them fleeing the church to find someone (or something) that will listen or care. Tragically, but understandably, most of these precious souls walk away and want nothing to do with worshiping our glorious God.

Omission by Silence

A less obvious—but just as effective—manner in which the children were kept away from Jesus was through the silence of those standing around, as the disciples rebuked. Silence about abuse, and silence about how an institution responds to abuse, will inevitably facilitate an environment of abuse. Perhaps the most stark modern-day example of this is the Penn State tragedy. Not only did those who know about the sexual abuse of young boys by Jerry Sandusky remain silent, but still others remained silent upon hearing of the institution's failure to take prompt corrective action. The consequence of these silences was years of ongoing sexual abuse and the untold destruction of many young lives.[25]

Tragically, such silence is common within the Christian environment. Second Samuel 13:1–22 provides the horrifying account of the rape of Tamar by her brother Amnon, both children of King David. Next to the sexual assault itself, perhaps the most egregious aspect of this story is the utter silence that dominated those who learned of the offense. When Tamar disclosed the abuse to her brother Absalom, he responded, "'Now hold your peace, my sister. He is your brother; do not take this to heart'" (2 Samuel 13:20). His instruction was apparently driven by the fact that the perpetrator was her brother. Even worse was the response of King David, who was the one responsible for sending his daughter to Amnon's house: "When King David heard of all these things, he was very angry" (2 Samuel 13:21). He was angry—but remained silent and did nothing.

These types of responses are still all too common within the modern church. Whether it's a notable pastor, a staff member, an influential church member, or a well-respected member of the community, the identity of the alleged perpetrator still drives many in the church to remain silent about suspected abuse. Not long ago I was speaking with someone regarding a physician within a Christian community who sexually abused numerous children. Though many were suspect of this individual's bizarre behavior with children, they remained quiet due to the fact that he was a physician who was "needed" within the community.

In *This Little Light*, Christa Brown recounts that after being repeatedly sexually victimized by her youth pastor, she finally gained enough courage to report the abuse to the church music minister. Upon hearing her disclosure, the music minister made young Christa promise that she would not tell anyone else of the abuse. Just a few short weeks later, the church announced that the offending youth pastor had accepted a "calling" to another church.[26] Not only did the church's silence allow the offender to escape legal responsibility and to move to a new church of unsuspecting victims, but it also loudly conveyed to Christa that she was worthless. Again, this silence was premised upon the fact that the perpetrator was a youth minister and was most likely rationalized with the lie that exposure of this offender would hurt the "cause of Christ."

Decades of addressing child sexual abuse within the faith community prompted attorney Jeff Anderson to remark, "Every institution protects the powerful among them and puts the institution above the well being of kids. It's about power and preservation. The more powerful the institution is, the less child protection and harder for them to do the right thing."[27] A silence that covers abuse and the failed response of the church to abuse loudly communicates worthlessness to the one being abused. Not only does such silence cause further harm to the survivor, but it also enables the continued victimization by perpetrators. Silence frees perpetrators to move between Christian environments, victimizing and destroying young worshipers along the way.

Whether the robbery of worship is through rebuke or silence, the common thread is the church's failure to respond to abuse in a manner that draws people to Jesus. Ultimately, these forms of robbery are rooted in a Christian culture that is all too often focused upon the institution, rather than the gospel. A self-focused institution will go to great lengths to protect its comfort and reputation at the expense of the individual, which is the very antithesis of the gospel. Little thought is given to the impact that such actions will have upon the abuse survivor. Such institutions will promote a culture of silence, if it means that the ministry will be able to protect itself and continue forward with its ministry objectives. The fact that God's worship is being robbed along the way makes little difference.

THE RESTORATION OF WORSHIP: PROTECTING AND RESPONDING WITH EXCELLENCE

It is the worship of our great God, and the realization that Satan's purpose is to rob God of that worship, which must drive the heart and soul of every Christian in confronting child sexual abuse. Satan's tragic agenda would be too overwhelming but for the glorious fact that it is by the work and power of God alone that we tackle this evil. As John says, "In him was life, and the life was the light of men. The light shines in the darkness, and the darkness has not overcome it" (John 1:4–5).

Child abuse can never truly be addressed apart from God. He is the only true source of protection and healing; without God there can be no worship. So how does God go about using us to preserve and restore worship, as it relates to children and abuse?

Worship is restored when God enables us to understand and confront child sexual abuse with excellence. We must begin by taking concrete steps to educate our Christian communities about the tragic reality that child sexual abuse robs souls of life and faith, which ultimately robs God of worship. First, the souls of victims may be lost, as they are left with a distorted and deceitful perspective of God. Second, the souls of perpetrators are at risk, as we all too often allow them to slither through God's house, abusing his little ones with little or no consequences. Failing to confront perpetrators not only enables continued abuse, but it also demonstrates a failure to care about the eternal judgment of their souls. Third, the soul of the larger community is at stake, as the general public too often views the church as an institution far more interested in protecting itself than in protecting the bodies and souls of children. Christians must understand that this is not just a tragic human-interest issue—it involves the glory of our great God.

Understanding and Educating with Excellence

If the Christian community hopes to address the evils of child abuse authentically, they must first understand and teach people the inescapable spiritual connections between worship and abuse within the training grounds of tomorrow's Christian leaders— seminaries. At the very minimum, every seminary should require at least ten hours of instruction on child abuse and how to prevent and respond to it. If tomorrow's pastors and leaders fail to grasp these truths, we cannot expect them to be understood by the wider Christian community. The National Child Protection Training Center has taken the lead to develop such a curriculum for mainline seminaries. GRACE (Godly Response to Abuse in the Christian Environment) is currently in the initial stages of developing such a curriculum to be implemented within evangelical seminaries.

Additionally, we must begin writing and teaching these truths at every level of Christian culture, in a manner that ensures that this sinful crime remains on the radar screen of every Christian. This can be accomplished through Sunday sermons, Sunday-school and youth-group curricula, small-group Bible studies, and even community church-wide gatherings. What a testimony it would be to communities if every church came together for the purpose of understanding and educating one another on this issue.

We must also educate the Christian community about the prevalence of child abuse and those who perpetrate such abuse. Christians must understand that abuse is not an issue that happens elsewhere, but is alive and well in every community. Every Christian should be well aware of the following statistics:

- Child sexual abuse is seventy-five times more common than pediatric cancer.[28]
- One out of five girls, and one out of seven boys, will be sexually abused by their eighteenth birthday.[29]
- According to the Department of Justice, there is one child molester per square mile in the United States.
- One in seven children between ages ten and seventeen have been sexually solicited online.[30]

We must also educate the Christian community about those who offend. In addition to the five exploitations described above, every Christian should have a basic understanding of the following common characteristics of many offenders:

1. Offenders can be the least suspected people. Unfortunately, many in our faith community still believe that they can spot a child molester simply by appearance. Parents are most often on the lookout for the creepy-looking guy who hangs out at the park or outside of the school. All adults *should* be concerned and take action to protect children when they see such a person. However, do not allow that limited stereotype to identify those in our community who may be a danger to

children. When selecting a jury, I often asked prospective jurors, "Can you tell me what a burglar looks like?" This question often helped jurors understand that child molesters cannot be identified by appearance or social status. In my years as a child sexual abuse prosecutor, I prosecuted physicians, computer programmers, financial advisors, teachers, and even a child sexual-abuse investigator! We must teach our faith community that our protective antennae should be focused on behavior, not looks or economic status.

2. Offenders often prey upon trusting and vulnerable young people. In order to sexually victimize a child, an offender must first gain access to the child. As a result, offenders spend much time planning and executing what is commonly known as the "grooming" process, in which the offender gains access to the child in order to develop a trusting and/or authoritative relationship. Once such a relationship has been created, the perpetrator is often free to abuse. Access to such children is obtained by the already existing position of the offender to the child or the child's family (family members, friends, coaches, youth pastors, etc.); or by the intentionally created position whereby an offender targets a child and begins to lavish that child with attention, gifts, and "love." This can include an adult who takes an interest in a troubled child, a child from a broken home, or a child he or she has similar interests with. Both categories of access assist offenders to target vulnerable children, who trust and obey them. Again, we must teach our faith community to keep its antennae up so that children who fall into either category are carefully watched and protected.

3. Offenders have many victims. One study indicates that child molesters who sexually victimize females outside of the home averaged approximately twenty different victims. The same study found that child molesters who sexually victimize males outside of the home averaged approximately one hundred fifty different victims![31] The reality is, those who sexually victimize children likely have victimized dozens of other children during their lifetime. Not only does this open our eyes to the prevalence of this tragic epidemic, but it should also prepare us to respond to individuals within our faith community who are caught engaging in criminal behavior against a child, demonstrate outward remorse, and beg for restoration, claiming that this was the only child they victimized. Based upon these statistics, the offender is most likely lying—which means they are continuing to deceive in order to reestablish trust and access to children.

The purpose of providing such startling information is not to frighten, but to awaken a generation that all too often fails to grasp the gravity and reality of child sexual abuse within our own faith community. The above is just a sample of the common types of behavioral characteristics found among those who sexually victimize children. Clinical psychologist Anna Salter's *Predators, Pedophiles, Rapists, and Other Sex Offenders: Who They Are, How They Operate, and How Can We Protect Ourselves and Our Children* (New York: Basic Books, 2003) is a great resource that identifies and explains how these offenders think and act. Every parent and pastor should read this book.

Preventing with Excellence

We must minimize the opportunities for abuse within our respective communities. One survey found that only 22 percent of respondents were required by their church to receive child-protection training.[32] If we truly view this as an issue of God's worship, then every church and Christian institution must adopt policies and procedures that will protect children, along with providing child-protection training to all its members. Generally, such policies and trainings should be developed by individuals with experience and expertise on the myriad of issues related to abuse. Organizations such as GRACE (www.net grace.org) and The National Child Protection Training Center (www .ncptc.org) provide assistance and consultation in developing effective child-protection policies. At a minimum, these policies should address such basic issues as the following:

- Background screenings for all church workers and volunteers; this must not be limited to simply criminal background check

- Parameters related to adult-child contact on and off church property, including physical contact, in-person interactions, electronic communications, and privacy issues
- Similar parameters related to child-child contact

In addition to child-protection policies, Christian institutions can foster an environment of safety by offering personal safety classes to children and youth. Such classes should

- Teach younger children that the parts of their body covered by a bathing suit are not to be touched by an adult.
- Teach older youth ways to guard against becoming too "attached" to a non-parental adult, including, but not limited to, being alone with adults.
- Educate older youth about how sexual offenders think and act.
- Instruct children of all ages what to do if they are inappropriately touched or simply uncomfortable around a certain adult or peer.
- Explain to all youth the difference between sinning and being the victim of a sin. A prosecutor friend once told me about a 13-year-old girl who had kept her abuse secret for eight years because the only thing she knew about sex outside of marriage was that it was "sinful." Perpetrators often point to biological reactions as evidence that the victim is equally "sinful," and the victim quickly accepts this falsehood. Consequently, many victims fear disclosing abuse, believing that they are responsible.
- Identify and make available qualified resources for youth who have been abused.

Once we take steps to educate and prevent with excellence, we must minimize opportunities for abuse by exhorting our members to keep their antennae up. This simply means to be constantly applying what has been learned, whether it relates to offender behavior or to church-adopted child-protection policies. To ensure that any concerns are properly expressed and addressed, institutions should develop a protocol for communicating such concerns.

Responding with Excellence

Our response to abuse should mirror the gospel in all aspects. The gospel tells us that our identity is in Christ alone, and that our reputation and all that we possess belongs to God. Another way of putting it is that apart from Christ's accomplishment, we have no reputation and we possess nothing. This gospel-centered perspective gives us great freedom to expend ourselves on behalf of abuse survivors, regardless of the earthly consequences. By doing so, we acknowledge God's holiness, his sovereignty, and our dependence upon the exclusive power of the gospel. Let's explore some practical ways to respond to child sexual abuse with gospel-centered excellence.

Rejecting the culture of rebuke and silence. As discussed earlier, a culture that promotes the rebuking or silencing of those who disclose abuse is one that is more concerned with self-preservation and reputation than the heart of the gospel. The gospel is all about a God who was not silent in the face of sin and who not only publicly embraced the sick and hurting, but ultimately gave his life for them. Responding to abuse with a gospel-centered perspective should propel us to embrace the hurting, encourage disclosures, and promote transparency, regardless of the earthly consequences. Any other response cannot be reconciled with the gospel.

Being prepared to respond. Develop a policy that provides a specific protocol for the way the institution will address abuse disclosures. The priority of any such protocol should be the protection and support of the alleged victim. A few key aspects of such a policy should include the following:

- Making sure allegations have been reported to law enforcement
- Ensuring that the child does not have contact with the alleged perpetrator while on church property or at church events
- Assigning a leader to maintain communication with the child's family, with the purpose of shepherding them with encouragement, assistance, and prayer

- Assisting the complainant's family in locating and paying for a qualified counselor. Such a counselor must be well-versed about child sexual abuse and the use of religion in the abuse of children, and experienced in helping children cope physically, emotionally, and spiritually
- Developing a support network within the church during the criminal prosecution process. Those within this network should be exhorted to refrain from "taking sides," but simply provide encouragement to the family during a difficult season
- Making sure measures have been taken to protect all the children, and communicating such measures to all of the members
- Being prepared to provide support and assistance to other abuse survivors within the community that suffer secondary effects after learning of an abuse allegation
- Shepherding the alleged perpetrator and the perpetrator's family if he or she is a member of the body (I highly recommend that churches only obtain such an understanding from a qualified and experienced professional or organization. Organizations such as GRACE can provide such assistance.)

A response protocol that is premised upon the protection and support of the alleged victim is a strong first step in welcoming these hurting souls into the arms of Jesus.

Obeying the law. In order to effectively carry out its responsibility of protecting children, most states have laws that mandate certain citizens to report suspected neglect or abuse. Christians are not exempt from obeying these laws, nor any other laws that are designed to protect children. Romans 13 clearly indicates that the civil government plays a role in God's design for society and his people. A primary purpose of criminal law is to punish those who intentionally commit inherently wrong actions that harm another. If that is the case, there can be no greater responsibility of the civil government than to punish citizens who violate laws designed to protect society's most vulnerable members—children. It is imperative that Christian institutions educate their members about these laws and give the spiritual directive to obey them. There can be little debate within the Christian community that the protection and survival of children is a God-ordained responsibility that we cannot neglect or excuse.

Being teachable. Sometimes the very words and/or actions that we think will bring much needed comfort and peace to abuse survivors actually produce more pain. Christians often have a misguided belief that being a Christian automatically makes one an expert at providing comfort to those experiencing life's deepest pains. Christa Brown best illustrates this by recounting an e-mail she received from a woman who was attempting to encourage her by talking about "God's love." Christa's response follows:

Dear [addressee]:

When I read your email, my hands shook so much that I spilled my coffee. My chest began to pound. I started being short of breath. I felt literally sick. I had to get up and take a walk with headphones to try and shift my brain into a different mode. That's what talk of God's love can do to me. It's a physiological response.

I do not believe you intended to inflict any hurt on me, and to the contrary, I expect that you intended to offer some comfort and hope. But, from my perspective, it is as though your email brandished in front of me the very weapon that was used against me. It is as though you're telling me that I should pick up that very same sword that was once used to eviscerate me and should fall on it all over again. I can't do that. My love of God, my faith, my own extraordinary desire to live the will of God… those are the very parts of me that were transformed into weapons that savaged and destroyed me. As a result, that part of my brain, that part of me that was once able to turn to God, to put things in God's hands, to believe that God would take care of me…all that part of my brain is inaccessible. It is electrically charged and it is the land of the predator… it is a ravaged land that is there within my own head.

I think it is somewhat analogous to a person who has a stroke. The person's brain tissue is damaged by the physical trauma of oxygen deprivation, and because of that trauma, a part of their brain doesn't get the connections right anymore. It is as though it is short-circuited out and (depending on what part of the brain is affected) the result may be that they can't form words anymore even though their thought-making process is still intact. My brain has also been damaged by trauma, although it was a severe psychological trauma rather than a physical brain injury.

Sometimes, with rehab work, people who have had strokes can learn to attach words to thoughts again, but they do so consciously and with great effort. In effect, they work at rewiring their brains around the place of trauma. In some ways, I think I am engaged in an analogous process...The extent to which I may or may not be able to do so remains to be seen....

Another possibly useful analogy is to think about a victim of torture whose torturer always played Beethoven while he beat and brutalized the victim. Years later that victim of torture is unlikely to much appreciate the music of Beethoven, and he may feel great anxiety when he hears the music, even if he is merely at a shopping mall. And perhaps he won't even realize why he is becoming so short of breath or why he is feeling the need to leave the mall immediately. The music is just background noise. But on some level his brain is still processing it as something that linked to degradation, pain and fear. The sort of talk of God's love that is in your email is the sort of talk that transports me to the torture chamber that is in my head.[33]

Ultimately, only our sovereign God can provide authentic comfort and peace to those suffering from the ravages of abuse. He is the One who can truly identify and empathize with the abused and is able to demonstrate authentic love and encouragement. Christians must understand and acknowledge that they are helpless to provide such comfort apart from the wisdom God graciously imparts to us. We must further acknowledge that he usually imparts such wisdom when we yearn to learn from those God places in our paths, those who have a greater understanding and experience with abuse issues. Resting in this reality will free us to learn how to truly love, comfort, and serve those who are hurting.

THE GOSPEL: THE INDISPENSABLE ELEMENT

Ultimately, an authentic missional response to child sexual abuse must be centered upon, and fueled by, the gospel. The gospel is about a God who didn't remain silent in the face of sin, but he took self-sacrificial action in order to openly confront sin and redeem those he loves, for his ultimate glory. A gospel-centered response to child sexual abuse begins with understanding that silence is not an option. We must be willing to openly confront abuse and give of ourselves so that those impacted can experience the healing and transformative power of Jesus. The church must willingly struggle alongside of survivors, even to the point of sacrifice. If we are unwilling to sacrifice our agendas, our finances, or even our reputation, on behalf of these precious souls, then we have failed to grasp the powerful countercultural reality of the gospel.

The gospel is also about the ultimate pursuit by God of a hurting and hopeless people. Such a glorious truth must empower and encourage each of us to pursue abuse survivors God has placed in our path.

Not only do we worship a pursing God, but the gospel is all about a God who is approachable to the hurting. He is approachable because he listens to the cries of hurting people and empathizes with their deepest pains. Judging, condemning, and blaming those who approach us will only result in further hurting those whom we have been called to love and serve. Only the power of the gospel enables an approachable spirit to be the common thread that makes up the fabric of the Christian community.

The gospel further reveals that God's relationship with us is eternal—he never lets us go. This beautiful truth must drive us to embrace the possibility that our relationship with abuse survivors is long-term and often will require a significant investment of time, energy, and resources. We must never let them go. Individuals and churches who initially reach out to provide assistance often find themselves growing frustrated and impatient with the myriad of issues associated with those who have survived childhood sexual abuse. We must take courage that the God who never lets us go will graciously provide us the ability and strength to love and serve for a lifetime.

CONCLUSION

What is the Christian response when we learn of the prevalence of child sexual abuse in our culture? Shall we respond as the priest or Levite, making up seemingly "godly" reasons why we must walk by (see Luke 10)? The gospel calls each of us to action towards the hurting, driven by our adoration and love for God. A missional response to child sexual abuse can only occur when all of us in the Christian community take concrete steps to restore worship by protecting our children and by responding to this deadly sin in a manner that draws survivors into the arms of Jesus.

9.

GOD SCATTERS TO GATHER THROUGH HIS PEOPLE:
A Missional Response to Migrant Churches

ELIAS MEDEIROS

Diaspora and the creation of "migrant churches" is a global phenomenon with significance for all Reformed churches around the world. It has been vitally important throughout the history of redemption and contemporary history, and it is especially crucial in Christian missions today. "Any evangelical congregation, denomination and institution that is indifferent to this historic moment in regards to 'Diaspora' missions will regret it later. The 'plane' of missions to, through and beyond the Diasporas is on the move.... There will definitely be turbulence (theological, strategic, and ethical [biblical, ecclesiastical]) but the plane will land safely for the Glory of God, the edification of His church, and the salvation of the unconverted."[1]

The missional relevance of this topic is clear, and there is substantial academic and practical material already. Therefore, we will limit our discussion to four main topics: the theological/biblical basis for such ministry, the growing trend of diasporas, the need to evangelize and minister to peoples in diasporas, and practical suggestions to mobilize churches in reaching out to peoples in diasporas.

THE THEOLOGICAL/BIBLICAL BASIS

The term "migrant church" can easily be misunderstood. However, we have examples of migrant churches throughout the history of the church—churches that migrated as a whole from their place of origin to a foreign ground. In this chapter I will discuss migrant churches as churches to be planted or organized among or by migrants, but not limited to that specific ethnic or migrant population. Therefore, the expressions "migrant churches," "churches in diasporas," and "diaspora churches" are used interchangeably in this discussion.

The motivation to become involved with and committed to evangelizing, discipling, and planting churches among diaspora peoples—as well as to work with them, through them, and beyond their immediate geographical location and ethnicity—must be grounded on theological/biblical convictions. Our theological considerations begin with the doctrine of the Trinity: God the Father, the Son, and the Holy Spirit.[2]

Nothing in history happens by chance. The will and the work of God the Father, the Son, and the Holy Spirit are clearly revealed in Scripture, from creation (Genesis 1–2) through consummation (Revelation 22). A historical overview of the Old and the New Testament attests that diaspora is intrinsically related to redemptive history and sovereignly planned, executed, and carried out by the Father, Son, and Holy Spirit.

Every geographical move of every human being who ever lived happens within the overall will and sovereignty of God. God creates nations (Genesis 25:23; Psalm 86:9–10); he creates languages and cultures (Genesis 11:1, 6–7, 9); and he determines the location, the moves, and the timing of our habitations. Acts 17:26–29 implies that he not only uses diaspora, but that he designs, conducts, and employs such diasporas for his own glory, the edification of his people, and the salvation of the lost everywhere. Every dispersed person and people group has a place and a role to play in God's redemptive history.

God sent his Son from his place of honor and glory (Philippians 2:4–12) to be the incarnate Word dwelling among man (John 1:1–14).

While still a baby, Jesus was taken by Joseph and Mary from Jerusalem to Egypt because of life-threatening circumstances—a case of diaspora. Christianity is the only religion in which God himself was a "migrant." This fact has missional implications for those whom the Son sends in the world (John 17:18). To be missional is to think, speak, act, and live as one sent by the migrant Son.

The diaspora work of the Spirit is emphasized throughout the book of Acts, immediately following the promise of the Spirit in Acts 1. Indeed, one might appropriately say that the spreading of the gospel to all the nations is empowered by the telling of the mighty works of God in all the various languages (Acts 2:9–11); Peter gives the official Old Testament interpretation of this remarkable event by his sermon in Acts 2:17–36, citing the book of Joel. The Holy Spirit, promised by the Father and the Son, was sent to empower each believer everywhere as a witness of the Lord Jesus Christ, and to endow every member of the body of Christ with gifts for service everywhere.

Most of the New Testament books were written from outside Jerusalem, by servants of the Lord living and ministering in a diaspora context. Two books in the New Testament were written specifically to believers in diaspora, James and 1 Peter. James, the brother of Jesus, wrote to Jewish believers living among the nations: "James, a servant of God and of the Lord Jesus Christ, [t]o the twelve tribes in the Dispersion: Greetings" (James 1:1). Peter also wrote to both Gentile and Jewish believers living among the nations—"Peter, an apostle of Jesus Christ, to the pilgrims of the Dispersion in Pontus, Galatia, Cappadocia, Asia, and Bithynia" (1 Peter 1:1, NKJV). Peter actually uses two different words in his letter to emphasize that those to whom he is writing are in diaspora: 1) pilgrims—"one who comes from a foreign country into a city or land to reside there by the side of the natives"; and 2) strangers—"a foreigner, one who lives in a place without the right of citizenship." The same word is used in Luke 24:18 (NKJV): "Then the one whose name was Cleopas answered and said to Him, "Are You the only stranger in Jerusalem, and have You not known the things which happened there in these days?"

The biblical texts assume missional participation, both of those who are purposely sent out to the nations (Matthew 24:14; 28:19–20; Mark 16:15, 19–20; Luke 24:45–47; Acts 1:8) and of those who have been dispersed for other immediate reasons (political, economic, educational, ethnic—see Isaiah 49:6 and Daniel 12:2). The expansion of the early church in the book of Acts, the final gathering of God's people spread throughout the world and from among all the nations at the second coming of Christ, and the grandiose worshipful celebration in heaven (Revelation 5:8–10) all presuppose the significant role and ministry of the priesthood of believers (1 Peter 2:9–10).

Diaspora, therefore, is a missional activity decreed and blessed by God under his sovereign rule, to promote the expansion of his kingdom and the fulfillment of the Great Commission (Matthew 24:14; 28:17–20). God's sovereign ruling over human history and dispersion is explicitly stated by Paul in his speech to the Athenians: "And he made from one man every nation of mankind to live on all the face of the earth, having determined allotted periods and the boundaries of their dwelling place, that they should seek God, in the hope that they might feel their way toward him and find him. Yet he is actually not far from each one of us, for "'In him we live and move and have our being'; as even some of your own poets have said, 'For we are indeed his offspring'"" (Acts 17:26–28).

From the fall of man to the present day, diasporas have been an indispensable means by which God has accomplished his redemptive purposes. The history of the expansion of the Christian church—past, present, and future—cannot be explained apart from the historical reality of God's sovereignty, his ruling over the nations, and the moving of his people everywhere.

THE GROWING TREND OF DIASPORAS

Scripture as well as secular history make it clear that the history of mankind is a record of peoples on the move—peoples in diaspora. Recent studies indicate that this process is accelerating. The total number of international migrants has increased over the last ten years from an estimated 150 million in 2000 to 214 million persons in 2010.[3] The full reality is even more striking when "hidden" migrants, related family members, and extended families are taken into consideration.

People already in diaspora today would constitute the fifth-largest country in the world. And, even more significantly, according to a Gallup Poll published on April 12, 2012, "About 13% of the world's adults— or more than 640 million people—say they would like to leave their country permanently. Roughly 150 million of them say they would like to move to the U.S.—giving it the undisputed title as the world's most desired destination for potential migrants since Gallup started tracking these patterns in 2007."[4] And according to another Gallup survey conducted in 119 countries during 2009 and 2010, "More than one in four adults worldwide (26%) say they would like to go to another country for temporary work….This figure is nearly twice the 14% worldwide who say they would like to migrate permanently to another country if they could and translates into roughly 1.1 billion adults."[5]

The desire to leave one's place of origin for temporary work elsewhere characterizes many Christians as well. "Christians living in the Diaspora context represent the largest self-supporting contingency of missionary force which has been located within many of the so-called 'unreached peoples' and accessible to practically all people-groups of the world today."[6]

Over the past 30 years, there has been an escalation in the number, scope, and impact of migrant populations. For example, 1.1 million Arabic-speaking Muslims live in Argentina; 110,000 Han Chinese live in Cuba and 312,000 in the United Kingdom; 143,000 Spanish Jews are in Israel; 104,000 Punjabi-speaking Sikhs reside in Sri Lanka; and 117,000 Bengali Muslims reside in the UAE (United Arab Emirates).[7] Consider, as further evidence, the situation in Europe: "Africans alone make up 31% of the population of Marseilles, France, for example, and 15% of Parisians…. In London, 40% of the city is made up of ethnic minorities, many from the Commonwealth who, by legal or illegal means, have taken up residence there."[8]

These are just few examples of global diasporas today. The fact is: Every reader of this chapter lives near individuals and families who are living outside their place of origin.

The implications of these statistics are extraordinary. Christians in Argentina can reach out to more than a million Arabic-speaking Muslims; Cuban Christians may be able to minister to more than 100 thousand Han Chinese without leaving home; Christians in Sri Lanka have the opportunity to evangelize and to plant churches among more than 100 thousand Punjab-speaking Sikhs without the need for a passport; and so forth. Unfortunately, most Christians have not been actively, intentionally, and intensively engaged even with migrants who live just across the street. Using a new term gaining wide acceptance in missional circles, such people groups who live in our neighborhoods are "*unengaged*, which means that no one church, no one mission agency... has yet taken responsibility to tell them of our great God and Saviour, Jesus Christ."[9]

There is no question that diasporas are global, intensifying, and escalating on a large scale. It is also clear that our world is a world of diasporas—in effect, a borderless world. But the most important question is, How will we, as the church of the Lord Jesus Christ in the world, moving among the peoples, react to all of these people on the move? Some churches invest resources and personnel to send missionaries to China, while seeming to forget the Chinese around them. Will we simply use these migrants as maids, employees, and so forth? Will we patronize them? Or will we genuinely welcome them in the name of Jesus?

The Illegal Immigrant Issue, the Diasporas, and the Migrant Churches

Those ministering in the context of the diasporas, and who are involved with the leadership of migrant churches, take the topic of illegal immigration seriously. I have personally participated in such discussions in Germany, France, Portugal, Brazil, Philippines, the United States, and other countries. We recognize that how we treat immigrants is not just a political and moral matter; it is a serious theological and ecclesiological concern. In other words, we should never take this topic lightly, nor approach it unbiblically. How then should we deal with this subject?

The answer to this question is not simple. Those of us who are directly involved with such discussions understand its complexity, as well as the naiveté of single-handed answers. What follows are personal recommendations and perspectives I support, as the authors being cited express a biblical/theological Reformed evangelical view on this sensitive question.

I would recommend the guidelines contained in the "Evangelical Statement of Principles for Immigration Reform"—endorsed by more than 150 influential North American leaders representing reputable evangelical denominations, institutions, and organizations—which urged "[American] leaders to work together with the American people to pass immigration reform that embodies... key principles." They called for a solution that: 1) "respects the God-given dignity of every person"; 2) "protects the unity of the immediate family"; 3) "respects the rule of law"; 4) "guarantees secure national borders"; 5) "ensures fairness to taxpayers"; and 6) "establishes a path toward legal status and /or citizenship for those who qualify and who wish to become permanent residents."[10]

Focus on the Family president Jim Daly, one of the signers, states elsewhere, "The question is, what can the Christian community do to engage this community of workers coming from other countries without proper documentation and what can we do to encourage them to do the right thing?"[11] It sounds pragmatic, but this question leads us to consider the biblical teaching on dealing with the aliens, sojourners, and foreigners in our midst. From our theological and biblical perspectives, we must view them as people created in God's image—as people God cares for; and as people whom God commands *us* to love and to care for.

From an ecclesiological standpoint, we ought to remind ourselves that the church of Jesus Christ welcomes all sinners. Second, everyone who comes to the saving knowledge of the Lord Jesus Christ, believes in him alone, and is baptized becomes a visible member of the church. Third, all believers are expected to grow in the grace and the knowledge of the Lord Jesus Christ, which implies dealing with all areas of their lives—including law-abiding citizenship for the glory of God, the edification of his people, and the salvation of the lost across the street and around the world. No group of people or individuals should ever be demonized or targeted as our enemies.

Such biblical principles lead us to go beyond fairness. "A concern for fairness," wrote Chuck Colson in 2006, "isn't the most important reason that Christians ought to oppose this demonization of 'the strangers in our midst.' As theologian T. M. Moore recently wrote… 'God defends strangers.'" Besides that, "God expects His people's 'attitude toward the strangers and sojourners in their midst' to reflect His own concern."[12]

Does it mean, then, that we "ought not be concerned about the massive lawbreaking?" Of course not. Colson is right when he affirms that "the rule of law is a Christian contribution, coming out of the Reformation, and it requires respect for law, just as the Bible does." It means "that Christians must work to see that the immigration debate generates light instead of heat. We must insist that the illegal-immigration issue be addressed without treating millions… as a kind of fifth column. That is the very least we can do if we are obedient to God's command to welcome strangers. And that's a fact I got from the highest possible Source."[13]

We, as children of God and members of his body, "are explicitly called to love even our enemies (Luke 6:35), but I think we err, especially in contemporary political discourse… in turning people so quickly into enemies in the first place," states Matthew Soerens. Further, Soerens clarifies, "That's not to say that we should water down our convictions—if they are firmly grounded in Scripture and rooted in the truth, we should be passionate and tireless advocates. But even if we are firmly convinced of the justice of our cause, we must renounce uncharitable and unloving toward that end."[14] In other words, the question is not "what would Jesus do," but what did Jesus teach and do as revealed in the Scriptures?

THE NEED TO EVANGELIZE AND MINISTER TO PEOPLES IN DIASPORAS[15]

As argued above, Christians in diaspora—as well as Christians interacting with those in Diaspora—must constantly seek to ground all of their discussions (expositional, historical, strategic, and experiential) in careful scrutiny of the Word of God. This will surely involve consideration of at least one very specific biblical teaching—the Great Commission.

We must never make the mistaken assumption that everyone in all of our churches fully understands and lives out Christ's command to make disciples of all the nations. This biblical command should regularly and forcefully be brought before all of God's people. The question must constantly be asked if we really *are* making disciples of all the nations. As Donald McGavran has argued, "The purpose of missiology [and I would add 'Diaspora' missiology] is to carry out the Great Commission. Anything other than that may be a good thing to do, but it is not Missiology."[16]

The migration trends described above mean that the missiological opportunities before us are greater than ever before in the history of mankind.[17] Diaspora missions may be understood simply as applying the Great Commission—making disciples of *all* nations—to the remarkable demographic realities of our twenty-first-century world. This is missions *to* the diasporas, *through* the diasporas, and even *beyond* the diasporas, in obedience to Jesus's command in Matthew 28.

Missions to the diasporas. Many people groups previously presumed to be "unreached" from the 10/40 window are now accessible because of the global trend of migrant populations moving from south to north, and from east to west. Congregations in receiving countries—often industrial nations in the West—can practice "missions at their doorstep" by reaching newcomers in their neighborhoods without crossing borders geographically, linguistically, or culturally. God is moving the diasporas geographically, and the church must not miss any opportunity to fulfill the Great Commission by speaking and living the gospel in the midst of those who are now newly accessible.

Missions through the diasporas. Christians who are themselves migrants, and thus part of the diasporas, must seize their new opportunity to fulfill the Great Commission. Christian believers in diaspora are one of the most strategic "missionary" forces in the history of missions, and yet few churches or missions agencies seem to be taking adequate account of this fact. After all, Paul always started preaching in the synagogues where he could find his fellow Jews in the Diaspora. As already stated, Peter and James wrote specifically to the church living in the context of diaspora. The history of the church throughout the centuries further supports this methodology. Reformers such as John Calvin, the Puritans, and other evangelical groups had tremendous kingdom impact while living in diaspora. Missions *through* the diasporas is an essential part of fulfilling the Great Commission.

Missions beyond the diasporas. Equally important among strategic concerns of missions in the context of diaspora is the need to mobilize self-supporting Christians living in diaspora to evangelize other people groups in their immediate context and among other members of the host society. This is what we would call "missions beyond the diasporas." After acquiring the language and making cultural adjustments, diaspora Christians are able to contribute positively to existing local congregations and in the planting of new ones. Immediate and adequate biblical and cross-cultural continuing education must be made available to all members of the body, so that all are equipped for ministry (Ephesians 4:11–14). Thus, discipleship and education are imperative to enable Christians in diasporas to impact other ethnic groups within their reach and to foster their theological thinking in dialogue with other Christian thinkers in diaspora. Theologizing in the context of diaspora will hugely enrich our Christian tradition and our entire missional pilgrimage.

Yes, this approach to missions is different from some of the traditional paradigms, but Christian denominations and organizations failing to seize this *kairos* missions moment in the history of the church will miss an incredible opportunity. Instead of concentrating solely on sending Western missionaries to other parts of the world, we may now, for example, maximize the potential of expatriates from their homeland to return as "missionaries." We may creatively employ many of these "self-supporting diaspora missionaries"; perhaps this could be called "reverse missions."

The reality is that Christians living in diaspora context potentially represent the largest self-supporting missionary force in the history of the world. They include members of the so-called "unreached peoples," and collectively they have access to practically all people groups of the world today. There is such amazing potential here! So how do we begin to realize that potential?

PRACTICAL AND EFFECTIVE WAYS TO MINISTER TO PEOPLES IN DIASPORAS

We start by recognizing and openly affirming the need to broaden our traditional missions paradigms so that those paradigms include vigorous strategies that help us become "bridges of God."[18] What follows are some tentative initial suggestions about practical and effective ways that we can minister to, through, and beyond the diasporas.

The following seven steps were recommended in 2009 by T. V. Thomas, during the Lausanne Diasporas Strategy Consultation in Manila.[19] Thomas has been ministering among peoples in diaspora—also referred to here as People on the Move—and lecturing on this subject for many years. Under each of his seven steps, Dr. Thomas provides additional, specific suggestions. He rightly introduces his practical guidelines with this comment: "With so many people from so many origins moving in so many directions and landing in so many destinations, planned or unplanned, it could be concluded that we are fast becoming a 'borderless world.' The Triune God in His sovereignty is moving people so that they may seek Him and know Him. Reaching the *People on the Move* is both an urgent necessity and an amazing opportunity for Christians and Churches. This certainly is a new paradigm in the mission of the contemporary Church."[20]

Step #1—Help the Church Embrace the Vision for the Diaspora Peoples

1. Each diaspora group provides both an accessible mission field and a potential mission force.

2. People on the move are more open to listen and are often receptive to the gospel.

3. The primary agency for the evangelization of the people on the move is the church of Jesus Christ in its local and global presence.

4. The gospel fits into any culture and background, but the church has to use the necessary means in order to reach out to the respective diaspora group.

5. Evangelization of the *People on the Move* calls for focused intentionality, urgent passion, and strategic practical action.

6. Reaching an individual or a group with the gospel can have far-reaching consequences for kingdom advancement.

Step #2—Ensure the Right Attitudes

Attitudes are important and powerful in life, relationships, and ministry. The following are seven questions that will help you and your congregation to assess your readiness to reach out to diaspora people:

1. Do you have a patronizing attitude toward other cultures, races, and ethnic groups?

2. Are you racially prejudiced or ethnocentric?

3. Has the influx of people from other cultures, races, and ethnic groups paralyzed you, or excited you to evangelize them?

4. Do you have a loving burden for the "strangers" in your midst (Leviticus 19:33–34; Deuteronomy 10:19)?

5. Are you ready to embrace diversity of culture and ministry to all cultural, racial, or ethnic groups?

6. Have you embraced loving hospitality as a vital spiritual principle of Christian life and ministry (Matthew 25:35; Romans 12:13; Hebrews 13:2; 1 Peter 4:9)?

7. Are you an active part of a nurturing community who worship and learn together, love and serve each other (Acts 2:42–47; 1 Peter 1:22; 3:8; 4:8–11)?

Step #3—Explore Your Neighborhood

Increasingly, diaspora people are moving into all kinds of environments. Often, people are unaware of the changes taking place in their everyday world. Here are some questions to help diagnose who really is your neighbor, in your work, residential or leisure world:

1. Who are the diaspora people in your neighborhood?
2. What are the lands of their origin?
3. What is the size of each diaspora group?
4. Why did they come? Or, what factors brought them here?
5. What is the heart language or mother tongue of the diaspora people(s)?
6. What generations are represented among them?
7. What are their religious affiliations?
8. Have they established worship places?
9. Are there some Christian believers among them?
10. What are their educational levels?
11. Where are they vocationally/professionally?
12. What is their receptivity level to the gospel?
13. What are their felt/immediate needs?
14. How can you meet these felt/immediate needs and begin to build meaningful relationships with them?
15. Who else can you partner with to reach them?

Step #4—Engage in Holistic Ministry

1. Treat all people with mutual respect, dignity, and generosity.
2. Work collaboratively with people of all backgrounds, [when Bible truth will not be compromised, on issues of common concern], e.g., youth issues, drug abuse, housing, unemployment, racism, etc.

3. Encourage various diaspora groups to work together to face common challenges and serve their communities.
4. Pursue partnerships with other churches and Christian agencies which share expertise, materials, personnel, prayer, and resources for training.
5. Work intentionally in partnership with governments and non-governmental agencies (NGOs) whenever possible, where Bible truth and practice are not compromised.
6. Approach ministry with extreme creativity and flexibility.
7. Extend ministry to diaspora people on existing ministry initiatives.
8. Seek to provide advocacy services and legal expertise for those who are victims of injustice—the refugees, the sinned against, the trafficked people, the powerless, etc.
9. Provide material, emotional, and psychological support, and trauma counseling for the vulnerable.

Step #5—Equip for Effective Ministry

1. Help the local church realize that it is a landing place for diaspora people and a launching pad for diaspora ministries.
2. Make believers aware of the scope and the available avenues of ministries to diaspora people.
3. Keep believers informed of timely and true information about challenges and progress of ministry.
4. Ensure spiritual growth and vitality are regularly experienced by believers
5. Mobilize intercession.
6. Provide training to increase cross-cultural competence of believers.
7. Equip believers to share their personal testimony succinctly.
8. Enhance believers' skills in cross-cultural hospitality.
9. Train Christians to engage in culturally sensitive evangelism and discipleship.

10. Provide appropriate culture-sensitive and language-specific resources for effective outreach and discipleship.
11. Expose key language-specific resources available on the Internet for evangelism and discipleship
12. Explore ways to open doors and use contact points for the gospel to them.

Step #6—Encourage Building Genuine Relationships

1. Identify with the people of the diasporas and get involved with them on a personal level.
2. Take risks and build genuine cross-cultural relationships.
3. Provide loving hospitality to care for their felt and immediate needs.
4. Get to know the diaspora peoples and their original cultural contexts.
5. Find believers who can communicate with them in their mother tongue or heart language.
6. Seek to expose your faith, but not to impose your faith on them.
7. Pray for guidance of the Holy Spirit to share the good news of Jesus with them.
8. Ensure Christianity that is shared is Bible-based, but also culture-based.

Step #7—Empower the Diaspora Christians of Churches for Mission

1. Present to diaspora Christians or churches the vision, advantages, and opportunities for mission.
2. Instill a missionary vision, and foster an environment of mission.
3. Plan relationship-building opportunities with the diaspora to implement the Great Commission locally.
4. Identify and train diaspora leaders.

5. Cooperate with mission agencies to provide theological training in the respective mother tongue.
6. Employ distance learning and electronic means to train potential Christian workers.
7. Network partnerships with Christians and churches in countries of origin.
8. Cultivate partnerships with host country churches to engage in mission.
9. Create focused prayer networks for ministry effectiveness.
10. Link with national, regional, or global Christian diaspora networks when possible.

I pray that this brief discussion of God's "scattering to gather" will motivate every reader to begin reaching diaspora people with God's good news. Those who try it will experience a thrilling kingdom adventure! Diaspora people are winnable for our Lord Jesus Christ—and are already winning others to Jesus!

10.

DOGMA MEETS DIVERSITY IN EUROPE:
A Missional Response to Secularity

ROBERT CALVERT

According to Greek mythology Zeus, the chief of the gods, kidnapped the daughter of the king of Phoenicia, Europa, by approaching her in the shape of a bull. When Europa sat upon the bull, it took her to the island of Crete, where Zeus revealed his true identity. One French translation interprets this abduction story as the stealing of the European soul to God.

Is there now any sense of interaction between the soul of Europe and the presence of the living God? If there is such a thing as a European soul, it surely today has been shaped by pagan, Celtic, Jewish, and Muslim spirituality. However, the true "god" of the soul of Europe in the twenty-first century is one of secularity.

If secularism is the philosophy of "the death of God," and secularization the process by which people lose faith, then secularity is the paradigm which undergirds and creates the framework for such an age. Glenn Smith defines this for us, "Secularity in counter distinction to secularism or secularization refers to the conditions of beliefs or the shift in our understanding on which our society is grounded."[1]

We are now a bit more than one hundred years removed from the ground-breaking World Mission Conference in Edinburgh in 1910, and in the context of that historical perspective, I will seek to describe the secularity that now defines Western Europe.

The era of labor-intensive industrialization (urbanization) developed in Europe at the end of the nineteenth century; this is often known as the "muscle" period. The middle of the twentieth century could be described as the era of capital-intensive industrialization (metropolitanization), otherwise known as the "machine" period. Toward the end of the twentieth century, the whole world, led by Western technological revolutions, entered the era of information-intensive industrialization (globalization) otherwise known as the "mind" period.[2] Through all of these changes, "religious" or "spiritual" perspectives continued to be present, but the nature of those perspectives changed radically.

Charles Taylor, author of a mammoth text on the subject, traces the spiritual values of secularity back to the deism which was so influential in seventeenth and eighteenth centuries in Great Britain and France (as well as America). Taylor argues that deism rejected the theistic commitments common to Judaism, Islam, and much of Christianity, and instead drew its concepts of God's nature and existence from reason and personal experience rather than from biblical revelation. With this deistic epistemology, the spirituality that developed was what Taylor calls the current "age of authenticity"—an individualistic era in which people find their own way or do their own thing. Use of one's own reason and experience to find whatever god there might be ultimately meant that intellectual autonomy became, in effect, a kind of god, and the ultimate arbiter in all matters of concern. Thus, deism led to atheism and many abandoned faith in God, at least as he is traditionally understood.[3]

But interestingly, this "galloping pluralism on the spiritual plane" (Taylor's phrase) seems to have produced a thirst for something more than self-sufficiency and reason—something that looks and sounds like a kind of "communal worship." The context for understanding secularity, therefore, is actually the extraordinary cultural, ethnic, and religious pluralism that dominates most Western European and North American environments—pluralism which has already been described from the perspective of "migrant churches" by Elias Medeiros in our previous chapter.

To build on Dr. Medeiros's analysis, more than a third of the population of Leicester, England is non-white. Leicester also has the highest percentage of residents of Indian origin of any city in Britain (23.5 percent), and more than 50 percent of schoolchildren of five years of age are non-white. Leicester elected its first Muslim mayor in May of 2012, and soon it will be the first non-white-majority city in the United Kingdom.[4]

Many of these immigrants to Leicester arrived in the 1970s; among them were Gujarati Hindus fleeing Idi Amin's regime in Uganda, others of African origin, and large groups of Caribbean and Chinese immigrants. Leicester boasts of its diverse character and has become a model for multiracial, multicultural, and multireligious existence. There are at least twenty-one mosques, at least eighteen Hindu temples, six Sikh Gurdwaras, two Buddhist temples, two synagogues, one Jain temple, and a large number of Christian churches of all denominations in Leicester today.

The Leicester experience symbolizes the shift in religious identity being seen throughout Western Europe. Grace Davie, a sociologist of religion, describes it as "believing without belonging"—a kind of religious nominalism that is quite different from our typical understanding of secularism, in which large percentages of populations are not less religious but differently so.[5] Raymond Bakke adds, "Mission is no longer about crossing the oceans, jungles and deserts, but about crossing the streets of the world's cities"[6]—a point made quite powerfully by Dr. Medeiros in our last chapter.

In this religiously pluralistic context, being "missional" requires a global perspective among globally minded congregations that work in partnership with multiple agencies, social services, churches, and other religious groups. Modern cities such as Leicester are culturally, ethnically, and religiously cosmopolitan. Its citizens adhere to different beliefs and convictions that are drawn from different traditions. The claims of the Bible have to compete with the Qu'ran, the Hindu Vedas, the writings of Buddha, the Jehovah Witnesses' New World Translation, and *The Book of Mormon*—often all at once.

Claims for the Bible's authenticity must therefore be presented in an intellectual marketplace where there are many competing religious truth claims. In this environment, Andrew Kirk argues, "Although it is imperative that Christians argue for the probity and reliability of the Bible against unreasonable skepticism and misrepresentation, in the last analysis, living with consistency the good news of Jesus and the Kingdom of God, in the power of God's Spirit, is the most cogent demonstration of the reality of what we declare to be true."[7]

But, in addition to the number of different faith groups, the church in Western Europe and Great Britain must come to grips with the fact that there may soon be, at least in a few cities and regions, a non-Christian majority religious presence—most likely Islam.[8] Philip Jenkins reminds us how close we already are to that situation, "If Western Europe's 15 million Muslims represented a single nation, they would be the sixth largest country of the European Union, more populous than Belgium."[9]

Davie suggests that religious pluralism offers two scenarios for the Christian church. Followers of secularization suggest that "growing religious pluralism necessarily undermines the plausibility of all forms of religious belief," whereas rational choice theorists (mostly in North America) "argue precisely the reverse: religious pluralism enables the religious needs of increasingly diverse populations to be more adequately met."[10] Those Christians and churches that would be "missional" in such a context must think carefully about both of these possibilities, and be ready and able to craft strategies that take both into account.

I will describe two strategic missional initiatives now underway in the world port of Rotterdam, where I minister. Our city's population is largely non-Dutch; it is said that half of all babies born in the city have at least one parent who was not born in the Netherlands. Rotterdam's ethnic and religious pluralism is illustrated in a guide to non-Dutch churches, which details the stories of 113 churches that intentionally seek to serve primarily immigrants.[11] Such service is massive. In order

to create a means of dialogue and distribution of services, the municipality of Rotterdam instituted a new platform for ideological and religious
organizations in April of 2008. Its objectives include the "stimulation of
mutual dialogue on the need to participate in society."[12] The impetus
for this platform came from evangelical Christians networking in city
hall; the council now includes representatives of Christian denominations, various non-Christian religions, and secular humanists.

If we are going to be missional in the kinds of pluralistic cultures
that now dominate Western Europe and North America, we can no
longer afford the luxury of working in isolation. The sheer complexities of the task, realities of globalization, and limitations of resources
all call for a renewed commitment to multilevel partnerships—even
partnerships that include members of other religious communities or
those who do not identify with any faith community.

In addition to seeking the welfare of the community God has placed
us in, by forming such partnerships, we must realize and act upon the
insight of Roland Robertson, a sociologist of globalization: "Religious
factors will almost certainly be intimately involved in those variegated
strategies for relating individuals and national societies to the emerging
global order."[13]

Religion appears to have a special role in reinforcing individual
and community identity within pluralistic cultures. Gerrie ter Haar
has concluded that, for African Christians in the Netherlands, "Their
adherence to Christianity constitutes the most important element of
their social identity."[14] In this age of migration, religion has become a
key factor in global change and the creation of transnational societies.
Religious identity helps to deal with the pain of being uprooted and
alienated—and in this way, religion has a key role in providing meaning and purpose. Faith can offer a basis for forming personal values
and identity in an era when social-economic forces give rise to loss of
roots, indifference to local space, and lack of community. In the clash
between religious forms of the West and the rest of the world, there is
potential for new kinds of religious community. Indigenous Christian
churches must do all they can to support the development of such communities of migrant Christians.

It has been often stated that Christianity in Europe is in decline. In 1900, 71 percent of the world's Christians lived in Europe; by 1960 this figure had dropped to 46 percent, and by 1990 to 30 percent. Declining institutional churches are characterized as having large numbers of nominal Christians, false security in apparent large numbers, the inability to change quickly, inflexible structures, and inhibitions against experimentation.[15] These are challenges of which any European or North American church must be aware. The two strategies mentioned above—broad participation by Christians in projects that benefit everyone in an area, and intentional nurturing of migrant Christian communities—may not eliminate those challenges, but they dramatically improve the likelihood that the challenges will be met and overcome.

Further, even in the context of such challenges, there can be *and there have been* numerous examples of what one must call at least a revitalization (and possibly even a revival) of Christian worship and witness in Evangelical and Renewalist churches in Europe; the publication of Mission Praise (http://www.missionpraise.com) is one of many signs of a new thirst to express spiritual desire and experience. Over the last fifty years, some historic institutional churches in Europe have developed new and sometimes radical approaches to worship. Taize (France), Wild Goose (Scotland), and the Thomas Mass (Finland) are just three examples. We must all be aware of such approaches, and be willing to learn from those utilizing these approaches.

The contours of the religious map of Western Europe are not so much being *with*drawn as being *re*drawn. Christian and evangelical identity is being shaped by the missional opportunities which the dogma/diversity context presents to us. Some more specific examples of missional ways to respond to the dogma/diversity context include the following:

- In eastern Europe, the Orthodox Church is facing the same kind of religious pluralism and secularization, and has adopted some remarkable new strategies of living missionally before the watching world. In the Greek port of Piraeus (near Athens) and in the city of Vollos to the north, Christian students have been involved in cleaning up the beaches with black bin-liners; and evangelical and Orthodox leaders have worked together to distribute materials which include both environmental messages and portions of the New Testament in modern Greek.

- In southern Europe, governments of nations previously considered Roman Catholic are intentionally broadening their religious alliances. In a city on the north side of Lisbon, the newly elected mayor bypassed the traditional Roman Catholic church in order to visit an Assemblies of God congregation composed primarily by members of the migrant church. That particular congregation had, in the space of just a few years, grown from thirty to three hundred members, and it is likely that the fundamental reason for both the growth and the visit was that everyone in the municipality knew this new church for its holistic care to drug addicts and the elderly.

- Back in Western Europe, in the center of Antwerp, a Dutch couple, Jaap and Ina Hansum, has formed an informal partnership with a group of Turkish young people. The resulting "Bible-house" has become a kind of spiritual home for a number of Muslim families who immigrated to Belgium from southern Turkey. On the basis of this kind of "deed witness," one of the young Turkish men who had gotten into difficulty with the police asked the Dutch evangelist, rather than the imam, to visit him in prison. The Hansums clearly recognize that demonstrating care for those to whom they desire to witness is the essential foundation of such witness.

- In central Europe, churches in atheistic societies are bearing witness to the gospel through community-building. The soulless housing blocks in eastern Europe pose an enormous missionary challenge. What may be the largest housing estate in Europe is four metro-stops long in the south of Prague. One pastor there has had the joy of building a new church in the grounds of an asylum-seekers' center. The invitation to do so came from its atheist director, who was moved by how much better her children performed after regular visits from church members.

- In northern Europe, when the Iron Curtain came down in 1990, a new synergy developed in Berlin when Christian ministries from both sides of the wall—one that provided care for elderly in the east, and an addiction ministry in the West—came together. As a result of this partnership, the five hundred employees of the two ministries now make up the largest single city mission in all of Europe. Across a metropolis of four million people (many of whom are from eastern Europe, Turkey, and Asia), sixteen churches now serve as mission or preaching stations. In addition, the city mission owns three hotels in the city; it is seeking to reach German professionals who are not already confessing Christians and has also developed programs with Turkish and Arabic peoples. In doing so, they are bearing witness to the love of Christ with people of other faiths.

These are just a handful of examples of how the evangelical church in Western Europe is thinking and acting missionally in the context of dogma and diversity.

The Lausanne Committee for World Evangelization set forth a remarkably accurate road map for the church of the twenty-first century at its urban ministry consultation in Pattaya, Thailand. It states, for everyone in European cities to hear, we as European Christians must

(a) Recover prayer in personal and corporate life.

(b) Clarify the goal and message of large-city evangelism.

(c) Promote biblical and practical inter-church cooperation, and cooperation between church and parachurch groups.

(d) Reverse Christian defeatism by the renewal of stagnant churches and by calling Christians back to the cities.

(e) Restore a family *koinonia* atmosphere in the urban church.

(f) Regain credibility for the message through identification with, and response to, people's social and intellectual needs.

(g) Research the city: hidden peoples, existing ministries, and the forces that shape it—historical and current, especially the place and role of mass media.

(h) Plan for awakening by training city workers, both for their own city and other regions, and by anticipating new church and service group forms, planting them where needed.

(i) Permeate all city structures, for the transformation of people and structures of society.[16]

Thirty years after the Pattaya Consultation, we may want to reaffirm some of these calls, but also highlight other approaches such as those mentioned above. The participation of the European church in such violence as the Crusades should also not be forgotten, as evangelical Christians seek today to call the church back to humility, integrity, and simplicity. The challenge of secularity is to make the case for (the truth of) Christ in societies that are pluralistic and globalized, and to make the peace of Christ in societies that are broken and divided. Evangelical Christians, who need to engage rather than escape the challenge of this secular age, are to be empowered to this by the astonishing announcement that "in Christ God was reconciling the world to himself" (2 Corinthians 5:19).

11.

THE MISSIONAL CHALLENGES OF ISLAM:

A Very Diverse People, Religion, and Culture

JOHN LEONARD

If we read today the section about Islam in the report of Commission #4 of the 1910 Edinburgh Missions Conference ("The Missionary Message in Relation to the Non-Christian World"),[1] two things are clear. First, some things have changed very little since that commission reported. The report could be read today with only a few alterations, and would still accurately describe large parts of the Islamic world. What has not changed is how diverse Islam, its peoples, religion, and cultures are. It is because of this diversity that I have subtitled my contribution to this volume "A Very Diverse People, Religion, and Culture."

Second, *Everything* has changed with regard to the relationship between Islam and the rest of the world. At the turn of the twentieth century, there were 200 million Muslims. At the turn of the twenty-first century, there are 1.57 billion Muslims, making up 22 percent of the world population. Muslims can be found on every inhabited continent and every country on earth. There are 973 million in the Asia-Pacific region; 315 million in the Middle East and North Africa; 241 million in Sub-Saharan Africa; 38 million in Europe; and 4.6 million in the Americas.[2]

The largest concentration of Muslims is found in a belt that runs along North Africa through the Middle East, north into the Stans (Afghanistan, Kyrgyzstan, Kazakhstan, Turkmenistan, Tajikistan, Uzbekistan), across India and China, then south through the Malay Archipelago. This area of the world is sometimes referred to as the 10/40 window. Most Muslims are not Arab and do not speak Arabic, but come from many cultures, peoples, and languages. The most populous Muslim country, Indonesia, with a population of just over 200 million, is in Asia. Even among Arabic-speaking Muslims (estimated at about 225 million) there are different dialects that make it impossible for many Arabs to understand one another. For example, Middle-Easterners have a difficult time understanding the colloquial Moroccan dialect.

Muslims take great pride in the Umma (the community of believers). They share a core set of beliefs based upon the Quran and the Hadith, that "Faith is to affirm your faith in Allah, His angels, His Books, His Messengers and the Last Day, and to believe in the Divine Destiny whether it be good or bad" (Sahih al-Bukhari, 1:2:48). Along with these six beliefs there are five practices, or pillars, that all Muslims are required to practice. In the Hadith, Mohammad said, "Islam is based on five principles: The confession, prayer, giving to the poor, the pilgrimage, and the fast" (Sahih al-Bukhari, 1:2:7). Some Muslims add a sixth obligation: Jihad, or struggle. This is one of the points of controversy between Muslims. For many Muslims, this is a personal inner struggle to submit to God, while for others the struggle is a battle against all who oppose Islam.

Muslims would like to believe, and have others believe, that Islam is one religion and one people, but in reality it is a divided religion. There is the major division between Sunni and Shiite Muslims, which are further divided into several smaller groups. There are also smaller heretical groups that identify with Islam such as the Ahmadiyya from India and the Nation of Islam in America.

Muslims practice Islam for a variety of reasons, and in a variety of ways. Some scholars suggest that the majority of Muslims practice a form of folk Islam, which is a mixture of animistic practices and Islam.[3]

Phil Parshall suggests that as many as 70 percent of Muslims practice folk Islam.[4] Sufism is a mixture of Islam and mysticism, where Islamic practices represent ways of encountering the divine. The Wahhabi sect is a reformist group that purged Islam of all forms of superstition, using force when necessary, to keep fellow Muslims on the right path. There are other Muslims who are deeply pious men and women who try to bring their entire lives under submission to God; they are well versed in their religion, carefully applying Islam to all of life.

There are also, of course, militant Muslims who believe Islam is continually at war with non-Muslims. The good news is that Muslim fundamentalists may only make up as much as 5 percent of the Islamic community. The bad news is that with a total global Muslim population of more than a billion, the actual number of fundamentalists could be as high as fifty million.

Other Muslims are cultural Muslims. They are mainly concerned with raising and caring for their families. Islam is important to them because it maintains family, community, and national solidarity, but they are not committed to Islam theologically. They keep the fast and will attend mosques on important religious days. They say that they don't drink alcohol or eat pork, and typically they don't. And then there are secular Muslims who consider all religions to be impediments to life in the modern world. Although most would never come right out and say that they don't believe in the teachings of Mohammad, they do all they can to avoid the more inconvenient aspects of Islam. They are more nationalistic than religious when it comes to questions about Israel and Western intervention into the Muslim world.

Not only is there a huge variety of different worldviews among Muslims and an equally huge variety of motivations for practicing Islam, there are also many different combinations of these factors, all of which together geometrically increases the different types of Muslims. Understanding how diverse and different Muslims are is one of the challenges Christians face. We cannot have just one response to this very different community. We must understand the individual Muslim with whom we are speaking, and we must shape our message to him or her individually. We must be careful not to stereotype Muslims. They need a Christian response that answers the questions they are asking. Islam in all its variety poses multiple challenges and requires a variety of well-thought-out answers.

A century ago the world was vastly different. The West was intoxicated with progress. Epistemologically, our theories were grounded in evolutionary thought, which "proved" Western superiority. We believed that Western technology would ameliorate mankind's condition, and this became "the white man's burden." The task we gave ourselves was to parent the rest of mankind toward the benefits we had obtained. Our military might and our belief in cultural evolution made it easy for us to colonize the world for the good of native peoples, while at the same time enriching ourselves with their resources and their labor.

In 1910, at the World Missionary Conference in Edinburgh, there was great exuberance. Drinking from the same fountain as Western society, Christians believed that progress would make Christianity the world's religion. The president of the conference, John R. Mott, had called for the evangelization of the world in his generation. The leaders of the conference believed that God had given them technology as the tool for this task and colonial rule as the means for reaching the world for Christ. Cultural and religious evolution caused the West naively to believe that the peoples of the world would throw off their primitive and superstitious ways, embracing the modern West and its Christian religion, and that this "embrace" would bring "primitive peoples" into the twentieth century. Little did they know that these things would in fact function as barriers, and that the 1910 World Missionary Conference would not be the starting point of the twentieth-century missionary movement but its high-water mark.

Samuel Zemwer gave a series of lectures at Princeton Theological Seminary in 1915 entitled "The Disintegration of Islam." In those lectures, he predicted, "Like all other non-Christian systems and philosophies, Islam is a dying religion; from the outset it had in it the germs of death—neither the character of the Koran nor of its Prophet have in them the promise or potency of life that will endure."[5] Again, at the turn of the twentieth century, Zemwer's prediction seemed a sure bet.

Muslims struggled with the dilemma of what Mohammad had promised and the reality of their lives.

They believed that as long as they followed Mohammad's teachings they would be a great and victorious civilization, but in 1900 they were a conquered and impoverished people. Muslim countries that were not already under Western colonial rule soon would be, after World War I. There was nothing of any value in the Muslim world. The golden age of Islam, where Muslim scholars kept alive the science, mathematics, and philosophy of the Greeks, had long since past. They lagged far behind the West in every field of knowledge. It seemed, both literally and figuratively, that the greatest contribution the Arab world could or would ever make to modernity was the Arabic numeral "zero."

But in one generation, all this would change. Oil would be discovered in Iran in 1905. In 1944, the largest oil reserves in the world, estimated at 300 billion barrels, would be discovered in Saudi Arabia. After World War II, the Muslim world would throw off the shackles of Western colonialism. But what path would they follow? What future would they choose for themselves?

Colonialization brought the best and the brightest of the Islamic world to the West to be educated, indoctrinating the next generation's leaders in Western ways. Instead of creating a unified consensus, however, these young leaders were pulled in many different directions. Some believed Western democracy would be best for them. Others were convinced that Marxism was the way of the future, and still others favored some form of Arab nationalism. Only a few could be heard calling Muslim peoples to turn away from Western capitalism, eastern Marxism, and the nationalism of the third world, and to look to Islam. One of those early voices was Hassan al-Banna, an Egyptian who founded the Muslim Brotherhood in 1928. He and his followers were convinced that only a return to a complete commitment to Islam would point the way forward for the Muslim people.

It took another generation for Muslims to determine that capitalism and Marxism were foreign systems that could not be planted in Islamic ground. The systems did not work, so many turned back to Islam—not to the backward, superstitious practices of the past but a new modern, intellectual, philosophical, and militant version of Islam. It would not be the political or military leaders but the clerics who set both religious and national agendas; it was not top-down transformation but bottom-up revolution. Muslims believed the tide was changing and were galvanized as a people by their ability to liberate themselves from colonial rule by the power and wealth that comes from petrodollars.

Islam was given further credence because of the perceived moral superiority of groups such as the Muslim Brotherhood, who provided social services for the poor and re-Islamized Muslim nations. They looked like saints in comparison to political leaders. For this new generation, colonization was not the controlling of the ground but the controlling of the mind. It wasn't enough to remove foreign rule from the nation; Western thinking also had to be erased from the minds of Muslim people.

All vestiges of Western influence had to be removed in small stages, and each victory raised Muslims' confidence. The shah of Iran, Mohammad Rezā Shāh Pahlavi, was easily overthrown by a religious cleric, the Ayatollah Khomeini, because he had "betrayed" Islam by aligning himself too closely to the West. There was also the taking and holding of American prisoners in Tehran, the expulsion of Americans from Beirut, and the defeat of the Russians in Afghanistan. Each of these victories emboldened Arab militants, but there was still one unacceptable loss and continuing defeat.

The shame that most Muslims, even to this day, feel must be set right is the liberation of Muslim lands from the one remaining Western colony on Muslim soil: Israel. That country's existence is a reminder that they feel must be corrected of Western domination of Islam and the Jewish betrayal of the prophet. The problem was that the organized armies of the Arab states could not win a victory over Israel or the West, but highly committed Muslims, working in transnational organizations such as al-Qaeda, proved they couldn't lose. They beat the Russians; they brought down the World Trade Center; and it is believed they will defeat the Americans in Iraq, Afghanistan, and Iran, and ultimately expel the Jews. "Allah Akbah!" We enter the twenty-first century wondering not whether Islam will survive, but how we can live in peace with Islam.

Colin Chapman, in the introduction to his second edition of the *Cross and the Crescent: Responding to the Islamic Challenge,* presents four dimensions of the challenge. They are numeric, economic and political, cultural, and intellectual and theological.[6]

THE DIMENSIONS OF THE CHALLENGE

Numeric

The numeric challenge is the result of Islam's extraordinary growth, which is primarily the result of higher birth rates, not conversion growth. Some consider the higher birth rates among Muslims more than a challenge; they consider it a threat, a Muslim conspiracy to take over Europe and India. Some alarmists are predicting a Muslim Europe and an Islamic India because they have taken the past birth rates among Muslims and applied those to present and future birth rates. If these rates continue, there will be huge demographic shifts. But evidence suggests that Muslims, particularly second-generation immigrants to Europe, are not having the same number of children as their parents, but similar to Europeans their age, prefer smaller families. Although the percentage of Muslims will increase, they will not overrun Europe or India.

But there is another important demographic fact: 40 percent of the Arab world is under fourteen years of age, while the West is graying. This is likely to produce a continued wave of immigration to Europe and North America. On the other hand, even though Islam is making progress in Africa through conversion and reproduction, it is likely that Africa will remain a Christian continent because of an equally strong conversion and birth rate among Christians.

Economic and Political

As long as the world is addicted to fossil fuels, nations must come and bow before the Islamic world. The oil embargo of the 1970s showed the world how dependent they were on Arab oil. Now awash in petrodollars, the Arabs are a force to be reckoned with in global financial markets. There are rumblings among Russia, China, and the Arab world about prying loose the U.S. dollar's hold on the petroleum market; if this happens, many parts of the global game will change.

Politically, Islam is on the move as a transnational movement. It is demanding that Sharia law be implemented across the Islamic world— even in states that in the past were considered secular. The British government is under growing pressure to authorize local Sharia courts to handle "smaller" criminal cases in coming years.

We should not be surprised by the Islamic world's outcry for Sharia. It is a response to the moral decay they see around them, especially in the West. Instead, we must find ways to work with Muslims and other religious groups in order to restore public morality. Most Muslims see globalization as destroying everything that is precious to them: family, morality, community—and they are looking for ways to protect themselves. Would it not be missional to stand with Muslims in that process?

Nor should we necessarily or automatically be afraid of the economic prosperity of the Islamic world. Christians must not fall victim to the myth of the limited good, nor to envy. The economic advance of one group doesn't always mean the economic decline of another. History and much economic theory suggest that the free exchange of goods and services strengthen mutual self-interest. The conundrum will be to allow for such enlightened self-interest while, at the same time, addressing the moral decay which such self-interest often produces.

Cultural

One way to see the Islamic and non-Islamic world is as two tectonic plates pushing against each other. Everywhere the Muslim world rubs up against the non-Muslim world, there is friction. That friction has only increased with the pressures of globalization. The West is convinced that newer is better, but much of the world is past-oriented in its values. How long will it take for the world to grow tired of fast food and theme parks? How soon before people begin to ask for what is permanent and not plastic, real and not recycled?

The West needs to be humbled. There is a fine line between backward values and enduring values. We would do well to learn from Islamic culture the value of family, community, and hospitality. As Christians, can we build or reestablish a culture built on the teachings of the Scriptures?

Intellectual and Theological

Islam is a total system of religion, philosophy, law, and culture. It is a system that presents to many a compelling alternative to Marxism and capitalism. It is a highly sophisticated theological system that answers the deepest questions about man, God, and existence. It is centuries of case law in pursuit of justice.

Again, we should not fear the rebirth of Islamic theology, for where Islamic theology and culture are fully lived out—for example, in Iran—there is a growing distrust in the power of external control for inward transformation. Instead, what the world needs to see is a different kind of civilization, where freedom and moral transformation go hand in hand. The answer to Islamic theology is not the individualistic and pietistic theology of evangelicals, but covenantal and Reformed theology—a theology that does not separate the world into the secular and the sacred but calls Christians to live the totality of their lives for the glory of God. It is, in fact, only a fully orbed Reformed theology, with its strong insistence on scripturally based world- and life-view, that can adequately respond to the intellectual and theological challenges of Islam.

During the last century, missions among Muslims have undergone dramatic transformation. In the Edinburgh report on Islam in 1910, it seemed that few Muslims were coming to faith in Christ. Today, we are seeing conversions on a regular basis. These conversions are occurring in the context of a wide variety of means. Some individuals are having dreams, others are watching Christian TV programs, and still others have Christian friends who have impacted their lives. House churches are springing up across the Islamic world. While there were few missionaries working among Muslim peoples at the turn of the twentieth century, there are now people from all over the world working in Muslim lands. A century ago missionaries hoped to see one conversion; now we *expect* to regularly see Muslims come to Christ. To assist this global effort to bring Muslims to Christ the WRF has adopted its Project on Ministry among Muslims.

The report by Committee IV, "The Missionary Message in Relation to the Non-Christian World," was the most anticipated report at the 1910 World Missionary Conference and the most studied and written about after the conference because it promised a new approach to reaching people of other faiths. The old method was to destroy the godless faith so that Christianity could be planted. The new method understood other religions as incomplete but still a product of the Spirit of God; thus all religions contained some elements of God's truth. It is the gospel and Christ that *fulfills* them—thus, the term that later developed, "fulfillment theology."

The positive aspect of this new approach was that it saw God as active in the entire world through his providence, but this approach was naïve about the rebellion in man's heart and about how we construct systems—particularly religious systems—to hide from the truth about God. A second positive aspect of the fulfillment theology approach was that it allowed encounters with other religions to be defined not by conflict but by dialogue. However, the new approach did not improve the conversion rate among people of other faiths because, to them, their faith did not seem deficient—Christianity did not seem to "complete" their beliefs.

At the Edinburgh conference, most of those who worked with Muslims could not find any way of building on the foundation of Islam. Temple Gairdner, quoted in the Commission IV report, writes: "How can that which denies the whole essential and particular content of the message be said to prepare for Him, or to be a half-way house to His kingdom? For that is what Islam does. ... But the whole theory of Islam is that it, the latest sent of all religions, does not so much abrogate Christianity with its Book, as specifically and categorically deny both as willful corruption and lies."[7] At Edinburgh, it could not even be said that animists who converted to Islam were closer to Christianity. Once they had become Muslim, there was less of a chance that they would become Christian. There are many points of contact between Islam and

Christianity, but those who try to see these as starting points quickly find that they become dead-ends. It is like playing checkers with all the pieces moved to the center of the board. There is nowhere for anyone to move.

In the more liberal movements of the church, "fulfillment theology" would transform evangelism into "dialogue." If God is at work through all religious systems, there is no need to convert, but to learn to look for the Christ within all religions. The Jesuit theologian Karl Rahner introduced the idea of the "anonymous Christian"—a person of another faith who, even if he rejected Christ but followed his conscience and lived out of the grace of God, is saved though Christ. The inclusivism of Rahner was just a short stop on the way to the religious pluralism of John Hick.

Evangelicals took a more pragmatic approach to Islam, a less combative tone, and began to apply the ideas of contextualization to their work among Muslims. In 1980, Phil Parshall published *New Paths in Muslim Evangelism: Evangelical Approaches to Contextualization*, which called Christians working with Muslims to contextualize the gospel to its Muslim audience.[8] This included taking off their shoes and sitting on rugs on the floor, using drums to call people to worship, and wearing traditional dress clothes. There seemed to be a responsiveness to a gospel that had shed its Western form.

The next generation of missionaries—believing that if a little is good, more had to be better—tried highly contextualized approaches. In these approaches, called "insider movements," Muslim converts are not called out of Islam but called to live for Christ within the Islamic system. This entire phenomenon is discussed in detail in this volume by John Nicholls in his excellent chapter on "Hidden Believers," which immediately follows this chapter. I would simply suggest here some questions which Dr. Nicholls explores in greater depth:

1. Has Christian conversion taken place, or are these Muslim followers of Jesus merely a sect of Islam?
2. Has a religious movement been formed that is neither Christian nor Muslim?

3. Should we give these movements more time to see what devel-
    ops from them, hoping they will become more orthodox?
4. Will a new religion be formed like Baha'I, that is a mélange of
    several religions?
5. Should we keep wooing such individuals towards a more or-
    thodox form of Christianity?

Finally, the church must think holistically about the challenges
(note: challeng*es*) the Muslim world presents to us. In holistic work, if
we are to obey Jesus, we must be as "wise as serpents and innocent as
doves" (Matthew 10:16). There are three distinct areas with which the
church must deal in its response to the Islamic world. Each will require
a different strategy and different objectives, but if we are to align ourselves with God's own mission these are the areas that we, the church
of Jesus Christ, must thoughtfully and carefully address:

- Muslims living in nations that are dominated by Islam
- Muslims living in nations where there are significant populations
  of both Muslims and non-Muslims
- Muslims who are living outside the Islamic world in predomi-
  natcly Christian countries

Islam is a global religion. We must work together with the wid-
est possible coalitions of nations, agencies, and religions to guarantee
the rights of all peoples. We need to use organizations like the United
Nations to protect all people's religious freedom. The United Nations
Universal Declaration of Human Rights states, "Everyone has the right
to freedom of thought, conscience and religion; this right includes freedom to change his religion or belief, and freedom, either alone or in
community with others and in public or private, to manifest his religion or belief in teaching, practice, worship and observance."[9] These
calls for freedom are not exclusive for either Muslims and Christians,
but apply to all nations and to individuals of all faiths. Organizations
such as the World Evangelical Alliance, of which the World Reformed
Fellowship is a member, and individuals such as Dr. Thomas Johnson

are providing leadership for the global evangelical church in insisting that religious freedom be assured to all.

In Muslim majority nations we must aggressively evangelize through sending missionaries and training national pastors. At the same time we must use radio and satellite TV. We must make sure that ancient Christian churches in Muslim lands are free to worship, and that new believers are not harassed or persecuted. Recently in Morocco, believers were arrested and missionaries expelled from the country. Churches in Indonesia are being burned. In such situations, we must bring pressure politically and economically when Christians are mistreated. We cannot allow this to happen. The more non-Western voices that cry out, the better. We must keep the church at large informed on the persecuted church through organizations such as Open Doors, Voice of the Martyrs, Persecution Project Foundation, and International Christian Concern. We must put pressure on all political leaders to uphold human rights—for *all* people.

In nations that are divided between Muslims and other populations, we must protect the non-Muslim population. The world must react quickly to genocide where Muslims are killing non-Muslims. In the Sudan, the world must not allow the Muslims in the north to eliminate the Christians in the south; the racial dimension of this conflict must also be addressed. Currently in Nigeria, Muslims are killing Christians across what is known as the middle belt, in Jos. There is evidence that the Muslim authorities are aiding in the killing of Christians, the burning of their homes, and the confiscating of their property. If we do not bring worldwide attention and pressure on what the Muslims of Nigeria are doing, Christians will either be killed or forced out of the country.

Where possible, we should call for international peacekeeping forces to protect the non-Muslim populations in these divided countries. We must also help the Christian population not retaliate with force, but seek justice and peace through the proper channel. If we do not stand with our brothers and sisters, they will die silently. We need Christian journalists to tell these stories to the world.

Finally, in Christian nations where Muslims are immigrating, we have the joy of sharing our life and faith with these, our guests. We must invite them into our homes and welcome them into our churches. Muslims will not be won to Christ by convincing arguments, but by missional Christian communities that live out the gospel. In this way Muslims will understand the difference between "Western" and "Christian."

The twenty-first century may look very dangerous—with nations like Iran obtaining nuclear capabilities and Muslim fundamentalist groups wanting to bring jihad to the non-Islamic world—but the church must not try and wage a modern crusade against Islam. Instead, we need a truly catholic church—a worldwide community of believers, who daily lay down their lives in loving service to one another and those around them. A universal community is needed that cannot be called white or Western or imperialist, but Christian. We need followers of Christ from every walk of life, believers who will spread over the earth like water, filling the deepest and darkest places on earth with the hope and light of the gospel. When that happens, the earth will be covered with the glory of God as the waters cover the sea. As Martin Allen reminded us in the opening chapter of this volume, The challenge is not Islam; it is same challenge Christ gave us two thousand years ago—to go and make disciples of all nations.

12.
A MISSIONAL APPROACH TO "HIDDEN BELIEVERS"

JOHN NICHOLLS

As John Leonard pointed out in the previous chapter, there is little new in the encounter between Christianity and Islam. At the World Missionary Conference of 1910, Islam was described by one speaker as "The Great Antagonist," and many of the reports grappled with strategic and practical aspects of mission to Muslims. Many of these aspects are still familiar to mission workers here in the twenty-first century. But the subject of this chapter is a more recent development: the Hidden Believer movement that developed as recently as the 1980s in parts of the predominantly Muslim world.

Hidden believers (HBs) have been described as Muslims who trust Jesus as Lord and divine Savior, believe Jesus died for their sins and rose again—but who insist this does not make them ex-Muslims or converts to the Christian religion. They want to remain within their Muslim community, honoring Jesus in that context.

HBs have also been described as "messianic Muslims" who remain legally and socially within the community of Islam; who reject or reinterpret those aspects of Islamic theology that are incompatible with the Bible; who share their faith with unsaved Muslims; who may (if they are an entire village) result in a "messianic mosque"; who are viewed as Muslims by the community; and refer to themselves as "Muslims who follow Isa the Messiah"; but who may still face rejection and expulsion from the community of Islam as theologically deviant.

Since the 1980s, a sometimes fierce debate has continued among practitioners of mission to Muslims. Much of the discussion is defined by the C1 to C6 "contextualization scale," developed in an attempt to describe the graded differences between traditional Christian groups whose "culture" and language are essentially alien to the Muslim communities in which they are placed, and other Christian groups that to a lesser or greater degree live within Muslim culture and use Muslim ("insider") terminology. In the C1 to C6 terminology, hidden believers are rated C5. (The category C6 is applied to what might be called "secret believers"—individuals who have come to faith in Jesus, but whose faith finds no corporate expression. They continue to live within Muslim families and within Muslim society.)

Some have tried to move the debate away from the C1–6 scale, asserting that the issue at stake is not so much one of contextualization but of *identity*. In more recent years, the debate has been sharpened by the fact that new versions of the Bible are being prepared within the HB context that significantly alter the text of the New Testament, deleting references to Jesus as the Son of God, and to God as Father. For many observers, this latter development has been a final and decisive factor in rejecting the hidden-believer strategy.

A cursory survey of the history and status of Christian missions to Muslims reveals several issues that underlie the HB debate—and which define the problem and solution for HB protagonists:

1. The identification of "Western" (especially the US and UK) with "Christian," as a single entity which is simultaneously active in military, political, economic, and missionary activity.

This may seem an obvious mistake to those whose thinking is rooted in Western liberal assumptions—that religion is a matter of private, individual choice; that multiple religions can flourish within the same political and social entity; and that church and state are distinct and separate concepts. But Islam does not make any such sharp distinctions, any more than do many other traditional cultures. The late Harvie M. Conn used to ask his students to suggest what the first chapter of the Confession of Faith of a Reformed Church in Japan might deal with.

The answer was "church and state"—seeking to demonstrate that you could be a Christian without ceasing to be Japanese.

C5 advocates place much importance on the avoidance of the term "Christian," and on the assertion that one can be a follower of Jesus and still remain within Muslim society. This concern is accentuated by the tendency of Islam to place what we might call "the world of Islam" above even the nation-state. For example, an Iraqi Muslim may be far more personally and passionately affected by a perceived "Western/ Christian" military operation in Sudan than a British Christian would be affected by a Chechen attack in Moscow. Anyone who engages with Muslims, whether in Lahore or London, will experience the reality of this problem. The HB movement is an attempt to avoid having this as a barrier to the spread of the gospel.

2. **The extent to which Western—especially, but not exclusively, American—social norms dominate the worlds of business, information technology, media, and the aspirations of individuals and families.** The idolization of individual choice, materialistic prosperity, change, and novelty as obvious virtues, and of personal glamour, are extremely pervasive, visually attractive, and inevitably corrosive of the moral values of conservative societies. The problem, as far as Christian missions are concerned, is that many missions, missionaries, and churches follow lifestyles that seem indistinguishable from what is seen on local television.

We in the West may be satisfied that we have established satisfactory boundaries between ourselves and "the unbelieving world," but to many who look at us from a different perspective, Christians don't seem all that different from the cast of *Friends*. Our pastors and missionaries often seem to be extravagantly wealthy—and far removed from the ascetic holy men to whom serious-minded Muslims look for spiritual wisdom and guidance.

3. **For some thirteen hundred years, Christians in Muslim lands have had to live with the discrimination of "Dhimmitude."** The *Merriam-Webster Dictionary* defines this as "a person living

in a region overrun by Muslim conquest who was accorded a protected status and allowed to retain his original faith." While outright persecution, massacres, and forced conversions have been intermittent or rare, the constant social pressure of discriminatory taxation, together with second-class political, military, and economic status have served to drain away the confidence and the evangelistic vision of Christian communities. Muslims tend to look down on Christians as being "lower caste," and Christians have, to varying extents, taken on the defensive mind-set of the underdog, eager to do nothing that might provoke further restrictions or persecutions. The Christians in many Muslim lands have thus become a barrier to evangelism. (Brother Andrew's book *Secret Believers*, with its fictionalized narrative of a Middle Eastern country, gives a useful insight into this problem.[1]). Muslim converts are not sought by such churches, and they are not welcomed if they come. Both sides, Muslim and Christian, have adopted a tribal mind set toward Christianity.

A single chapter cannot expect to deal exhaustively or conclusively with such a long-running and complex debate (and that is just one reason why the previous chapter by Dr. Leonard is crucial reading for anyone interested in this subject). But I trust that the present chapter will serve to provide wider information and insight, and identify an agenda for research and further discussion from a Reformed point of view. What follows is intended to prompt a discussion for defining that agenda.

EVALUATING AND RESPONDING TO THE HB MOVEMENT: A SURVEY OF BIBLICAL FOUNDATIONS

As Reformed Christians, our first priority is to evaluate any such movement as the hidden-believer movement by the teachings of the Bible. This involves more than searching for simple proof texts to support either side. We need to consider how HB fits with the great underlying and interweaving themes of the whole Bible, the whole counsel of God. What follows are some critically important questions that must be asked.

Does HB operate within the biblical definition and limits of contextualization? Terms such as "contextualization" and "culture" have become the common coinage of missiological debate, but it is vital that they reflect the boundaries evident in such places as 1 Corinthians 9:21: "To those outside the law I became as one outside the law (*not being outside the law of God but under the law of Christ*) that I might win those outside the law" (emphasis mine). Clearly, Paul wishes to guard here against an unlimited contextualizing, but where are the lines drawn?

The position of Jewish believers in Jesus, in the New Testament era, is often used as a justification for "messianic mosques" and other extreme forms of contextualization. But what exactly does the New Testament reveal of the relationship between Jewish and Gentile Christians? What evidence is there for apostolic approval of a distinctly Jewish form of evangelism or discipleship? And (in a somewhat wider and less authoritative sense) what can we observe and learn from the history of the Ebionites and other Jewish/Christian movements in the early centuries? In any case, on what grounds can valid parallels be drawn between "messianic Jews" and converts within any other religion, since Judaism in the New Testament era was an outcome of a genuine divine revelation and activity (albeit distorted by the accretions and interpretations of the Pharisees)—not the product of a human religiosity?

Does HB do justice to the biblical centrality of the covenant community? Reformed theology teaches that the biblical narrative leads inexorably from the call of Abraham and his family (Genesis 12) to the constituting of a separated worshiping and structured community at Sinai (Exodus 19–24). The unfolding revelation of Old and New Testaments shows how this community is shepherded and preserved through the Davidic kingdom and the upheavals of exile and return, until it is transformed and fulfilled through the saving work of Jesus. There is a fundamental continuity between the Old Testament and the New Testament, despite the various discontinuities.

Western Enlightenment individualism has seriously ignored the significance of community, and even of family (cf. the baptism of believers' children into the covenant community). How does HB do justice to the centrality of the one covenant community—a community that is sharply intolerant of any form of compromise with its rival religious/social communities (e.g., Revelation 2–3)? What is the identity of the children of HB adherents?

The New Testament does not present the believing community as a merely local phenomenon focused on believers' own needs. Rather, it is set in the context of God's eternal predestination as a central feature of God's ultimate purpose. In John 17, Jesus himself prays for the community as a visible evidence of the divine uniqueness of his work. This community is distinctive precisely because it overflows the cultural and historical differences between Jews and Gentiles. Can an HB community that is "hidden" within Islam be part of that world-convincing united community for which Jesus prays?

The doctrine of the Holy Spirit and his work are also relevant to this discussion. He has no fellowship with darkness. He convicts, guides, and empowers believers to a holiness that exceeds and is clearly distinguished from that of scribes and Pharisees. Above all, he is the anti-Babel Spirit who creates the one new humanity through union with Christ. How does the indefinitely continuing separation of HB adherents from others who are openly Christians within their same geographical setting sit with Paul's teaching of mutual ministry and the exercise of spiritual gifts (e.g., 1 Corinthians 12; Ephesians 4:15)?

Perhaps it also relevant here to point out that the New Testament contains a clear (if too often neglected) pattern, *internal to the one church*, for dealing with cultural differences arising (in part) from the differing cultural backgrounds of believers in Jesus. Is not Paul's teaching about the mutual responsibilities of those he calls weak in faith and those who are strong (Romans 14:1–15:13) a more relevant and better paradigm for addressing the cultural and contextual challenges facing Muslim-background converts? What justification is there for establishing separate churches for "weak" and "strong" believers? (Though here, as elsewhere throughout this debate, many of us need to look closer to home and hear the Lord's own challenge in John 8:7, "'Let him who is without sin among you be the first to throw a stone'"!)

Is the divine sonship of Christ an unavoidable offense? The gospels make it plain that it was Jesus's language of divine sonship that shocked and offended the Jewish leaders (John 10:32–39), and was a key contributing factor to his crucifixion (John 19:7). The apostle John states clearly that the purpose behind his composition of the fourth Gospel was precisely to bring people to believe that Jesus is the Son of God (20:31). If Jesus and John repeatedly asserted something that was an inflammatory offense to the (Jewish) people among whom they were ministering, and whom they were endeavoring to lead to faith, what justification is there for deliberately avoiding that truth when endeavoring to lead Muslims to faith? Or, turning the question around, why is the language of sonship (and Trinity?) so vital to the way we proclaim Christ that we must use it despite the outrage it may provoke?

The inevitability of suffering and the triumph of grace. The HB movement appears to be a response to the hostility and hardness that Islamic society has displayed toward the gospel. Followers of Jesus are not to seek confrontation unnecessarily (Romans 12:18)—but neither are they to put peace and personal safety before faithfulness to the gospel. Acts 4:23–31 describes a situation where the apostles were threatened with violent punishment if they continued to openly preach Christ. Their response was to pray—not for the binding of their enemies and their own safekeeping, nor for wisdom to avoid saying anything that might offend the dominant powers, but for "all boldness" in preaching the word.

While it is difficult for those of us who live under no real threat of physical persecution to make such judgments, we do know that many of our brothers and sisters throughout history—and around the world today—face precisely such threats. None relish such threats, but some have come to see that suffering is not only a common consequence of becoming a Christian but also a gift from God that can mysteriously and wonderfully advance the life of the individual believer and the worshiping community.

In Eastern Europe under communism, some believers developed a "theology of martyrdom" that sought to embrace suffering under the sovereignty of a wise and loving heavenly Father. How can we develop and apply such thinking and such piety today? How can we prepare and help our brothers and sisters to be "more than conquerors?"

Finally, as Reformed Christians, we have a strong alertness to the sovereignty of grace. God is moving all things together, and all things forward, toward consummation. The book of Revelation sets out in many places the ultimate reality of the church of God gathered from all nations and people groups, worshiping around the throne of God, in the presence of the Lamb of God—not just in the glorious future but in the imperfect present as well. In an age of methodologies and ministry models, statistics and case studies, how do we ensure that we do not lose sight of the certainty of God's triumph, and the fearlessness it instills?

THE ONGOING DEBATE

However negatively one may respond to certain aspects of the HB movement, we do well to remember that such debates must be carried on in the spirit of Christ, with a humility that is prepared to learn as well as to criticize, and an honesty about our own failings and inconsistencies. Our own opinions are too often formed in response to partial and distorted second-hand reports. We unwisely charge people with what we see as the "logical implications" of something they have said or done—and in accusing others of rending the body of Christ, we may be creating unnecessary rents ourselves.

There are many questions that we must put to ourselves as we debate within the worldwide community. These may include the following:

- What is the perspective on the HB movement of our brothers and sisters in countries such as Indonesia, Korea, and China—where the Christian church has been planted and has developed within a strongly non-Christian culture and has faced fierce opposition? How do they present the gospel? How do they disciple converts?
- In what ways have nineteenth-century Western Colonialism and twentieth-century economic imperialism harmed and distorted the presentation of the gospel to the non-western world? What

can we learn from the experience of the church through the ages—in the persecution period of the Reformation in Europe, the growth and decline of the ancient eastern churches, and the oppressions under twentieth-century totalitarian systems?

- What are the longer-term fruits of the Hidden Believer movement? Is it a helpful transitional phase; a useful, if limited stimulant; a universal solution; or a spiritual dead-end? How can Christian churches within Islamic societies sustain a bold witness for Jesus Christ and welcome Muslim-background converts into their gospel communities? What weaknesses of C1–C4 mission practice does HB spotlight, and how should we address them?

- What are the lessons of the hidden-believers debate for the evangelization of Muslim communities living in the midst of "Western" and other non-Muslim societies? What biblically-based guidelines are inspiring and controlling the surge in church-planting around the world? How are they avoiding, in their own settings, the dangers that some see in the HB movement?

- What about the pastoral perspective—where does all this leave Muslim converts in Bangladesh and other places? How can we find and express fellowship with C5 communities? How should we encourage our churches to pray?

The intent here is not to end the debate about hidden believers in the Islamic world, but to extend that debate into the light of biblical teaching. The gospel of Jesus Christ proclaims God's creation of a radically *new* community in lively union with Jesus Christ. If Western civilization is in many ways a grossly distorted parody of what Jesus came to achieve, then so is the *ummah* (the collective community of Islamic peoples). To rightly identify and edify the church in both its Western and its Islamic contexts is a vital task, especially in these days when the cities of the world bring all cultures into close proximity. The HB controversy gives the worldwide church an opportunity for gracious, serious, and profound discussion, as well as the opportunity to clarify and display that new and visibly united community that includes members from every nation, tribe, people, and language.

13.

A MISSIONAL RESPONSE TO HOMOSEXUAL STRUGGLERS IN THE CHURCH AND THE GAY COMMUNITY

JOHN FREEMAN

Homosexuality. I can't think of a word or concept today that produces a more emotional, prickly, and quick-tempered response, both throughout society and within the church. This can be an intensely explosive and volatile topic, and rightly so. While there are many reasons for this—explanations that go beyond the scope of this chapter—it's been my experience that beliefs about issues closer to the human heart generally are those we fight to validate and justify. Suffice it to say, we would have to look far and wide to find a more controversial issue in our present culture.

A majority of those reading this would probably agree and assume that homosexual desire and behavior is wrong—that is, sinful. The Word of God does, in every place and in all instances, condemn homosexuality as a practice of heart, mind, and body—as it does all sexual sin outside the pattern instituted by God in Genesis 1:27–28, where the pattern for biblical sexual expression is defined in the context of marriage of one man and one woman. At the same time I am beginning to see a much more confused ideology and theology concerning the biblical legitimacy of homosexuality, especially among the thirty-and-under age groups in our churches. (How and why that's occurred could be the basis of another whole paper.)

However, if we stop at just labeling homosexuality as sinful, we fall far short of presenting a redemptive and Christlike response to a growing dilemma for the household of faith—and more specifically in this case, those of the Reformed faith. Many of us are dealing with these deeply heart-wrenching struggles in our own lives and in the lives of those we love.

As one who has been involved in more than twenty-five years of ministry to believers wrestling against deep struggles regarding their sexual identity, as well as with those who have boldly identified themselves as gay or lesbian, I have seen a growing and very polarized response from leaders in the historic Reformed community. Two responses from two elders dramatically demonstrate where the challenges lie.

I was explaining to one elder who sat at the table with me the essence of our ministry and what we actually do for people who contact us for help. His verbal response startled me, to say the least: "I don't care—let them all go to hell." The anger and vehemence in his statement took me aback. In a conversation with another elder—this time about whether or not Christians could be gay and adopt both that label and identity—he looked me boldly in the face and said unwaveringly, "Gay Christians? What's wrong with Christians being gay?" It was not a question; it was a comment. Again, the reasons for these varied responses are intricate and complicated, and broader than the range of this chapter, but suffice it to say that both these responses are shallow, unhelpful, and, more importantly, less than biblical and redemptive in nature.

How are God's people, the church, to respond to a growing phenomenon that we can't escape as a culture or in our own personal lives? Almost everyone today either knows someone who is gay or lesbian or who has a relative impacted by homosexuality. In a real sense, homosexuality has embraced the culture and the culture (and some churches) has embraced homosexuality. This is just "what is" today. It's also a growing human dilemma for many in the Reformed community who are personally impacted by these problems, however much we would like to pretend otherwise. One very relative question is, Will we be part of the problem, or part of the solution?

Let's digest the first part of that question. I think we must own and take responsibility for some of the theological and ideological "mess" in which we find ourselves. By that I mean that, historically, we've either ignored this major human dilemma for many people, or we've separated or detached it from other types of sexual sin. We've expected some type of magical, spontaneous resolution about real questions of identity and sin issues to emerge from afar, rather than encourage our people to be honest about these embarrassing, shame-ridden, and very real problems. Even though we often think we have, we haven't assigned the issues the same significance that God has—that this is, and has always been, part of the fallen order of things...well, since the fall. Truly, nothing is new under the sun, although we've mistakenly let our people think, "Surely none of us would be struggling with 'that.'" Truth be told, many of us are struggling with it—especially our covenant children.

Additionally, we've relegated struggles with same-sex attraction and homosexuality to a category of "the other"—that is, different from and set apart from other sexual struggles and sin. Due to its nature, we've assigned it to that dark corner of the room where the light cannot shine.

One of my former seminary professors, Harvie Conn, once taught in our missions class on 1 Corinthians 6: 9–11, "Or do you not know that the unrighteous will not inherit the kingdom of God? Do not be deceived: neither the sexual immoral, nor idolaters, nor adulterers, nor men who practice homosexuality, nor thieves, nor the greedy, nor drunkards, nor revilers, nor swindlers will inherit the kingdom of God." He stressed the fact that living an unrepentant life regarding these things was something that could get you in much trouble, in this life—and the next. But he also stressed that this passage taught that you could get in trouble just as easily as a heterosexual sinner as a homosexual one—as well as for other more "acceptable," non-sexual sins.

We need to take *all* sin seriously, not just that which we find personally offensive or distasteful—or that with which we can't identify or see ourselves committing. All sin is an offense to God, whatever its nature, sexual or otherwise. Same-sex attractions are usually first felt and experienced at an early age by youth who don't ask for them and who didn't go around saying to themselves, "I think I'll be gay when I grow up." By placing same-sex attractions outside the realm of other "normal" sexual sin struggles, we've created a silent space that has fostered neglect, pastorally speaking. The culture, our own fallen hearts, and the strategies of the evil one have conspired to confuse, confound, and shipwreck our faith, and has led many of us to fail to understand and respond to this specific sin as Scripture commands us. Of this neglect, we must repent. We are now reaping the fruit of many years of not discussing and addressing these things, pastorally and proactively, at all levels of church life.

Does this mean that we turn the other way and ignore sin and disobedience? Absolutely not. It *does* mean that the motives of our own hearts in addressing this sin must be filled with genuine love and compassion, showing the kind of love and compassion that Christ shows to others who are caught in sins of a sexual nature in the Scriptures. Any kind of response by God's people must be redemptive in nature. We need to realize that those who struggle with and are captured by sexual sin are always among the brokenhearted. Whether recognized or admitted, emptiness and despair are often companions of not only homosexuality, but all sexual sin.

What are we, the church, doing to help reach, share the gospel with, and rescue those dealing with same-sex attractions and homosexuality? What might that look like?

First, any effort along these lines must be intentional. It requires a plan, a focus, and a strategy, just as it would to reach anyone caught in a life-dominating problems. We can no longer negate or deny the fact that our people, increasingly, are bringing a multitude of scars and open wounds regarding sex and sexuality into their relationship with Christ. Also, what is generally happening and being experienced by people "out there" is also impacting folks in the pew. No one escapes falling for the false appeal of sin.

Of course the primary place to begin is with the people in our own congregations. Intentionality in this area means introducing proactive education with all our youth. It's in the early years, usually around age ten today, when many of our youth are first wrestling with these things. Admittedly, twenty-five years ago most youth didn't have to be asking at age ten, Am I gay? Today they *are* asking that question, earlier and earlier. Biased and agenda-driven vehicles of the culture, which none of us can effectively escape—movies, television, the media, music, and the secular education system—force the question onto our youth all too soon.

We must equip and involve all those in youth ministry, starting in early middle-school ministry—including Sunday-school teachers, volunteer leaders, and especially youth staff—about these problem areas and issues. *Get this:* We want twelve-year-old Jimmy to be able to approach a trusted male in our youth ministry and admit, "I'm looking at pictures I shouldn't be on the computer and I know it's wrong." We want fourteen-year-old Suzy to be able to go to a trusted woman in our church and be able to confess, "I think I'm a lesbian. What do I do now?" Unfortunately, it's been my experience that most youth workers are woefully unprepared, and often left stunned and speechless at such revelations. Any youth worker or youth pastor not able and willing to address these issues head on, regularly and compassionately, should not be in youth ministry today!

If more of our churches were equipped to handle these real heart questions, we might not see so many of our churched youth gravitating toward, and influenced by, gay and lesbian student unions and homosexual organizations on high school and college campuses. We might not see so many of our youth genuinely seeking help for their questions and struggles from the Internet—only to be further taken in by falsehoods and bad theology concerning homosexuality. The "silent years"—when no preteen or teen talks about what's going on inside—must be intentionally addressed, over and over again, by our youth workers, along with varied and multiple permission-giving messages. The church must be seen as a helpful and safe place for youth to disclose these types of struggles.

Within the church context, we also want to offer concrete, pastoral help to those adults struggling with homosexuality. Many men and women sit silently in our pews weighed down by the shame, guilt, and embarrassment of either ongoing same-sex attractions or a homosexual past, which still impedes their personal relationships and their growth in Christ. Here again, repeated up-front permission-giving messages need be supplied from the leadership in all capacities, effectively communicating, we know and expect that these struggles might well be part of your experience—and we want to help. Together, we can handle this. Much too often contrary messages are given, both verbally and nonverbally, that say, We're fragile in this area; we can't handle it. This must cease if we expect our people to voluntarily seek help; we must expect the gospel to do its work.

Being spiritually mature in our leadership means the end of naivete. It means admitting, again, the gravity of the fall and realizing that everything is as it should *not* be—including, and especially, the sexual struggles of our people. Mature ministry takes people right where they're at—in various states of delusion and sin. Consider these stunning words by a megachurch pastor:

> Every effective church will have sexual strugglers as well as others dealing with many other life-dominating sins in it. When these people sit in our pews, they are all in various stages of dealing with their problems. Some are in denial that there is a problem. Some know their sin is against God's law, and live lives of hypocrisy and deception. Some are struggling with various degrees of success and failure to make the changes God requires. Others are regularly and effectively accessing the grace present in the Gospel in order to live changed lives. The challenge of the church is to assist sinners at all of these stages. We flush out the self-deceived; expose the dishonest; confront the rebel; offer forgiveness to the guilt-crushed; provide hope to the despairing; and support the surrendered. In addition, the church must invite in and hold the attention of those who formerly would never dared look to the church for hope or help.[1]

This means that we must proactively put structures in place within the church context to help those who are struggling. Today, many churches are successfully running Bible study/support groups or sexual integrity groups focused on these issues and problems, for their members and the community. These are places where men and women can begin to address, often for the first time, what has fueled their hearts and led them into ungodly sexual lifestyles. They can also learn, with the help of other caring and supportive people, to address ways in which they are still tempted to walk in unbelief—the lies they tend to believe about others and their own identity, their false "functional" theology, and the faulty thinking they live by on a day-to-day basis.

It's also the place where people begin to learn how to repent well. As one pastor put it, we must learn how to "kill that which is killing me, without killing myself." No one can do this on their own; it only comes with assistance from the community of believers   including lay members of the congregation and perhaps those with a special concern or heart for those who have these specific "besetting" sin struggles.

Any kind of intentional outreach must be both truth and mercy-based. This is, of course, necessary in ministering to those within the church, but is much more crucial for those outside the church. I'm thinking here both of those who are unbelievers as well as those who may be regenerate but in open rebellion, as well as those with deep scars and broken experiences with the church and "organized" Christianity. This too is representative of more people than ever today.

What is the implication for ministry, especially to those not of the household of faith—or to those disillusioned, abandoned, and outside the church family? It still means that we minister to people with both the truth and mercy of the gospel. We don't water down God's revealed will about the illegitimacy of any type of sex-out-of-bounds, including homosexuality. But we also do something that is most excellently mirrored and modeled through the Incarnation: we willingly, and joyfully, jump down into the trenches with others—in this case those pursuing or emerging from a gay identity or lifestyle.

Isn't that what Jesus did in leaving the riches of heaven and coming to earth for *us*? He left the most intimate, non-interrupted relationship ever devised, in order to taste and experience the mud, muck, and mire of humanity. Gospel ministry to those in trouble sexually, will do the same. Jesus did this for us; how can we not do it for others, especially in areas where the church has said "no way" and has had a hands-off and uninvolved mentality?

That hands-off mentality by the church, over the last fifty years, has contributed to the gay communities of our country becoming one of the fastest growing "people groups" in history. Many in the gay community now find friendship, support, encouragement, solace, and real community among their own. They take comfort in others who understand their struggles and plight, their past rocky and painful road to self-acceptance, as well as their current stresses—often with extended family and the church.

Here again, my former teacher Harvie Conn was helpful in giving me an understanding of the impact of groups left to fend for themselves in the face of adversity. I remember Harvie talking about how the church, for the most part, failed in its evangelistic efforts during the great immigration years of 1890–1920 when millions of Europeans came to America. These people groups of immigrants were considers "foreigners," and therefore not part of the mainstream of the church, or even targets for evangelism or ministry. As a result, Italians, Chinese, and Jews, for example, all became even more Italian, Chinese, and Jewish; they banded into insular, separate, and isolated communities where they could not only survive but thrive. In New York City, the Italians settled into "Little Italy"; the Chinese, into "Chinatown"; the Jews, into self-contained communities in Harlem and the Bronx. Looked at with suspicion as outsiders, and often feared and dismissed by the evangelical church, these and other ethnic and religious-based peoples became almost impenetrable as a community. Today's gay community and its structures are similar.

Showing mercy to and sharing the gospel with those involved (either actively or passively) in homosexuality will look different in different circumstances. I believe, however, that effective biblical methods include some crucial elements. Obviously, we need to be saddened and grieved at the fact that anyone would see homosexuality as the solution to life's confusion and hurts. Let me be blunt: *We need to be brought to tears—not only at ill-conceived ideas of where life may be found, but also at those in outright rebellion.* Why is it, then, that many believers respond to homosexuality and to homosexuals with anger and disgust? Is that truly Christlike?

In Luke 19:41, Jesus was brought to tears and "wept over" Jerusalem—over those who hated him, mistreated him, rejected the truth, had specific agendas regarding him, and would ultimately take his life. We must ask God to give us his heart for the sexually broken and shattered. Even if they don't see themselves that way, *we* surely must—and we must be moved to reach out with compassion.

Today most of our culture's views and perceptions of Christianity, especially when it comes to homosexuality, come from the ranting and ravings of television evangelists decrying the evils of homosexuality—and of gays and lesbians defending their lifestyle. Additionally, discussions of the legitimacy of homosexuality are often mixed and intertwined with the goals of conservative political parties. In other words, the gospel and politics get mixed together, resulting in a distorted view of Christianity. It can't be denied that this impacts the understanding and reception of the gospel message.

David Kinnaman and Gabe Lyons's book *unChristian* states that 91 percent of those surveyed between the ages of 16 and 29 say that Christianity is "anti-homosexual." Respondents claimed that Christians show excessive anger, disgust, and generally unloving attitudes towards homosexuals.[2] Clearly, the church is working from a public-relations deficit and distortion. For most people, Christians have nothing of value to say about this topic. We must work at overcoming and addressing these deficits—the places the gospel has not been accurately proclaimed in the marketplace. It's up to us to change that paradigm—yes, by admitting that sin is serious and destructive, but also by sharing the gospel and increasingly talking about God's "good gift" of sex and sexuality, even as we weep over and with people.

Another criterion to being effective in winning homosexuals to Christ is that we must deal with that person as a *person*, not as an *issue*. When we reduce people to their besetting sins or rebellion, we often react out of some deep motivation to set things right because our own sensibilities are offended. Sadly, I see this throughout the church today. I've been involved in many discussions with congregations about this issue where it becomes clear that most people's desire is for the homosexual to "just stop it," be like them, and become heterosexual—*not* to know Christ. Such a mind-set betrays our own fallen hearts and is misguided, unbiblical thinking.

Dealing with people as persons means that we see *them*—not the problem we want to fix or see changed. To do that, we must know who they are. Admittedly, this takes time and effort. But prayer, patience, and forbearance must be at the heart of any attempt to reach lost, hurting, confused, or disordered hearts of any kind! Our goal should not be that people are "set straight," but that they are won to Christ, either initially or in a deeper way—that they become true worshipers of the true God.

When believers proclaim the gospel to gays and to the culture at large in a loving, redemptive manner, punctuated with "grace and truth," it sets us apart and truly reflects the person of Christ. In such a heated and emotional debate, Christians have a responsibility to represent Christ to a fallen world and those in homosexuality in four specific and distinct ways:

1. Patiently listen. "Everyone should be quick to listen, slow to speak" (James 1:19, NIV). We should not be looking for loopholes in a debate or seeking a chance to criticize, shame, or find fault—or for the next thing to say to defend our position. We listen to understand the "heart thrust" of what the other person is saying. This is hard work. It is not natural. It takes practice. Learning how to patiently listen is a way we love people with Christ's love.

Loving biblically means we take time to observe—to see the world through the other person's eyes and experience. When we speak too quickly to force our views or to point out error, we don't "see" the person, just the problem we think needs to be corrected. We often respond out of that which disturbs us and makes us feel uncomfortable. The gospel, however, takes a deeper foothold when we enter the other person's world. We learn why people believe what they believe, what makes them who they are, what (or who) has hurt them in the past, and all that has hampered their "hearing." Treating people with respect, as image-bearers of God, helps deconstruct barriers.

Wasn't this Jesus's routine method of ministry? He dialogues with and engages the woman at the well (who may very well have been thinking he might just be the next better meal ticket). He compassionately, yet with spiritual authority, addresses the woman taken in adultery. He treats the sinful woman who poured perfume on his feet with respect. And for this, he was always being criticized for eating with and fellowshipping with tax gatherers and "sinners."

In loving by listening, we learn much more about people and discover why they have sought after other false gods. When we don't take time to get to know people, we tend to lump them into groups, label them on the basis of what we read in the news about "those" people, and mistakenly think that we understand them.

2. Personally repent. "'Do you think that these Galileans were worse sinners than all the other Galileans...? No, I tell you; but unless you repent, you will all likewise perish'" (Luke 13:2–3). Only a redeemed sinner, knowing he stands condemned apart from Christ's death on a cross, can reach a sinner who doesn't know he needs redeeming. Therefore, check your motivation before you engage someone. Are you doing it to reach a lost person with the enduring love that has found you out—a love that has exposed you as a cutthroat, a would-be fraud, and a depraved sinner who has been, through no merit of one's own, embraced by fatherly love? Are you doing it out of the awareness that, at heart, you're a sham, a misfit, a counterfeit, a phony, and that there is nothing good inside you to warrant God's love toward you? Do you really care about homosexuals, as men and women who desperately need to know the love of the Father—or would you rather they all just shut up and disappear?

Remember Jesus's words, "'he who is forgiven little, loves little'" (Luke 7:47)—or, stated the opposite way, "he who has been forgiven much, loves much." How we treat other sinners shows how aware we are of our own continuous need for the gospel and the work of Christ in our own lives. If we have no love for gays or lesbians, then we have not understood the forgiving love of Jesus in our own lives.

Where do we need to repent of our own bias and fears—of our own non-caring and hard hearts? What log is in our own eye that must be removed before we, in humility, can confront or challenge others? Where do *we* need the gospel? What temptations or sinful habits do we continually need saving from? Ongoing awareness of our own temptations and besetting sins—and marveling in the fact that our own record has been expunged through the work of the cross—must give us a heart of repentance ourselves.

3. Gently instruct.
"And the Lord's servant must not be quarrelsome but kind to everyone… correcting his opponents with gentleness" (2 Timothy 2:24–25). How do we talk with people who don't believe what we believe? An argumentative, win-at-all-costs approach does not conform to what Paul wrote Timothy. We must ask the Holy Spirit to instruct our own hearts as we seek to instruct others. Having a gentle manner does not mean becoming weak or vacillating in our own arguments; it means treating everyone with dignity and respect, even when they persistently disagree—or even are hostile. In fact, we need to expect hostility. Harvest USA staff member Dave White writes,

> When you interact with someone entrenched in sin, realize they will often be prickly and cantankerous. In pointing them to God away from their idols, you are taking from them the very thing they are hoping for or seeking "life" in. When you call someone to abandon his false hopes, it feels like you are stealing his canteen of water and leaving him stranded in a desert. In their fear, loneliness and despair they are prone to lash out at those now offering a new source of life. The way you respond to these attacks is critical for the gospel to take root.[3]

I have been involved in many conversations with gays and lesbians, especially on college campuses, as well as with those who are sympathetic to gay causes. I've learned that it's okay to let people beat up on us verbally. We can let them pound on our chests, figuratively. We, as God's people, are not that fragile and don't have to respond as if we are. I've learned that, after an episode of someone being in my face for calling into question a deeply felt belief, there is usually a silent moment—a breathing space—that I can now speak into with gentleness. It's then that I can often form a question, aimed at the heart, based on something the person has said—even if it was said in anger.

Bearing with people in gentleness gives an open door to the gospel that neither retreating nor using a like-mannered heated response ever will! This disarms and opens up hearts like nothing else can. The problem is that our own fear, unbelief, anger, defensiveness, self-righteousness, and uncertainty about what to say often gets in the way, so that often we never even get to that point!

Talking to those who are blind to the reality of their hearts, but who live in a world that supports and applauds spiritual rebellion, is both a privilege and a challenge. They are victims of their own sin, as well as caught in the lies and sins of others. But they are also accountable before a holy God for their continued choices to live on their own terms and for their refusal to submit to Christ. We must address both of these realities as we share Christ.

Gently instructing also means being grounded in the Scripture, not our own opinions. The real issue regarding what Scripture says about homosexuality is not about whether key passages are culturally relevant anymore, but whether Scripture, in its entirety, still has authority over all life. It should always be the truths of Scripture, and not our demeanor or presentation of it, that people reject.

4. Mercifully pursue, and then engage, the heart. "And have mercy on those who doubt; save others by snatching them out of the fire; to others show mercy with fear, hating even the garment stained by the flesh" (Jude 22–23). God calls us to be neither reclusive nor rude, but to move boldly into confusing, high-stakes situations with the gospel of his mercy. This means we bring the gospel where it is most needed. We pursue and engage the vocally anti-Christian pro-gay activist, the mild-mannered clergy who says the love of Jesus means

affirming homosexuality as God's gift, the out-and-proud lesbian in our office, the confused and scared teenager who fears he's gay and believes there is no other option to pursue, and the sexually abused woman who now sees a relationship with a woman as her only hope.

Showing mercy means practically caring for people in all their confusion, fears, doubts, and fallen thinking. It means being patient and persistent, holding our ground with those who say we are hateful bigots because we disagree with their beliefs. These are the characteristics of *missional ministry* to homosexual strugglers in the church and the gay community. As we do this, we are enabled to move into other people's worlds intentionally and with genuineness and authenticity, as servants and fellow sinners.

I once approached a man who was marching in a gay rally for two hours in pouring rain in South Florida's ninety-eight-degree heat and humidity. I said, "Sir, may I speak with you for a moment?" (He paused.) "What's so important to you that you would spend two hours, walking around in this heat and downpour? What point are you trying to get across here?" (The best kind of evangelism always begins with addressing the obvious, what's right in sight—what we hear and observe.) Subsequently, we had a two-hour conversation that ended with him shaking my hand and thanking me for stopping him—in spite of the fact that I shared the gospel and asked him to consider if God might have a different plan for his life. I listened to him, heard his concerns, and then engaged his heart with matters important to him—and to God. He actually invited me to a party with the other demonstrators that was being held afterward.

Engaging people on this level gets them into their story more quickly than anything else, and that's what we want. When people get into their stories, their personal histories and experiences, they become more open to us and to the gospel. Jesus was the master of this; therefore, we should try to be like the Master. His methods are often the most underutilized aspects of evangelism, and yet they make the deepest and most heartfelt impact, often leaving people wanting more!

You may be thinking, "Okay, this is all fine and good, but where do faith and repentance come in?" My answer is, "Everywhere!" People of the Reformed faith know that awareness of truth, and conviction of sin happen in hundreds of little ways and in many small steps before it becomes faith with a capital "F"—and repentance with a capital "R." Jesus pursues us in many ways, in the context of both little and big things: traumas, problems, life's hurts and disappointments, the loss of friendships or jobs—and even in life's successes, especially when we think we have it all and are happy but then realize we're not. God uses all that life brings our way—and especially, when it all comes crashing down around us—to get our attention and begin to question life decisions and choices. He uses all these same elements in the lives of homosexuals to bring them to Christ.

However, God rarely does this in a void. He uses other people—*his* people. I've seen this over and over again in the lives of those who come to our ministry—or any church-based ministry that offers help to those with out-of-control sexual desires and behaviors. In fact, that's the basis of one of Harvest USA's books, *Gay Such Were Some of Us: Stories of Transformation and Change.*[4] The twelve stories in that book all testify to the power of others who were part of the process of faith and repentance in each life.

The homosexual sinner needs and must experience what we all must experience. Thomas Chalmers had it right in his marvelous address, "The Expulsive Power of a New Affection." He explains how our sin, our habits and flaws, don't ever just disappear by a process of reason or mental determination (understanding them or trying harder). But while the bad affections of the heart—that by which we stand condemned, that which drives us into the dark places, that which corrupts, and that which robs us of true life—can't normally be destroyed, they may be dispossessed by something greater.[5]

Only when we are truly melted and moved by the sight, knowledge, and sense of God in Christ will our natural affections be changed. Only when we begin to understand God's love for us continually in Christ, through the riches of his grace, will the appeal of our sin begin to pale in comparison. Only when grace is understood, applied, and lived out to the point that we realize we "stand" in grace because of Jesus—that we don't crawl into it, creep into it, shuffle into it, or slink into it—then and only then will we see the deadly and life-robbing nature of all idols of the heart. These same truths are true for those struggling with homosexuality.

A Puritan prayer so rightly captures the essence of this—of what has to happen in every heart, gay or straight: "When thy Son, Jesus, came into my soul instead of sin he became more dear to me than sin had formerly been; His kindly rule replaced sin's tyranny. Teach me to believe that if ever I would have any sin subdued I must not only labour to overcome it, but must invite Christ to abide in the place of it, and he must become more to me than that vile lust has been; that his sweetness, power, life may be there."[6]

Those caught in fighting improper desires of homosexuality and those who have fully embraced homosexuality as a life and identity need the same thing—and are changed by these same truths. Do we have faith that this can happen? Do we believe the gospel still brings sight to the blind and releases the prisoners? Are we willing to be part of this salvage-and-rescue effort for the glory of Christ and the reclamation of sinners?

If we agree that we must be about this saving work, it will radically change how we "do church," how we begin to boldly address these problem areas among our own people—and how we will enter into and engage a lost and broken world.

CRAFTING AN EVANGELICAL, REFORMED, AND MISSIONAL THEOLOGY FOR THE TWENTY-FIRST CENTURY

A. T. B. MCGOWAN

This closing chapter draws together a number of themes and ideas I have explored over the past few years at various conferences and in various books. It also builds significantly on the WRF Statement of Faith (which can be found online at http://www.wrfnet.org/c/document_library/get_file?folderId=20&name=DLFE-46.pdf and as an appendix to the eBook version of this book). I appreciate the opportunity presented by this book to bring these various themes into a structured attempt to outline what an evangelical Reformed theology for the remainder of the twenty-first century might look like. This final chapter is divided into four main sections: first, the history of Reformed theology; second, the nature of Reformed theology; third, the method of Reformed theology; and fourth, the future of Reformed theology.

THE HISTORY OF REFORMED THEOLOGY

The intention of this first section is accomplish three things: first, to say a little about the Scottish Reformation of 1560; second, to highlight the need to look back and also to look forward when crafting a Reformed theology for the twenty-first century; and third, to emphasize the importance of understanding and critically evaluating our Reformed tradition.

The Scottish Reformation of 1560

The 2010 General Assembly of the World Reformed Fellowship marked the 450th anniversary of the Scottish Reformation. As a Scottish Reformed theologian, the Reformation of 1560 provides the foundation for my theology; therefore, an understanding of that event is crucial in any attempt to create a new Reformed theology for the twenty-first century. Let me begin, then, by highlighting three key benefits that the Reformation of 1560 brought to the life of the Church of Scotland: a Reformed theology, a Presbyterian system of church government, and a new form of church/state relationship.

First, in order to understand what we mean by Reformed theology, we must first reflect on the earliest history of the Reformation. The Reformation began with Martin Luther's rediscovery of the doctrine of justification and spread as he further developed his critique of medieval Roman Catholic theology and practice. For a time, the Reformation movement was united in basic theology, general principles and principal objectives.

There came a point, however, when there was a major split among the early Reformers—largely because of a disagreement over the doctrine of the Lord's Supper between Luther and Ulrich Zwingli. From this point on, the Reformation movement was divided into two main camps—the Lutherans on the one side, and those who came to be known as the Reformed on the other side. A generation later, John Calvin and John Knox were among the inheritors of this Reformed strand. The theology developed in the Reformed strand had much in common with the Lutheran strand, but was also quite distinct from it in a number of doctrinal areas.

The Church of Scotland became a church that was Reformed in theology. This theology was expressed first in the Scots Confession of 1560. In the post-Reformation period, partly due to the development of covenant theology and partly in response to Arminianism, other confessions were written. Of the churches that participated in the

Westminster Assembly, the Church of Scotland was the only one that adopted the Westminster Confession of Faith; the Congregationalists later adapted it to suit their purposes (The Savoy Declaration), as did the Baptists (The London Confession). From 1647 until the present day, the Westminster Confession of Faith has been the principal subordinate standard of the Church of Scotland.

A second benefit was a system of church government. Undoubtedly, the Presbyterian system of church government is one of Scotland's great gifts to the Reformed church. Indeed, Reformed churches all over the world look to the Church of Scotland as the "Mother Kirk (church)" from which they derive their Presbyterianism.

In the New Testament, elders were appointed in every place, and these elders exercised oversight and pastoral care of the young Christian churches. Between that time and the Reformation, a complex system of clerical oversight was established in the churches, with a hierarchy of clergy, including priests, bishops, archbishops, cardinals, and a pope. The Reformation provided a return to a simpler New Testament pattern. We find the beginnings of this in the earlier Reformers, in Zwingli, and supremely in Calvin.

However, it was John Knox and his associates who worked it out in a comprehensive and detailed manner, and in the context of a nation. In Scotland since 1560 there has been both a strong emphasis on biblical eldership and resistance to any notion of bishops or other hierarchical structures. During much of the seventeenth century, our forefathers had to battle against monarchs and parliaments who wanted to control the church through bishops.

The third major benefit coming out of the Scottish Reformation was a new form of church/state relationship. There are basically four ways in which church and state can be related. First, the state controls the church (Church of England). Second, the church controls the state (medieval papacy). Third, separation of church and state (Anabaptists, the United States). Finally, there is the Reformed position—that church and state owe duties and responsibilities to each other.

The beginnings of the last two positions are to be found in Martin Luther's "two kingdoms" doctrine. Luther argued that both church and state were ordained by God. The fatal weakness of Luther's position was that he believed they should operate in separate spheres. Calvin, however, argued that church and state owe duties and responsibilities to one another, and that the state has a duty to protect and guard the liberty of the church. However, he was not able to put this teaching into effect beyond the confines of Geneva. Again, it was John Knox who so developed this position as to see it in national terms and to argue for Reformed nations. He was followed by Andrew Melville, who was really the great architect of this principle as it worked out in Scotland.

This led to what is called "the establishment principle," whereby the Church of Scotland is in a unique relationship to the state—such that there can be no appeal against the General Assembly to the civil courts. Interestingly, this establishment principle is adhered to even by some of the denominations that have seceded from the Church of Scotland, such as the Free Church of Scotland.

The relationship between church and state in Scotland is unique, and it stands in marked contrast to the Anabaptist and voluntarist practices elsewhere in the Reformed world. Alongside that establishment principle was a system of parishes designed to ensure that the gospel reached to every corner of the land. This system is somewhat under threat today, due to the changes in European and UK law, but it is worth preserving and protecting.

Looking Back and Looking Forward

The second point to be made in this section is the importance of both looking back and looking forward, when crafting a Reformed theology for the twenty-first century. It is right that we should look back and celebrate the Scottish Reformation, but we must also recognize that *reformation can never be simply an event in the past but must also be an ongoing movement*. We must not only celebrate our Reformed heritage but also critically evaluate it to ensure that we build a Reformed church and a Reformed theology fit for purpose in the twenty-first century.

Many people in our Reformed tradition believe that to be Reformed means endlessly to restate and to defend the doctrinal formulations of the sixteenth and seventeenth centuries and fiercely to resist any change, progress, or development, even in the language used in our doctrinal statements. While our theology must remain true to its early roots, it must also take account of much that has happened since then.

Understanding and Evaluating Our Reformed Tradition

The third point of this section is simply to state two key principles. First, in order to craft a Reformed theology for the twenty-first century, it is vital to have a proper understanding of our Reformed tradition. It might be thought that this is self-evident, but unfortunately it is not. Many who stand within the Reformed tradition fondly imagine that the particular tradition in which they themselves stand is the true (or *only*) representative of Reformed theology. This myopia is astonishing, given the range of fine volumes available today that provide detailed historical descriptions of each of the main strands of Reformed theology. In any attempt to craft a Reformed theology for the twenty-first century, we must be sure that we understand the breadth and significance of our tradition, as it has found expression in many nations and in many churches.

The second principle is that we must be objective and honest in evaluating our Reformed tradition. There is an understandable reluctance to be critical of those who have gone before us, especially those whom we highly esteem and from whom we have learned a great deal. Yet, we must be prepared to submit our Reformed tradition to objective, honest scrutiny and evaluation. It would surely be astonishing if our forebears had all of the truth and had made no mistakes! This evaluation will often involve reading those whose views are quite different from our own, since as outsiders they may see things we have failed to see. This involves doing serious theology.

Unfortunately, many seminaries in our Reformed tradition are more like catechetical schools than true theological schools—that is to say, there are some places where people only read books that they know in advance are "sound" and with which they know they will agree. We must read and think widely and learn to evaluate the criticisms of our Reformed tradition made by those in other traditions. An intemperate rush to the defense, every time the Reformed tradition is criticized, is not in the spirit of Reformed theology. We must learn to admit our mistakes and be willing to accept criticism.

THE NATURE OF REFORMED THEOLOGY

There are also three points to be made in this second section. First, Reformed theology is a school of thought, not a strand of thought; second, Reformed theology must incorporate both a world- and a life-view; and third, Reformed theology must be rational but not rationalistic.

School—Not Strand—of Thought

Most readers of this book stand within the Calvinistic strand of Reformed theology; however, that represents only one strand within that broader school. It is therefore a matter of concern when certain Calvinists insist that a particular doctrinal assertion is Reformed and condemn others within the Reformed tradition who do not share their doctrinal conclusions. Often, these people believe themselves to have a monopoly on what is Reformed—a view that is quite contrary to the nature and history of Reformed theology.

Reformed theology has always been a school of thought with many strands. In the earliest days of the Reformation, scholars throughout Europe were developing Reformed ideas—Martin Bucer in Strasburg, Ulrich Zwingli and Heinrich Bullinger in Zurich, John Calvin and Theodore Beza in Geneva, Caspar Olevianus and Zacharias Ursinus in Heidelberg, to say nothing of Peter Martyr Vermigli who was everywhere! Add to this the theologians of Holland, England, and Scotland, and you have a fascinating school of thought. These various strands of Reformed theology did not always agree, and often came to contradictory conclusions. They also produced confessional statements which were quite different from one another in structure and content. For example, compare the Second Helvetic Confession with the Heidelberg Catechism, and then with the later Westminster Confession of Faith. Yet all were recognized as Reformed. There was a healthy debate between the strands, and no one strand was regarded as having all of the truth.

However, today some Calvinists believe they can tell us what is "truly Reformed." They believe that their particular strand of Reformed theology is the only one, and that the rest of us must accept it or suffer the consequences. This attitude is obvious in some of the language they use—on many matters they will tell us that their view is *the* Reformed position. Notice that definitive article!

Those who hold to the Reformed faith must resist insisting that only one strand of Reformed theology is acceptable. Like the early Reformers, we must learn to show respect for Reformed brothers and sisters who choose to express their theology in a different language and with different emphases.

World- and Life-View

Unfortunately, some have reduced Reformed theology to soteriology and, when asked to define Reformed theology, will speak about the five points of Calvinism. We need to see Reformed theology as both a worldview and a life-view.

One of the most significant but somewhat undervalued theologians of the early twentieth century was Professor James Orr of the United Free Church College in Glasgow. He was a friend of B. B. Warfield and wrote some of the articles in the original "Fundamentals" booklets, as well as some of the most significant early responses to German liberal theology. In 1891, Orr delivered the first series of the Kerr Lectures, later published under the title *A Christian View of God and the World*, outlining Calvinism not simply as a five-point soteriology but as a world- and life-view.

It is the Dutch who are usually credited in Reformed circles with having developed "world- and life-view" Reformed theology. In particular, mention is usually made of Abraham Kuyper's *Lectures on Calvinism*, which he gave as the Stone Lectures at Princeton in 1898. However, in his first footnote, Kuyper references Orr's earlier book, and a reading of Kuyper's work demonstrates the strong influence of Orr upon his own theology.

This understanding of Reformed theology is vital if we are to avoid our theology being reduced to a system of doctrines concerning the salvation of humans. In Scotland, we have drawn much of our Reformed thinking from the English Puritans and the American Princetonians. In doing so, we have tended to neglect the Dutch Calvinist tradition, especially the work of Kuyper and Herman Bavinck. For example, in the highlands of Scotland where I live, many people who become Christians are taught that they must now stop playing the fiddle or the accordion and stop taking an interest in Gaelic music and tradition; they must read only Christian books and go only to Christian meetings. All other music, painting, literature, sculpture, theatre, ballet, and so on are described as "worldly" and are to be avoided.

The Dutch do not see things that way. Instead, they argue that we must have a worldview that sees all of art as part of God's good creation, and that it must be redeemed and claimed. It is no coincidence that there is a great tradition of Dutch Christian painters, but few Christian painters in the English and Scottish traditions.

The Dutch Calvinist view is that Christians must engage with the nation and with the culture at every level. Kuyper himself was a minister, a theologian, the editor of a daily newspaper, the founder of a Christian university, the founder of a Christian political party and, ultimately, Prime Minister of Holland. He saw no conflict between these roles because he believed that every thought must be taken captive for Christ. In crafting an evangelical Reformed theology for the twenty-first century, we would do well to take heed of this important tradition—which, I believe, is much more biblical than the culture-denying escapism of the Anabaptist and Fundamentalist movements that have so influenced sections of the Reformed church.

When I was a student in the 1970s, it was Francis Schaeffer who encouraged us to develop a worldview—to think carefully about the social, cultural, and philosophical influences that were affecting human thought so that we could speak the gospel into those contexts. The argument was that, unless we understood the mind of the culture, we would not be able to communicate Christ. Today, I believe that the work being done by Dr. Peter Jones (www.truthXchange.com), highlighting the dangers of new spiritualities and the resurgence of various forms of paganism, is equally important and makes him the Schaeffer of our day. Jones explains clearly that a worldview is being communicated today that stands in marked contrast to biblical Christianity and often slips under the radar.

Rational, Not Rationalistic

The third point to be made here is that Reformed theology must be rational but not rationalistic. I believe we have a great deal to learn from Reformed Christians in the southern hemisphere in this area. Those of us who live and work in Europe and North America have often been arrogant and patronizing toward Christians in Africa, Asia, and South America, imagining that they must learn from us. The truth is, the leadership of the worldwide church has moved south; and it is the church leaders in Africa, Asia, and South America who are now standing up for biblical truth when so many churches in the northern hemisphere have capitulated.

For this reason, we must learn from our African, Asian, and South American brothers and sisters as we seek to craft an evangelical Reformed theology for the twenty-first century. In particular, we must learn from their understanding of spirituality, their strong doctrine of the work of the Holy Spirit, and their emphasis on the importance of the battle against demonic powers and evil spirits.

The Enlightenment has influenced those of us in Europe and North America more than we like to think, and we have often been guilty of rationalism. This realization came to me with particular force during the discussions of the WRF Theological Commission, as we sought to prepare a new statement of theology for the twenty-first century. Time and again, we Europeans and Americans would come up with a carefully worked-out doctrinal formulation—all very rational and logical—and time and again, our brothers from the southern hemisphere would gently correct us and show us our blind spots.

THE METHOD OF REFORMED THEOLOGY

This brings us to the third main section of this chapter—namely, the method of Reformed theology. There are three points to be made here.

First, we must be always reforming. Second, we must demonstrate humility and respect as we do our theology. Along with that, and third, we must be willing to learn.

Always Reforming

One of the slogans of the Reformed churches since the end of the seventeenth century has been *semper reformanda*—"always reforming." To be always reforming will involve a number of things, but above all it will involve the practice of constantly submitting our theological views to the bar of Scripture. We must not assume that every doctrinal statement we have inherited is true and is beyond criticism. We must regularly reexamine our doctrinal formulations, rather than simply restate and defend them.

Reformed churches have always said that they believe in the principle of *ecclesia semper reformanda* (the church always reforming), but there is often little evidence of this. Many Calvinists give the impression that theology stopped with Calvin—or, at the very latest, when the Westminster Confession of Faith was completed! Calvin would have been appalled by this attitude, and so would the Westminster divines themselves. We must be always reforming.

One of the theologians from whom I have learned most is the late Professor John Murray. On one occasion he wrote about the need to develop further the old covenant theology; however, his words have a more general import.

> Theology must always be undergoing reformation. The human understanding is imperfect. However architectonic may be the systematic constructions of any one generation or group of generations, there always remains the need for correction and reconstruction so that the structure may be brought into closer approximation to the Scripture and the reproduction be a more faithful transcript or reflection of the heavenly exemplar.[1]

On the negative side, to be always reforming means that we must not be afraid to admit mistakes or wrong emphases in the past, and to recognize that we do not have all the truth. On the positive side, it means freedom from the fear of thinking new thoughts and reconstructing old thoughts.

Humility and Respect

We must be humble as we state what we believe and avoid the arrogance that has so often characterized those in the Reformed tradition. We need to listen with respect to theologians from other traditions, perhaps especially those with whom we most disagree. Dialogue, particularly in an ecumenical context, has often been regarded negatively by those in the Reformed tradition; nonetheless, it is an important element of our witness to Christ. As we engage in dialogue we must display both honesty and humility. If we talk only to those who share our Reformed theology and shout across the barricades at everyone else, how do we expect to win people for Christ?

We need to develop an approach to theology that is gracious and shows respect. Reformed theologians have often been guilty of rudeness, disrespect, and an arrogant dismissal of those with whom we disagree. We talk about heresies quickly—*too* quickly—and are always ready to go to war (often within the camp), and yet are very slow to obey the scriptural injunctions about grace, kindness, gentleness, love, and respect.

Willingness to Learn

We must not dismiss theologians completely because of some areas of disagreement. The way some Reformed theologians have treated J. I. Packer and John Stott is disgraceful. I often find in students an unfortunate tendency to divide the world into good guys and bad guys, with the bad guys being dismissed without further discussion—and they get this attitude from their teaching elders. For example, we may disagree with Karl Barth on many issues, but his contribution to the battle against the old classical liberal theology should never be underestimated.

Instead of this negative attitude, we must develop a warm-hearted and welcoming Reformed theology. It is my contention that Scotland offers to Reformed Christianity a model of a warmhearted and wel-coming Calvinism. In general, Scottish theologians have rejected an overly rationalistic approach to theology. There has always been a strong emphasis on a theology that can be preached and includes a great deal of grace. Most of our best theologians have been or are preachers who serve with a love for the grace of God in the gospel. Thus, they are less likely to be hard-hearted and negative in their thinking. And while we have had our share of controversy and theological disputes over the centuries, in general Scottish theologians have not devoted their work to controversy and argument.

The Reformed faith has often received bad press today, precisely because so many of its proponents appear to be hard, negative, and angry most of the time! I have to say that I have friends in the US (and there are some much closer at hand) who are capable Reformed men, but who seem to spend their whole lives and all of their publications doing battle on the latest theological issue. They are perpetually at war with someone! The mantra of "defending the faith" can easily be used as a cover for a mentality that enjoys the battle and relishes a fight.

A warmhearted Calvinism entails a refusal to view the Reformed faith negatively. Let me give you an example: Some years ago at the Scottish Reformed Conference, an English minister presented a paper in which he explained what he understood to be the meaning of the word "Reformed." Unfortunately, the whole definition was in nega-tive terms—to be Reformed you had to be anti-Arminian, anti-Roman Catholic, anti-charismatic, anti-Billy Graham, and so on. Undoubtedly there are some in Scotland who identify with this and have taken a similar position, but I would suggest they have always been a small mi-nority and that the central tradition of Scottish Reformed Christianity has been warm, open, and engaging.

THE FUTURE OF REFORMED THEOLOGY

As we seek to craft an evangelical Reformed theology for the twenty-first century, there are certain areas which require some work—again, in three specific areas. First, we must recover some of Calvin's core themes; second, we must simplify some of our theological structures; and third, we must reemphasize the importance of the two key themes of sovereignty and grace.

Recovery of Calvin's Core Themes

Calvin's core themes have not exactly been lost in Reformed theology. However, they have often been overlaid with a thousand qualifications and explanations—in the process, dispelling the simplicity, clarity, and beauty of Calvin's own expression of them. I am thinking of such themes as the knowledge of God, the sovereignty of God, the grace of God, the fatherhood of God, the adoption of God, and the Word of God.

We must also recover Calvin's strong emphasis on the person and work of the Holy Spirit. Calvin was supremely a theologian of the Holy Spirit—something that could not be said of many of his successors. Similarly, his commitment to a theology of common grace has been largely neglected, except in the Dutch tradition. Above all, Calvin's high Trinitarian theology has not always been understood and appropriated within our tradition. Many modern Reformed theologians have seen the Trinity simply as a doctrinal formulation to be included somewhere in our doctrine of God. The way Calvin centered his whole theological system in the Trinity is a masterful example we ought to rediscover.

Simplification of Structures

The best way to explain what I mean by simplification of structures is to give an example. My main research interest over the years has been in the rise and development of covenant theology, particularly as it has impacted Scottish theology. It seems to me, however, that the whole edifice of covenant theology has become top-heavy and unsustainable in its present form.

The simplicity of Calvin's teaching on the one covenant of grace could usefully be recovered. Through the late sixteenth and seventeenth centuries the whole idea of the covenant was built upon so that we ended up with the Covenant of Works, the Covenant of Redemption, and the Covenant of Grace. The sheer complexity of this system renders it less useful than it could be. Also, the old federal theology has certain inherent weaknesses, some of which were highlighted by John Murray in his opposition to Meredith Kline's views. There is a real need to strip back some of the complexity and elaborations of federal theology and return to Calvin's simplicity. I have advocated what I call "headship theology," using Romans 5 and 1 Corinthians 15 as a means of regaining simplicity. This enables us to use the word "covenant" precisely as it is used in Scripture and by Calvin—namely, as an overarching concept to describe the relationship between God and his people.

The other area where we might simplify structures concerns a recovery of Calvin's *ordo salutis*. Reformed theology has so elaborated upon *ordo salutis* as to make it somewhat unfit for purpose. Calvin's *ordo salutis*, by contrast, was very simple: union with Christ leading to justification on the one hand, and sanctification on the other hand. The recent work of Richard Gaffin and others on the doctrine of union with Christ as the central element in salvation has been helpful, but it needs to be taken up by others.

Reaffirmation of Sovereignty and Grace

In all this work of recovery and simplification, we must reaffirm the vital relationship between two of the fundamental elements of Reformed theology: the sovereignty of God and the grace of God. When Reformed theology has placed too much emphasis on the sovereignty of God and neglected the love and grace of God, we have ended up with a cold, legalistic, determinist theology that has denied the free offer of the gospel. When Reformed theology has placed too much emphasis on the love and grace of God and neglected the sovereignty of God, we have ended up with a weak, liberal Christianity with no real sense of God's justice and judgment. Only when God's sovereignty and God's grace are held in proper balance will Reformed theology be true to the teaching of Scripture and true to its own best instincts.

CONCLUSION

I believe that the development of an evangelical Reformed theology for the twenty-first century requires a much closer relationship between the church and the academy. On the one hand, the church has often been suspicious of the academy, believing that so-called ivory-tower theologians have little concern for the church and dismissing arguments about academic freedom as an excuse for departing from the confessional position of the church. On the other hand, the academy has often viewed the church as failing to take seriously the important work theologians do in the areas of biblical, historical, systematic, and pastoral theology. The academy has accused the church of using it simply as a machine to churn out candidates for the ministry.

As a theologian who is also a minister of the gospel, having worked in both church and academy, I believe that the many misunderstandings and misrepresentations on both sides have been deeply damaging and must be overcome. The church must recognize the importance of the academy and support those who are engaged in serious academic study. The academy must, in turn, recognize that theology must be carried out in the service of the church.

When Karl Barth began to write his dogmatic theology, he called the first volume "Christian Dogmatics." He then began again, this time calling his finished work *Church Dogmatics*. This was a most significant move. In similar vein, many of the theologians in the Scottish universities used to wear their clerical collars when teaching, in order to demonstrate that they understood their theological vocation as an aspect of their calling to the ministry. We need to recover that sense of unity of purpose between church and academy.

This brings me to my final point—namely, future hope. I hope that Reformed theology will constantly reexamine its doctrinal formulations in the light of Scripture—the infallible Word of God—and that Reformed theology will be firmly rooted in the life of the church. I hope that Reformed theology will have its roots in the sixteenth century but its top branches firmly in the twenty-first century. I hope that Reformed theology will be recognized as a school of thought and not a single strand. I hope that Reformed theology will develop a world- and life-view, will be open to the leading and guiding of the Holy Spirit, and will avoid overly rationalistic formulations. I hope that Reformed theology will be respectful of those with whom we disagree, will show humility and respect, and will always be willing to learn. I hope that Reformed theology will learn from Calvin, but also from Bavinck and others. I hope that Reformed theology will hold on to the fundamental tenets of our system, while being willing to explore, experiment, and take risks. I hope that we will listen carefully to Martin Allen, when he says in the opening chapter of this volume, that such theology must have "a proper engagement in mission." Above all, I hope that Reformed theology will honor God and be used to explain the truth of the Scriptures to a fallen world, in order that more men and women and children may come to know our Lord and Savior Jesus Christ.

MISSIONAL IS MISSION CRITICAL

FRANK A. JAMES, III

This volume had its origins at the 2010 WRF General Assembly ("Continuing the Reformation: A Missional Theology for the 21st Century"), and this missional commitment found deep resonance later that same year at the Lausanne Congress in Cape Town, where it was embedded in "The Cape Town Commitment." I want to commend the WRF and the Lausanne movement for their commitment to the missional vision for the Church.

I am rather protective of this word "missional." It seems that everyone is now missional. An ever-increasing number of seminaries, church-planting organizations, missionary agencies, and churches have now appropriated the term on their websites. Lead largely by younger leaders, evangelicals have moved from suspicion to celebration of the missional. But we must not allow it to become a mere buzzword, the latest fad, or the lingo of trendy Christianity. To be missional takes courage. It requires a revision of what it means to live out the gospel in this messy postmodern world. It obliges us to contemplate the Trinity in deeper ways—just as God the Father sent the Son, and God the Father together with the Son sent the Spirit, so also the Triune God sends the church on a redemptive mission into the world. To be missional is to accept the challenge and responsibility to be his agents in advancing his mission.

To my Reformed sisters and brothers I want to stress that missional is not a static proposition; rather it is a dynamic way of living the gospel in a culturally complex world—not unlike the world of Jesus and the apostles. Isn't that part of what Paul is saying to the Corinthians: *"I have become all things to all people, that by all means I might save some. I do it all for the sake of the gospel..."*? (1 Corinthians 9:22–23) Missional is a humble recognition of our own finitude and fallenness; it is a quiet confidence in the redemptive power of the mission-Giver; and it is always authentic and generous as it engages this muddled world. The missional mind-set changes everything.

The missional idea has an infinite number of manifestations. As this volume demonstrates, it is connected to the world outside our front door—profoundly impacting how we engage urban ministry, poverty, social justice, sex-trafficking, child abuse, violence against women, and homosexuality. It also extends to every quarter of the globe, and in both cases it requires a new sensitivity to the resident cultural complexities and a commitment to work within such complexities. As Reformed Christians we are keenly aware of our own fallenness and that kingdom work is work in a fallen world. Luther was right: "we are beggars all."

As I assume the mantle of leadership at Biblical Seminary, it is gratifying to know that President Dave Dunbar is entrusting to me a school that made the missional turn before it became fashionable and at considerable cost. I am delighted that the subtitle of this book has taken the Biblical Seminary motto: *Following Jesus into the World.* That is what we all must do.

ENDNOTES

Foreword: What Do We Mean by "Missional"?

1. Christopher J. H. Wright, *The Mission of God: Unlocking the Bible's Grand Narrative* (Downers Grove, IL: InterVarsity Press, 2006).

2. The Cape Town Commitment, I.10. © 2011 The Lausanne Movement. Permission to quote and full text available at http://www.lausanne.org/en/documents/ctcommitment.html.

SECTION ONE: LAYING THE FOUNDATION

1. What a Missional Church Looks Like

1. Darrell L. Bock, *Acts* (Grand Rapids, MI: Baker, 2008), 66.

2. D. F. Wright, "The Great Commission and the Ministry of the Word," *Scottish Bulletin of Evangelical Theology* (Autumn 2007): 152.

3. Harry Reid, *Reformation—The Dangerous Birth of the Modern World* (St. Andrews: St. Andrews Press, 2009), 239–251.

4. Chris Green, *The Word of His Grace: A Guide to Teaching and Preaching from Acts* (Downers Grove, IL: InterVarsity Press, 2005), 48.

5. James Read, "More than the Spirit of Mission," *Scottish Bulletin of Evangelical Theology* (Spring 2009): 47.

6. Quoted in Philip Jenkins, *The Next Christendom* (New York: Oxford University Press, 2002), 43.

7. John Stott, *The Contemporary Christian: Applying God's Word to Today's World* (Downers Grove, IL: InterVarsity Press, 1992), 335.

8. David W. Smith, *Against the Stream* (Downers Grove, IL: InterVarsity Press, 2003), 109.

2. What's the Point in Believing and Doing the Right Things? A Missional Approach to Orthodox Belief and Moral Behavior

1. See, for example, Iain Hewitson, *Trust and Obey: Norman Shepherd and the Justification Controversy at Westminster Seminary* (Minneapolis: NextStep Resources, 2011); A. Donald MacLeod, *W. Stanford Reid: An Evangelical Calvinist in the Academy* (Montreal: McGill-Queen's University Press, 2004); and Section Five of the WRF Statement of Faith.

2. Quoted in Samuel T. Logan, Jr., "The Doctrine of Justification in the Theology of Jonathan Edwards," *The Westminster Theological Journal* 46 (1984): 26ff.

3. Ibid., 26.

4. Edwards, *Works*, vol. 1 (Kindle edition, published by B & R Samizdat Express), locations 39753–39765.

5. Ibid., locations 28869–28887.

6. Ibid.

7. Norman Fiering, *Jonathan Edwards's Moral Thought and Its British Context* (Chapel Hill, NC: The University of North Carolina Press, 1981).

8. Edwards, *Works*, vol. 1, locations 29010–29026.

9. Ibid., locations 29048–29075.

10. Ibid., locations 29618–29625.

11. Ibid., locations 29631–29650.

12. Ibid.

13. Ibid., locations 29696–29703.

14. Ibid., locations 29834–29840.

15. Ibid., locations 30839–30846.

16. Ibid., locations 30973–30986.

17. Ibid., locations 30979–30998.

18. Ibid., locations 31478–31490.

19. Ibid., locations 31712–31725.

20. Ibid., locations 32082–32088.

21. Ibid., locations 29417–29422.

22. "The World Reformed Fellowship: A Brief Case Statement," http://www.wrfnet.org/web/guest/aboutwrf/casestatement#affirmations (last accessed 1/18/13).

23. Edwards, *Works*, vol. 1, locations 33045–33083.

24. Ibid., locations 33659–33703.

25. Ibid., locations 33729–33786.

26. Ibid., locations 33914–33927.

27. Ibid., locations 34306–34326.

28. Christopher J. H. Wright, *The Mission of God's People: A Biblical Theology of the Church's Mission*, Kindle edition (Grand Rapids, MI: Zondervan, 2010), locations 466–476.

29. Edwards, *Works*, vol. 1, locations 23335–23348.

30. Ibid., locations 33909–33929.

31. The Cape Town Commitment, I.10.

3. The Book of Romans and the Missional Mandate: Why Mission and Theology *Must* Go Together

1. Krister Stendahl, *Der Jude Paulus und wir Heiden: Anfragen an das abendländische Christentum* (München, Chr. Kaiser, 1978), 42–49.

2. Emil Weber, "Die Beziehungen von Röm. 1–3 zur Missionspraxis des Paulus," *Beiträge zur Förderung christlicher Theologie 9* (1905) Issue 4, Gütersloh: C. Bertelsmann, 1905.

3. Z. B. Walter B. Russell III, "An Alternative Suggestion for the Purpose of Romans," *Bibliotheca Sacra* 145 (1988), 174–184; Paul S. Minear, "The Obedience of Faith: The Purpose of Paul in the Epistle to the Romans," *Studies in Biblical Theology 2/19* (London: SCM Press, 1971), 91–110; Nils Alstrup, "The Missionary Theology in the Epistle to the Romans," in *Studies in Paul: Theology for the Early Christian Mission* (Minneapolis: Augsburg, 1977), 70–94; Krister Stendahl, op. cit.; L. Grant McClung, "An Urban Cross-cultural Role Model: Paul's Self-image in Romans," *Global Church Growth* (Corunna/USA) 26 (1989) 1: 5–8; Gottlob Schrenk, "Der Römerbrief als Missionsdokument," in *Studien zu Paulus, Abhandlungen zur Theologie des Alten und Neuen Testaments 26* (Zuricj: Zwingli-Verlag, 1954), 81–106; Charles Van Engen, "The Effect of Universalism on Mission Effort," in *Through No Fault of Their Own?: The Fate of Those Who Have Never Heard*, William V. Crockett, James G. Sigountos, eds., (Grand Rapids, MI: Baker Book House, 1993), 183–194; Karl Müller, "Das universale Heilsdenken des Völkerapostels nach dem Galaterùund Römerbrief," *Studia Missionalia 9* (1955/56): 5–33; Chris Schlect, "Romans as a Missionary Support Letter," *Credenda Agenda 6*, no. 31994: 9; Robert L. Reymond, *Paul: Missionary Theologian* (Geanies House, Great Britain: Christian Focus Publications, 2000), 208–213.

4. Alstrup, op. cit., 70.

5. Reymond, *Paul: Missionary Theologian*.

6. A. F. Walls, "The First Chapter of the Epistle to the Romans and the Modern Missionary Movement," *Apostolic History and the Gospel: Biblical and Historical Essays Presented to F. F. Bruce on his 60th Birthday,* W. Ward Gasque, Ralph P. Martin, eds., (Grand Rapids, MI: William B. Eerdmans, 1970), 346–347.

7. Anders Nygren, *Der Römerbrief* (Gottingen: Vandenhoeck & Ruprecht, 1965), 53–54.

8. Russell III, "An Alternative Suggestion for the Purpose of Romans," 175.

9. Schrenk, "Der Römerbrief als Missionsdokument," 81.

10. Thomas Schirrmacher, *Der Römerbrief* (Hänssler: Neuhausen, 1994).

11. Adolf Schlatter, *Gottes Gerechtigkeit: Ein Kommentar zum Römerbrief* (Stuttgart: Calwer Verlag, 1993), 383.

12. C. E. B. Cranfield, *A Critical and Exegetical Commentary on the Epistle to the Romans*, 2 vols. (Edinburgh: T & T Clark, 1989; 1979 revised reprint), vol. 1, 18–19.

13. Much of the text in this section is adapted from my Foreword to Trevor McIlwain and Nancy Everson's *Auf festen Grund gebaut: Von der Schöpfung bis Christus* (Hänssler Verlag: Neuhausen, 1998), 9.

14. See Lois McKinney, "Why Renewal Is Needed in Theological Education," *Evangelical Missions Quarterly* 18 (April 1982): 93–94; and Harvie M. Conn, Samuel F. Rowen (eds.), *Missions and Theological Education in World Perspective* (Farmington, MI: Associates of Urbanus, 1984).

15. Paul A. Beals, *A People for His Name: A Church-Based Missions Strategy* (Pasadena, CA: William Carey Library, 1995), 199.

16. David Bosch, "Missions in Theological Education" in *Mobilmachung für die Mission: Wie können Mitarbeiter für den Missionsdienst gewonnen werden?*, Horst Engelmann (Wiedenst: Missionshaus Bibelschule, no year, approx. 1983), xxxi–xxxii.

17. Ibid., xxx–xxxi.

18. Following Beals. op. cit., 201.

19. Compare Thomas Schirrmacher, "Mission unter unerreichten Volksgruppen," 23–26; and "Vorwort," 11–12, in *Gebet für die Welt*, Patrick Johnstone (Hänssler: Holzgerlingen, 2003).

20. This paragraph corresponds to a definition that was produced by leading evangelical missions leaders and missiologists at a conference of the Lausanne Committee for World Evangelization in March 1982.

21. The following text is a reworking of my "Gemeinde und Mission im Römerbrief," *Evangelikale Missiologie 16* (2000) 3, 109–110.

SECTION TWO: THE CHURCH REACHES THE WORLD

4. A Missional Response to Poverty and Social Injustice

1. P. J. Buys, *Calvinism Does Not Teach Apartheid*, Potchefstroom: IRS study pamphlet no. 55.

2. Simon Usborne, "F.W. de Klerk: The Day I Ended Apartheid," *Sunday Independent*, February 2, 2010. http://www.independent.co.uk/news/world/africa/fw-de-klerk-the-day-i-ended-apartheid-1886128.html (last accessed 2/8/13).

3. Ibid.

4. Peter Goodspeed, "History or Hate Speech? Apartheid-Era Songs Open Old Wounds," *National Post*, April 2, 2010.

5. Cornelius Plantinga, *Not the Way It's Supposed to Be: A Breviary of Sin* (Grand Rapids, MI: Eerdmans, 1995), 10.

6. B.K. Waltke, "Righteousness in Proverbs," *Westminster Theological Journal* 70, no. 2, 2008:237.

7. Oxford Declaration on Christian Faith and Economics, Oxford Conference on Christian Faith & Economics, 1990, www.esa-online.org (last accessed 2/8/13).

8. Alexander Strauch, "Strengthening the Love of the Christian Family," *Emmaus Journal* 2, no. 1, 1993:59.

9. B. B. Warfield, *Faith and Life: "Conferences" in the Oratory of Princeton Seminary* (New York: Longmans, Green, and Co., 1916), 50.

10. As quoted by Strauch, 60.

11. Rodney Stark, *The Rise of Christianity: A Sociologist Reconsiders History* (Princeton, NJ: Princeton University Press, 1996), 78.

12. Quoted by John Battle, "A Brief History of the Social Gospel," *WRS Journal* (June 1, 1999): 8.

13. "The Micah Declaration on Integral Mission," http://www.micahnetwork.org/sites/default/files/doc/page/mn_integral_mission_declaration_en.pdf, 1 (last accessed 1/21/13).

14. Jeffrey D. Sachs, *The End of Poverty: Economic Possibilities of Our Time* (New York: Penguin, 2005), 18.

15. *Recht in Overvloed: Gerechtigheid en professionaliteit in de ontmoeting tussen arm en rijk*, G.J. Buijs and G. Verbeek, eds. (Budel: Damon. 2005), 12, 26.

16. Ibid, 12, 25.

17. Sachs, *The End of Poverty*, 82.

18. Ibid, 21.

19. Ibid, 189.

5. What Is God's Global Urban Mission?

1. Translation by Leslie C. Allen, *Word Biblical Commentary: Psalms 101-150, Volume 21* (Nashville, TN: Thomas Nelson Publishers, 2002), 210.

2. Frank Frick, *The City in Ancient Israel*, quoted in Harvie M. Conn and Manuel Ortiz, *Urban Ministry: The Kingdom, the City, and the People of God* (Downers Grove, IL: InterVarsity Press, 2001), 83.

3. Miroslav Volf, "Soft Difference: Theological Reflections on the Relation between Church and Culture in 1 Peter," http://www.yale.edu/faith/resources/x_volf_difference.html (last accessed 1/21/13).

4. Thomas Schreiner, *The New American Commentary: 1, 2 Peter, Jude, Volume 37* (Nashville, TN: Broadman, 2003), 124.

5. John R. W. Stott, *The Message of Acts: The Spirit, the Church, & the World* (Downers Grove, IL: InterVarsity Press, 1990), 293.

6. Rodney Stark, *The Rise of Christianity: How the Obscure, Marginal Jesus Movement Became the Dominant Religious Force in the Western World in a Few Centuries* (San Francisco: Harper, 1997), 161–162.

7. Richard Fletcher, *The Barbarian Conversion: From Paganism to Christianity* (Berkeley: The University of California Press, 1999).

8. Philip Jenkins, *The Next Christendom: The Coming of Global Christianity* (New York: Oxford University Press, 2002), 94.

9. Ibid.

10. See Harvie M. Conn, *Evangelism: Doing Justice and Preaching Grace* (Phillipsburg, NJ: Presbyterian and Reformed Publishing, 1992).

6. A Missional Approach to the Health of the City

1. WRF Statement of Faith, Section Ten, paragraphs 3–4.

2. Cornelius Plantinga, Jr., *Not the Way It's Supposed to Be: A Breviary of Sin* (Grand Rapids, MI: William B. Eerdmans Publishing, 1995), 7.

3. Herman N. Ridderbos, *The Coming of the Kingdom* (Phillipsburg, NJ: Presbyterian and Reformed Publishing, 1975), 44.

4. Henri J. M. Nouwen, Donald P. McNeill, and Douglas A. Morrison, *Compassion: A Reflection on the Christian Life* (New York: Doubleday, 1983), 27.

7. A Missional Response to Global Violence Against Women

1. "Elie Wiesel's Acceptance Speech, on the occasion of the award of the Nobel Peace Prize in Oslo, December 10, 1986," http://www.nobelprize.org/nobel_prizes/peace/laureates/1986/wiesel-acceptance.html (last accessed 1/22/13).

2. Amnesty International, "End the Cycle of Violence," http://www.amnestyusa.org/our-work/issues/women-s-rights/violence-against-women (last accessed 1/22/13).

3. Audrey Hector, "Sexual Abuse of Children," http://christiananswers.net/q-eden/childsexualabuse.html (last accessed 1/22/13).

4. Chuck Colson, Domestic Violence within the Church: The Ugly Truth," *Religion Today*, October 20, 2009, http://www.religiontoday.com/news/domestic-violence-within-the-church-the-ugly-truth-11602500.html (last accessed 2/2/13).

5. "Gendercide," *The Economist*, March 4, 2010, http://www.economist.com/node/15606229 (last accessed 1/22/13).

6. Stephen Lewis, "Lend a Hand," *The Globe and Mail*, May 25, 2000, A15; cited in Ruth Compton Brouwer, *Modern Women Modernizing Men: The Changing Missions of Three Professional Women in Asia and Africa, 1902–69* (Vancouver, BC: University of British Colombia Press, 2002).

7. "Women and HIV/AIDS," http://www.avert.org/women-hiv-aids.htm (last accessed 1/22/13).

8. Julia Dahl, "'Honor Killing' under Growing Scrutiny in the U.S.," http://www.cbsnews.com/8301-504083_162-57409395-504083/honor-killing-under-growing-scrutiny-in-the-u.s.

9. See "Background Information on Sexual Violence Used as a Tool of War," http://www.un.org/en/preventgenocide/rwanda/about/bgsexualviolence.shtml; and the website Stop Rape Now: UN Action Against Sexual Violence in Conflict, http://www.stoprapenow.org (both last accessed 1/22/13).

8. Worship and Children: A Missional Response to Child Sexual Abuse

1. The author wishes to thank Duncan Rankin and Victor Vieth for their invaluable comments and suggestion regarding the material in this chapter.

2. Quoted in Wess Stafford, *Too Small to Ignore: Why the Least of These Matter Most* (Colorado Springs: Waterbrook Press, 2007), 1.

3. Ibid., 2.

4. "Child Maltreatment 2009," U.S. Department of Health and Human Services, Administration for Children and Families, Administration on Children, Youth, and Families (2010), http://archive.acf.hhs.gov/programs/cb/pubs/cm09/cm09.pdf (last accessed 1/22/13).

5. D. H. Russell, *The Epidemic of Child Sexual Abuse in the United States* (Newbury Park, CA: Sage, 2000).

6. Noemi Pereda, Georgina Guilera, Maria Forms, and Juana Gomez-Benito, "The Prevalence of Child Sexual Abuse in Community and Student Samples: A Meta-Analysis," *Clinical Psychology Review* 29, no. 4 (2009).

7. Recent years have seen a rise in Internet websites that are devoted to reporting and exposing issues of child abuse within the faith community, including www.bishopaccountability.org, www.snapnetwork.org, www.stopbaptistpredators.org, www.mksafetynet.net, www.thehopeofsurvivors.com, www.speakingtruthinlove.org, and *Child Abuse Survivors News*, found at http://paper.li/allgodschilddoc/1307357916.

8. Anna C. Salter, *Predators, Pedophiles, Rapists, and Other Sex Offenders: Who They Are, How They Operate, and How We Can Protect Ourselves and Our Children* (New York: Basic Books, 2003), 12.

9. John Calvin, *Commentaries on the Epistle of Paul the Apostle to the Hebrews*, translated by John Owen (Grand Rapids, MI: Baker Book House, 1998), 338.

10. John M. Frame, *Worship in Spirit and Truth* (Phillipsburg, NJ: Presbyterian and Reformed Publishing, 1996), 37.

11. Frame, "Some Questions about the Regulative Principle," http://www.reformed.org/misc/index.html?mainframe=/misc/frame_regulative_principle.html (last accessed 1/22/13).

12. John Piper, "Jesus and the Children: Pondering Children as Pride Detectors," http://www.desiringgod.org/resource-library/taste-see-articles/jesus-and-the-children (last accessed 1/22/13).

13. The Barna Group, "Evangelism is Most Effective Amongst Kids" (2004), http://www.barna.org/barna-update/article/5-barna-update/196-evangelism-is-most-effective-among-kids (last accessed 1/22/13).

14. The Centers for Disease Control, "Adverse Childhood Experiences (ACE) Study," http://www.cdc.gov/ace/findings.htm (last accessed 1/22/13).

15. Lawson, Drebing, Berg, Vincellette, and Penk, "The Long Term Impact of Child Abuse on Religious Behavior and Spirituality in Men," *Child Abuse & Neglect* 22, no. 5, 1998: 369, 376–377.

16. Salter, 44.

17. Ibid., 42.

18. Ibid., 36.

19. Laurie Goodstein, "Vatican Declined to Defrock U.S. Priest Who Abused Boys," *The New York Times*, March 26, 2010.

20. Donna Eshuys and Stephen Smallbone, "Religious Affiliations among Adult Sexual Offenders," *Sexual Abuse: A Journal of Research and Treatment* 18, no. 3 (July 2006): 279–288.

21. Christa Brown, *This Little Light: Beyond a Baptist Preacher Predator and His Gang* (Cedarburg, WI: Foremost Press, 2009).

22. Salter, 45.

23. Ibid., 29.

24. "The Abel and Harlow Child Molestation Prevention Study" (2002), http://www.childmolestationprevention.org/pdfs/study.pdf (last accessed 1/22/13).

25. See Bill Moushey and Robert Dvorchak, *Game Over: Jerry Sandusky, Penn State, and the Culture of Silence* (New York: Harper Collins, 2012); and Victor Vieth, et al., "Lessons Learned from Penn State," *Centerpiece* (National Child Protection Training Center, 2012), http://www.ncptc.org/vertical/Sites/%7B8634A6E1-FAD2-4381-9C0D-5DC7E93C9410%7D/uploads/Vol_3_Issue_3__4.pdf (last accessed 1/22/13).

26. Brown, 22–24.

27. Ruben Rosario, "Amid the Penn State Outrage, Victims Have Been Forgotten," http://www.andersonadvocates.com/Posts/News-or-Event/980/Pioneer-Press-Ruben-Rosario-Amid-the-Penn-State-outrage-victims-have-been-forgotten.aspx (last accessed 1/22/13).

28. "A Snapshot of Pediatric Cancers," National Cancer Institute, Washington, DC: U.S. National Institutes of Health (2008).

29. S. R. Dube and others, "Long-Term Consequences of Childhood Sexual Abuse by Gender of Victim" *The American Journal of Preventive Medicine* 28 (2005): 430–438.

30. Janice Wolak, Kimberly Mitchell, and David Finkelhor, "Online Victimization of Youth, Five Years Later," Crimes against Children Research Center (2006), http://www.missingkids.com/en_US/publications/NC167.pdf (last accessed 1/22/13).

31. Abel and Harlow Child Molestation Prevention Study.

32. Daniel H. Grossoehme, "Child Abuse Reporting: Clergy Perceptions," *Child Abuse & Neglect: The International Journal*, 22, no. 7 (July 1998): 743–747.

33. Brown, 215–216; used by permission.

9. God Scatters to Gather through His People: A Missional Response to Migrant Churches

1. Lausanne Committee for World Evangelization, *Scattered to Gather: Embracing the Global Trend of Diaspora* (Manila, Philippines: LifeChange Publishing, 2010), 28.

2. The following section was an integral part of a position paper written and presented by Enoch Wan and I during the Lausanne Diasporas Strategy Consultation held in Manila on May 4-9, 2009. The article was later published in *Scattered to Gather*, 12–18. This whole section is used and adapted here with the written permission of LifeChange Publishing, Inc.

3. International Organization for Migration, "Facts and Figures: Global Estimates and Trends," http://www.iom.int/cms/en/sites/iom/home/about-migration/facts--figures-1.html (last accessed 1/23/13).

4. Jon Clifton, "150 Million Adults Worldwide Would Migrate to the U.S.," http://www.gallup.com/poll/153992/150-Million-Adults-Worldwide-Migrate.aspx (last accessed 1/23/13).

5. Julie Ray and Neli Esipova, "More Adults Would Move for Temporary Work Than Permanently," http://www.gallup.com/poll/153182/Adults-Move-Temporary-Work-Permanently.aspx (last accessed 1/23/13).

6. Sadiri Joy B. Tira, "Filipino International Network: Strategic Model for Filipino Diaspora Glocal® Missions," *Global Missiology*, October 2004.

7. Finishing the Task, "The UUPG [Unengaged, Unreached People Group] List," http://finishingthetask.com/uupgs.php?sort=Country (last accessed 1/23/13).

8. David F. Wells, *Above All Earthly Pow'rs: Christ in a Postmodern World* (Grand Rapids, MI: Wm. B. Eerdmans Publishing, 2005), 92–93.

9. Finishing the Task, "The Task," http://finishingthetask.com (last accessed 1/23/13).

10. "National Association of Evangelicals, "Evangelical Statement of Principles for Immigration Reform," http://www.nae.net/images/content/Evangelicals.Ad.Politico.pdf (last accessed 1/23/13).

11. Sarah Pulliam Bailey, "Exclusive: Focus on the Family's Jim Daly on a New Stance on Immigration Reform,"*Christianity Today*, http://www.christianitytoday.com/ct/2012/juneweb-only/exclusive-jim-daly-on-immigration.html (last accessed 1/23/13).

12. Chuck Colson, "Defending the Strangers in Our Midst: The De-monizing of Immigrants," http://www.breakpoint.org/commentaries/5473-defending-the-strangers-in-our-midst (last accessed 1/23/13).

13. Ibid.

14. Matthew Soerens, "God Loves the Minutemen (and He Expects Me To, Too)," http://faithandimmigration.org/blog/god-loves-minute-men-matthew-soerens (last accessed 1/31/13).

15. This section was also written and presented by Enoch Wan and me during the Lausanne Diasporas Strategy Consultation, and published in *Scattered to Gather*, 24–30; used with the written permission of LifeChange Publishing.

16. Quoted by David J. Hesselgrave, *Paradigms in Conflict: 10 Key Questions in Christian Missions Today* (Grand Rapids, MI: Kregel Publications, 2006), 316.

17. Enoch Wan, "Diaspora Missiology," *Occasional Bulletin of EMS* (Spring 2007), 3.

18. *The Bridges of God* was the title of one of Donald McGavran's first published books in 1954, which became a reference in the history of the Church Growth Movement. For a short version, see McGavran, "The Bridges of God," in *Perspectives on the World Christian Movement: A Reader*, Ralph D. Winter and Steven C. Hawthorne, eds., (Pasadena, CA: William Carey Library, 1999), 323–338.

19. *Scattered to Gather*, 29–35; used with the written permission of LifeChange Publishing. I have adapted or suppressed a few of the original terms.

20. Ibid, 29.

10. Dogma Meets Diversity in Europe—A Missional Response to Secularity

1. Glenn Smith, "Thinking After... Acting Again: God's Global Urban Mission in an Era of the Autonomous Self and Globalization," http://www.citywithoutwalls.net/glenn_smith_thinking_after.pdf, 3 (last accessed 1/24/13).

2. Craig van Gelder, "Secularization and the City: Christian Witness in Secular Urban Cultures," in *Discipling the City: A Comprehensive Approach to Urban Mission*, Roger Greenaway, ed. (Eugene, OR: Wipf and Stock, 1992).

3. Charles Taylor, *A Secular Age* (London: Belknap, 2007).

4. Soeren Kern, "UK: Leicester Has Elected Its First Muslim Mayor," http://halalfocus.net/uk-leicester-has-elected-its-first-muslim-mayor (last accessed 1/24/13).

5. Grace Davie, *Europe: The Exceptional Case: Parameters of Faith in the Modern World* (Maryknoll, NY: Orbis Books, 2002), 19; see also Davie, *Religion in Britain since 1945: Believing without Belonging* (Hoboken, NJ: Wiley-Blackwell, 1994), 69ff.

6. Raymond Bakke, *A Theology as Big as the City* (Downers Grove, IL: Inter-Varsity Academic, 1997), 13.

7. J. Andrew Kirk, *Mission under Scrutiny: Confronting Contemporary Challenges* (Minneapolis: Fortress Press, 2006), 88.

8. Philip Jenkins, *God's Continent: Christianity, Islam, and Europe's Religious Crisis* (New York: Oxford University Press, 2009), 117.

9. Ibid., 115.

10. Davie, *Europe: The Exceptional Case*, 15.

11. Robert Calvert, "Ecclesial Patterns among Migrant Churches in Rotterdam," http://www.google.com/url?sa=t&rct=j&q=&esrc=s&frm=1&source=web&cd=4&sqi=2&ved=0CFMQFjAD&url=http%3A%2F%2Fwww.communitas.co.za%2Fartikels%2FCalvert.doc&ei=GYIWUOCeFMyN6AH8nIHYDg&usg=AFQjCNHjMUxazwaStxT_97_2t28yzwoqFw (last accessed 1/24/13).

12. "Uitnoding Oprichtingsbijeenkomst," *Platform van Levensbeschouwelijke en Religieuze organisaties in Rotterdam*, 9 April 2008, Stadhuis Rotterdam.

13. Quoted by William R. Garrett, "Thinking Religion in the Global Circumstance: A Critique of Roland Robertson's Globalization Theory," *Journal for the Scientific Study of Religion*, 31 (1992): 301; quoted in *A Global Faith—Essays on Evangelicalism and Globalization*, M. Hutchinson and O. Kalu, eds. (Sydney: Centre for the Study of Australian Christianity, 1998), 30–31.

14. Gerrie ter Haar, "The African Diaspora in Europe—Some Important Themes and Issues: Religious Communities in the Diaspora," in *Strangers and Sojourners,* Gerrie ter Haar, ed. (Leuven: Peeters Publishers, 1998), 45.

15. Peter Brierley, *Future Church: A Global Analysis of the Christian Community to 2010* (Toronto: Monarch Books, 1998), 43–44.

16. *Consultation on World Evangelization,* "Lausanne Occasional Paper 9: Christian Witness to Large Cities" (June 1980), http://www.lausanne.org/en/documents/lops/54-lop-9.html (last accessed 1/24/13).

11. The Missional Challenges of Islam: A Very Diverse People, Religion, and Culture

1. Vinoth Ramachandra, "'The Missionary Message in Relation to Non-Christian Religions': The Edinburgh 1910 Commission IV Report and Beyond" (30 April, 2005), http://www.towards2010.org/downloads/t2010paper04ramachandra.pdf (last accessed 1/24/13).

2. Pew Forum on Religion & Public Life, "Mapping the Global Muslim Population," http://www.pewforum.org/Muslim/Mapping-the-Global-Muslim-Population(23).aspx (last accessed 1/24/13).

3. Richard D. Love, "Church Planting Among Folk Muslims," *International Journal of Frontier Missions*, 11, no. 2 (April, 1994): 87.

4. Phil Parshall, *Bridges to Islam: A Christian Perspective on Folk Islam* (Grand Rapids, MI: Baker Book House, 1983), 2.

5. Samuel Zemwer, *The Disintegration of Islam* (New York: Fleming H. Revell, 1916), 7.

6. Colin Chapman, *Cross and the Crescent: Responding to the Islamic Challenge*, 2nd ed. (Leicester, England: InterVarsity Press, 1996), 9.

7. W. H. T. Gairdner, *The Reproach of Islam* (London: The Student Volunteer Missionary Union, 1910), 311–312.

8. Phil Parshall, *New Paths in Muslim Evangelism: Evangelical Approaches to Contextualization* (Grand Rapids, MI: Baker Book House, 1980).

9. United Nations, The Universal Declaration of Human Rights, Article 18.

12. A Missional Approach to "Hidden Believers"

1. Brother Andrew, *Secret Believers: What Happens When Muslims Believe in Christ* (Ada, MI: Revell, 2007).

13. A Missional Approach to Homosexual Strugglers in the Church and the Gay Community

1. "When Homosexuality Comes to Church," *Harvest News* (Summer 1992), 1.

2. David Kinnaman and Gabe Lyons, *unChristian: What a New Generation Really Thinks about Christianity... and Why It Matters* (Grand Rapids, MI: Baker Books, 2007).

3. David White, "Developing Christ's Heart for the Brokenhearted," *Harvest News* (Fall 2004), 2.

4. David Longacre, ed., *Gay Such Were Some of Us: Stories of Transformation and Change* (Boone, NC: Upside Down Ministries, 2009).

5. Thomas Chalmers, "The Expulsive Power of a New Affection," http://manna.mycpanel.princeton.edu/resources/doc/158/raw (last accessed 1/25/13).

6. "Contentment," *The Valley of Vision: A Collection of Puritan Prayers and Devotions*, Arthur Bennett, ed. (Carlisle, PA: Banner of Truth, 2003), 163.

Conclusion: Crafting an Evangelical, Reformed, and Missional Theology for the Twenty-First Century

1. John Murray, *The Covenant of Grace* (London: Tyndale Press, 1954), 5.

CONTRIBUTORS

Martin Allen studied at St. Andrews University, New College, Edinburgh and Covenant Seminary in St. Louis. Thereafter, he ministered in one congregation in the Church of Scotland near Glasgow for more than thirty years; in that time, a further church was planted. He chaired the Crieff Ministers Fellowship for fifteen years, and served on various theological groups before retiring in 2007. He is married to Ann, with two sons and two grandchildren.

John H. Armstrong (e-book only) is the founder and president of ACT3 Network, a mission for empowering leader and churches for unity in Christ's mission. He is an adjunct professor of mission at Wheaton College Graduate School and the author/editor of twelve books, one of which is the much-discussed book *Your Church Is Too Small: Why Unity in Christ's Mission Is Vital to the Future of the Church* (Zondervan, 2010). His primary mission is to mentor young leaders to practice unity in Christ's mission (visit www.act3online.com).

P. J. (Flip) Buys is associate international director of the World Reformed Fellowship. He also serves as associate professor in the research unit of the faculty of theology of North-West University in Potchefstroom, South Africa. He served for almost forty years as pastor, cross-cultural missionary, church planter, community developer, and theological educator in previously disadvantaged and extremely poor areas in South Africa. He was the founder of Mukhanyo Theological College, Mukhanyo Community Development Centre, and Mukhanyo Christian Academy (a school serving mostly HIV/AIDS orphans). He and his wife Hanneke have one granddaughter, Hannie.

Robert Calvert is the minister of the Scots International Church in Rotterdam in the Netherlands, and has a passion for urban ministry. He regularly lectures in this field and has founded organizations for uprooted peoples and for new immigrant churches. He obtained his D.Min. at Eastern Seminary Philadelphia in 2000 and is completing a Ph.D. on migrant churches at Utrecht University. Since 2002, he has coordinated a network for practitioners in urban ministry that organizes consultations across Europe.

Matthew Ebenezer (e-book only) completed his Ph.D. from Westminster Theological Seminary and is an ordained minister of the Reformed Presbyterian Church of India. He served for more than twenty years as faculty member and vice/acting principal at the Presbyterian Theological Seminary (PTS), Dehra Dun, India. He now teaches church history and practical theology at New Theological College, Dehra Dun, and the PTS. He has lectured and taught in South and Southeast Asia.

John Freeman is president of the organization Harvest USA. He began his ministry there as a volunteer while in seminary, and has maintained a deep burden to see those who struggle with sexual addiction experience change through Jesus Christ. John has guest-taught at classes and seminars at Westminster Seminary, Reformed Seminary, and Cairn University. He also has contributed to *Harvest News*, *Tabletalk*, and the faith page of *The Philadelphia Daily News*. He received a 2008 Amy Award for his contributions to the latter. A native of Chattanooga, Tennessee, John is a graduate of the University of Tennessee and Westminster Theological Seminary. John and his wife, Penny, have been married for more than thirty years and have three grown children.

Craig R. Higgins (e-book only) (D.Min., Trinity Episcopal School for Ministry) is the founding and senior pastor of Trinity Presbyterian Church, a multi-site church in the Westchester suburbs of New York City, which was one of the first church plants of Redeemer Presbyterian Church in Manhattan. He serves on the board of directors and as North American Regional Coordinator of the World Reformed Fellowship. Craig and his wife Ann live in Rye, New York, and have three children.

Frank A. James III is the President of Biblical Theological Seminary in Hatfield, PA. He formerly served as Provost and Professor of Historical Theology at Gordon-Conwell Theological Seminary. He has two doctorates, a D.Phil. in History from Oxford University and a Ph.D. in Theology from Westminster Theological Seminary/Pennsylvania. He is one of the founding members of the Reformation Commentary on Scripture (with Intervarsity Press) and has authored and edited nine books, including *Peter Martyr Vermigli and Predestination: The Augustinian Inheritance of an Italian Reformer* (Oxford University Press) and his latest book, *Church History: From Pre-Reformation to the Present* (Zondervan), is scheduled for publication in fall 2013.

Mark Johnston (e-book only) is senior pastor of Proclamation Presbyterian Church (PCA), in Bryn Mawr, Pennsylvania. Originally from Northern Ireland, he studied in Westminster Theological Seminary in Philadelphia, before returning to Ireland as a church planter. In 1994, he was called to Grove Chapel, in London, before moving to the United States in 2010. Mark serves on the board of Banner of Truth Trust and has written several books including, *You in Your Small Corner: The Elusive Dream of Evangelical Unity*.

Timothy Keller is the senior pastor of Redeemer Presbyterian Church in New York City, which he started in 1989 with his wife Kathy and their three sons. Since then, the church has grown to a weekly attendance of six thousand and helped plant nearly two hundred churches around the world through Redeemer City to City. He is the *New York Times* best-selling author of *The Reason for God, The Prodigal God,* and *The Meaning of Marriage*.

Diane Langberg is a member of Calvary Presbyterian Church (PCA) in Willow Grove, Pennsylvania, and plenary speaker at the WRF General Assembly in Johannesburg. She is a world-recognized authority on sex-trafficking and violence against women, setting up training programs to assist Rwandans in working with victims of trauma. She also owns her own Christian counseling practice, employing about fifteen other counselors. Among Dr. Langberg's many books are *Counsel for Pastors' Wives* (1988), *On the Threshold of Hope* (1999), *and Counseling Survivors of Sexual Abuse* (2003).

John Leonard is a graduate of Belhaven College in Jackson, Mississippi, Reformed Theological Seminary in Jackson, Mississippi (M.Div.) and Trinity Evangelical Divinity School in Deerfield, Illinois (Ph.D.). John is an ordained minister in the Presbyterian Church in America, and served with Arab World Ministries in France from 1988–1998. He is associate professor of Practical Theology and director of the Harvie Conn Center for Global Urban Mission at Westminster Theological Seminary in Philadelphia. He planted, and now pastors, the Creshiem Valley Church in Philadelphia.

Samuel T. Logan, Jr., has been International Director of the World Reformed Fellowship since 2005. He attended Princeton University (B.A.), Westminster Theological Seminary in Philadelphia (M.Div.), and Emory University (Ph.D.). He served at Westminster from 1979–2007, and is now President Emeritus. He was visiting fellow at Christ's College, Cambridge in 1988–89, and special counsel to the president at Biblical Seminary in Hatfield, Pennsylvania, from 2007–2013. He is a minister of the Orthodox Presbyterian Church. Dr. Logan's publications include *The Preacher and Preaching, Sermons That Shaped America, Confronting Kingdom Challenges*, and numerous articles on Jonathan Edwards.

A. T. B. McGowan is minister of Inverness East Church of Scotland, professor of theology in the University of the Highlands and Islands, and honorary professor in Reformed doctrine at the University of Aberdeen. He chairs the Theological Commission of the World Reformed Fellowship and is president of the Scottish Evangelical Theology Society. His most recent books are *The Divine Spiration of Scripture: Challenging Evangelical Perspectives* (Nottingham: IVP, 2007) and *The Person and Work of Christ: Understanding Jesus* (Milton Keynes: Paternoster, 2012).

Elias Medeiros (Ph.D. Intercultural Studies) is Harriet Barbour Professor of Missions and missions department chairman at Reformed Theological Seminary (RTS) in Jackson, Mississippi. He is an ordained minister of the Presbyterian Church of Brazil. Prior to coming to RTS in 1993, he worked as a rural church planter in the Amazon jungle and as an urban church planter in Northeast Brazil; pastored churches in the state of Paraiba, Brazil; taught at the Presbyterian Seminary in Brazil; and worked as academic dean at the Evangelical Missions Center in South Brazil. He is a member of the Global Diaspora Network Advisory Board of the Lausanne Committee, and he has been married to Fokjelina, a beautiful Dutch lady, for the past thirty-eight years.

John Nicholls was born in London in 1949 and grew up in a church with close links to the East African revival. He studied at Bradford University, the Free Church of Scotland College in Edinburgh, and Westminster Theological Seminary (D.Min.). He joined the London City Mission (LCM) in 1993 as director of training and recruitment, and became chief executive in 2004. He retired from the LCM in 2013, and now serves as associate pastor of Smithton Free Church (Inverness). He is co-author (with Irene Howat) of *Streets Paved with Gold*, a history of the LCM. He is married to Sarah; they have two children and three grandchildren.

Robert M. Norris (e-book only) has served as the pastor of Fourth Presbyterian Church in Bethesda, Maryland for the last thirty years. Rob studied at Kings College, London, and the University of St. Andrews, Scotland. Prior to his time at Fourth Presbyterian, he served as assistant minister at The City Temple, London; taught at London Bible College; was chaplain at the City of London University and St. Bartholomew's Hospital, London; and then served as executive pastor at First Presbyterian Church of Hollywood. California.

Henry Luke Orombi (e-book only) provided leadership and service to the ten million- member Anglican Church of Uganda until his retirement in December of 2012. He was a plenary speaker at the Third General Assembly of the WRF, and was one of the leaders of the global Anglican Communion who organized and directed the Global Anglican Future Conference (GAFCON) held in Jerusalem in June of 2008. He currently serves on the Primate's Council of the Fellowship of Confessing Anglicans, and was chairman of the Africa Host Committee of Lausanne III, held in Cape Town, South Africa, in October 2010.

Susan M. Post is the Executive Director of Esperanza Health Center and a Doctor of Ministry graduate of Westminster Theological Seminary. Susan enjoys the blessing of living, worshiping, and serving in ministry in her Hunting Park neighborhood of North Philadelphia.

Ron Scates (e-book only) has been senior pastor of Highland Park Presbyterian Church (PCUSA) in Dallas, Texas, for the past twelve years. Before that, he served at First Presbyterian Church of San Antonio, Texas, for ten years and at Central Presbyterian Church of Baltimore, Maryland, for eleven years. He is married to Anne, and they have five children. He is a graduate of Trinity University in San Antonio and Union Theological

Seminary in Richmond, Virginia (D.Min.). He serves on the boards of the World Reformed Fellowship, the Presbyterian Hospital System, the Presbyterian Children's Homes and Services, and is on the advisory board of the U.S. Lausanne Committee for World Evangelization.

Thomas Schirrmacher is director of the International Institute for Religious Freedom (Bonn, Cape Town, Colombo). He is also speaker for human rights and chair of the Theological Commission for the World Evangelical Alliance. Dr. Schirrmacher is professor of the sociology of religion at the University of the West (Timisoara, Romania), and president of the Martin Bucer European Seminary and Research Institutes (Bonn, Zurich, Innsbruck, Prague, Istanbul, Sao Paulo).

Basyle (Boz) Tchividjian is a former child-abuse prosecutor who currently teaches "Child Abuse and the Law" and several other courses at Liberty University School of Law. Professor Tchividjian is also the founder and executive director of GRACE (Godly Response to Abuse in the Christian Environment; www.netgrace.org). Professor Tchividjian is the third eldest grandchild of Reverend Billy Graham, and wrote the book *Invitation—Billy Graham and the Lives God Touched* (Multnomah, 2008).

Christopher J. H. Wright, Langham Partnership's International Director, is an Irishman living in London, with his heart firmly planted in the Majority World. Chris, with wife Liz alongside, has pastored a local parish church, taught at a top seminary in India, served as president of a key Christian college, and authored twenty books including *Old Testament Ethics and The Uniqueness of Jesus, The Mission of God,* and *The Mission of God's People.* Chris was chair of the Lausanne Theology Working Group from 2005–2011, and chair of the Statement Working Group at the Third Lausanne Congress, 2010, which produced The Cape Town Commitment. He is also chair of the Theological Resource Team for Tearfund (UK).

David Zadok (e-book only) is pastor of Grace and Truth Congregation in Israel and field director of Christian Witness to Israel. He has been serving the body of Christ in Israel for more than two decades. David earned his B.A. in computers and business administration from San Diego State University. He is a graduate of Westminster Seminary in California and the Institute of Reformed Baptist Seminary at Westminster Seminary. He is a retired major in the Israel Defense forces.